The Fearless Baker

The *Fearless* Baker

Simple Secrets for Baking Like a Pro

Erin Jeanne McDowell

Photographs by Jennifer May

A Rux Martin Book

Houghton Mifflin Harcourt

BOSTON   NEW YORK   2017

Library of Congress Cataloging-in-Publication Data is available.
ISBN 978-0-544–79143-5 (hbk); 978-0-544-79144-2 (ebk)

Book design by Rachel Newborn
Food and prop styling by Erin McDowell
Cover prop styling by Barbara Fritz

Printed in China
TOP 10 9 8 7 6 5 4 3 2 1

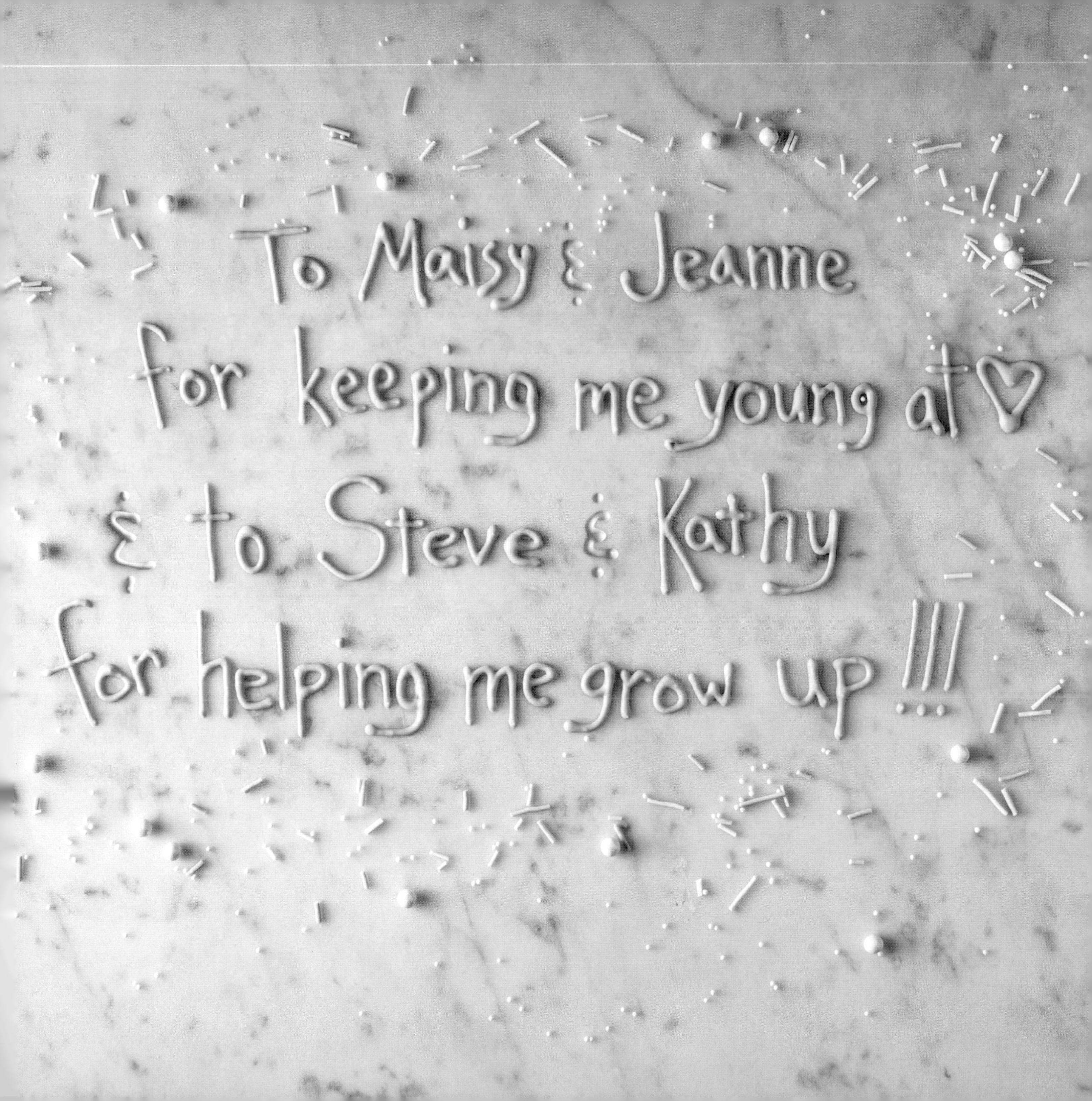

To Maisy & Jeanne
for keeping me young at ♡
& to Steve & Kathy
for helping me grow up !!!

Table of Contents

FOREWORD BY ROSE LEVY BERANBAUM 9

Introduction 11

1 **Cookies & Bars** 21

2 **Cakes** 77

3 **Pies & Tarts** 165

4 **Pastries** 247

5 **Custards & Creams** 319

RESOURCES 369

ACKNOWLEDGMENTS 371

INDEX 373

Foreword by Rose Levy Beranbaum

When I learned that Erin McDowell was writing her first baking book, my immediate response was *Yes!* quickly followed by *Of course!* I had met Erin when she was involved in the baking and styling of the photographs for my book *The Baking Bible*. We spent two intense weeks in a rented studio in upstate New York, baking, styling, discussing, and getting to know each other. Not only did Erin make delicious, nourishing lunches for the entire team every day, her sunny disposition helped set the tone. I taught her how to make a special border on a tart (see page 186), and she demonstrated how to make the most luscious, voluptuous ganache and buttercream swirls on cakes.

Reading through this book, I am struck by how eager Erin is to explore new ideas and inspirations and how open she is to learning. One of the secrets to being a great baker is to have love in one's heart and love for the profession. And one of the secrets to being a great baking author is having a true desire to share. Erin is gifted with both. Her written instructions are a model of clarity and a perfect reflection of her delightful and joyful spirit. And her writing style is so friendly, fun, and unpretentious that it makes baking more approachable than ever.

I didn't have to test recipes from this book in order to sing Erin's praises, because having seen her in action, and having tasted the results, was proof enough of her expertise. I tested four of the recipes just because they were so alluring I couldn't resist. The rhubarb cheesecake (page 350), which imaginatively replaces lemon juice with rhubarb puree, is topped with stunning ribbons of rhubarb. It's exceptionally delicious, and it leaves a surprisingly bright, fresh finish in the mouth despite the richness of the cream cheese. Chocolate puff pastry is something I'd never actually made before, but when I saw the photo for this book (page 307), I couldn't resist the challenge. Yes, it is "hard," as Erin realistically indicates at the top of the recipe, but it is an empowering experience, and success is guaranteed if one follows her excellent instructions. And her technique for making puff pastry results in the best palmiers I've ever made—or eaten.

Erin writes, "This book is intended to educate you on the whys and hows of baking in an approachable way. If you understand those basics, you can become fearless—and potentially tweak your own recipes to suit your whims, the way I do." I relate to this goal 100 percent. In fact, this is shades of the young me, at the start of my own cookbook-writing odyssey.

It is inspiring to see the fine and exciting work of this prize representative of the new generation of bakers. I am honored that she claims to have used my books as a launching pad to her baking education. And I am certain that Erin Jeanne McDowell will continue to march to the beat of her own drummer and rise to ever greater heights of discovery and baking excellence.

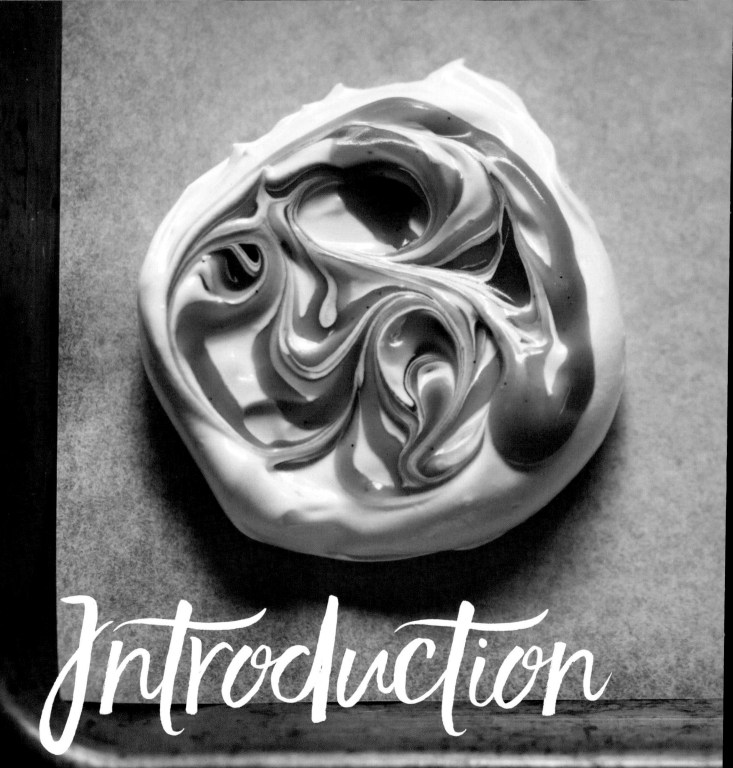

Introduction

You can (and should!) go bake right now. Pick up a recipe, assemble the ingredients, put them together, and create something *amazing*. I constantly remind folks that baking is nothing to be afraid of. But it scares a lot of people, and for lots of different reasons.

Baking has a reputation for being "by the book." Your oven temperature must be spot on, your measurements should be precise, and you better follow that dang recipe—*or else*. Meanwhile, over in savory land, people are adding a pinch of this and a splash of that like it ain't no thang. While baking will never have that same "fly by the seat of your pants" sort of vibe, there is flexibility to be found within those strict-sounding recipes—you just have to know where to look.

See, most recipes tell you *how* to do something, not *why*. When you understand the reasons behind what you're doing, baking suddenly becomes much more approachable. You'll begin to realize that it's OK to reduce the sugar in your grandma's pound cake recipe or make a chocolate version of your favorite custard pie. Some things, however, remain true: You should take care when measuring your ingredients, you can't make ingredient swaps willy-nilly—that sort of thing. But for every hard-and-fast rule, you can make tons of tweaks, nips, and tucks to get you from point A to point B as smoothly, easily, and (most important) deliciously as possible.

As a professional who creates recipes and specializes in making desserts look good for the camera, I get loads of baking questions. Lots of people ask me, "What's the *best* way to do . . . ?" I certainly have my own favorite methods, but that doesn't mean others won't work too. The best advice is to try detailed techniques from sources you trust—but then not to be afraid to experiment with new things! A recipe may tell you to chill something for thirty minutes, but you may have better luck if you refrigerate it overnight. Another recipe may tell you to roll out a dough on a floured surface, but you may prefer to do it between two sheets of parchment paper. In this book, I do my best to spell out my favorite methods, along with some others I know work. This is my way of showing you some of the right times to be flexible, because you'll always have the most success if you do it in a way that feels good/right/natural to *you*!

This book is intended to educate you on the whys and hows of baking in an approachable way. If you understand those basics, you can become fearless—and potentially tweak your own recipes to suit your whims, the way I do. This book isn't about shortcuts, but I do give you some really good ones. It doesn't focus on easy recipes, but there are definitely plenty of those too. This is a practical book for sweets lovers from someone who adores them! I'll show you the whys and hows, along with a healthy dose of creativity, tips, tricks, and style, to get you past fear and into your kitchen, baking up a storm.

Within the recipes, you'll find information about how you can substitute other ingredients into a recipe, ways you can tweak methods, and more. Just look for the handy label "Why It Works"—these tips not only apply to the specific recipe, but can also help you understand how to apply the knowledge you gain to others in your repertoire.

So take this book into your kitchen. Drop jam on its pages and throw enough flour around until some puffs come out when you close it at the end of the day. Let's bake together and make something crazy delicious!

WHAT THE PROS KNOW

Before you dive into these recipes, there are a few things that can help you from the get-go. This is stuff that the pros know and don't even think about but that can help you start seeing baking in a different—and easier—light.

Make Things Ahead. This may be the primary difference between professional bakers and home cooks. The pros churn out multiple components for a variety of desserts all day long. They often make a batch of one thing (a type of cake, a frosting, a fruit filling) and use it in multiple ways. It can be helpful to take a page from their book. Each of my recipes lets you know what components (or even the whole thing) can be made ahead. When I make layer cakes, such as the one on the cover of this book, I often bake the layers and make the frosting in advance so that when it comes time for assembly, that task is all I have to think about. It's a great way to give yourself a head start and enough time to avoid mid-baking freak-outs.

Look for Visual Cues. Good recipes give not only a suggested time frame for baking/chilling/resting and what have you, but also visual cues to help you determine when something's ready. These will help you nail recipes every time.

You Don't Have to Make Everything from Scratch. When you have the time, preparing all the components yourself can result in seriously impressive desserts. But for the hundreds of times real life gets in the way, it's OK to take some shortcuts. Take the Lemon Ricotta Turnovers on page 310—if you go through all the effort of making your own puff pastry, you don't have to make your own lemon curd too (or the other way around!). The recipe for Dulce de Leche Ice Cream Pie (page 206) includes a recipe for homemade dulce de leche, but ice cream pies are also quick and easy, so if you want to use the jarred stuff, that's fine. Do whatever you can manage—and when you do make it all from scratch, celebrate a little (you rock!).

Edible Garnishes Will Rock Your Socks Off. Whether you're talking about some chopped fresh mint on a tart, a handful of chocolate sprinkles on a cupcake, or a few adorably tiny cookies around the edge of a frosted cake, edible garnishes rule. Not only are they cute and yummy, they can help cover up mistakes in a way that makes them look as if you made them totally on purpose.

BASIC RECIPES YOU SHOULD KNOW AND MASTER

Whether you're a beginner or a frequent baker, some recipes are super-versatile, and these are called for in some form or another over and over again throughout this book. So no matter what your skill level, this list is a great jumping-off point.

If you can make meringue, you can make gorgeous Pavlovas (page 274), piled with fruit and whipped cream. You can also make cookies (page 53), incredible frostings (like the buttercream on page 149), toppings for pies and tarts (page 219), and even cute decorations for cakes.

If you can make shortbread, you can make cookies (page 40) or use the dough as a base for elaborate bar cookies (page 74) or as a crust for a tart.

If you can make pâte à choux, you can make cream puffs (page 277), éclairs, and crullers. Pâte à choux is so versatile that you can prepare one batch and turn it into different sizes and shapes, then finish them with an array of fillings for an incredible dessert spread.

If you can make pastry cream, you're ready to fill everything from cakes to pies and tarts to pastries. It's also the base for some types of mousse and soufflés (page 357). Plus, with just a few simple tweaks, you're moments away from other fillings like Diplomat Cream (page 341) and Chiboust (page 341).

If you can make pie and tart dough, any pie or tart is within your reach. You can also make variations like hand pies (page 199), galettes (page 200), and savory potpies. Understanding the method for these doughs also makes it easier to make things like Biscuits (pages 258 to 263) and even Puff Pastry (page 301).

If you can make sponge cake, you're set to make layer cakes of any sort. You can also make roulades (page 145) and other variations once you've got the technique down.

If you can make pound cake, you're on the road to delicious cupcakes, Bundt cakes, loaf cakes, and more.

If you can make brioche, you can use it as the base for tons of desserts, from free-form tarts (page 288) to flaky faux-laminated pastries (page 295) to Danishes (page 293).

HOW TYPES OF FLOUR DIFFER AND WHY IT MATTERS

Understanding flours will help you know when and how to replace or fiddle with various flours in your favorite recipes. Different types of flour contain different protein levels. The percentage of protein can indicate how much structure the flour will provide for the finished baked goods. Simply put, the more protein a flour has, the stronger it is.

All-Purpose Flour: The standard for many cookie, cake, pie, tart, and pastry recipes. It has a relatively average protein content of 9 to 11 percent.

Whole Wheat Flour: Made by milling the entire wheat kernel, this has a high protein content (11 to 13 percent), plus the ability to absorb more liquid, which is why it usually appears alongside another flour in a recipe.

Bread Flour: This has a high protein content (11 to 14 percent), which is ideal for bread doughs, because it can take intense mixing and shaping.

Cake Flour: A low protein level (7 to 8 percent) makes this flour ideal for cakes and other lighter, more tender baked goods. Most cake flours also have added starch to help prevent caking.

Pastry Flour: Similar to cake flour, but without the addition of starch, with a low protein level (7 to 9 percent).

Whole Wheat Pastry Flour: I'm a big fan of this one, which has a protein content of 8 to 10 percent, close to all-purpose flour, so it makes a better whole wheat substitute than regular whole wheat flour in many recipes.

Rye Flour: With a protein content of 8 to 10 percent, rye flours can vary in coarseness, color, and flavor. They are some of the most striking flours in terms of flavor and color, and they don't readily form gluten strands, making them a great addition to delicate baked goods like cookies and cakes.

Semolina Flour: A coarsely ground durum flour with a protein content of 12 to 14 percent.

Graham Flour: A coarsely ground whole wheat flour (11 to 13 percent), this is used to make graham crackers. Its texture makes a great addition to other baked goods.

THE FOUR BASIC TYPES OF BAKING INGREDIENTS AND WHAT THEY DO

At its most basic, baking uses four categories of ingredients: stabilizers, liquefiers, leaveners, and inclusions.

Stabilizers: Flour and eggs are both considered stabilizers. They provide structure to a recipe through the gelatinization of starch (flour) and the coagulation of protein (eggs). What this means: Altering the amount or type of stabilizers in a recipe can mess things up. You can make changes, but only if the ratios stay on point.

Liquefiers: Fats, sugar, and liquids (such as milk and cream) are considered liquefiers. In addition to making a batter or dough more liquid (of course!), they promote other reactions as a result (including browning, spreading, and tenderizing). If you alter one liquefying ingredient in a recipe, you'll likely need to modify other ingredients too. If you decide to use honey in place of some of the sugar, you may need to tinker with the fat and/or liquid amounts to make sure your dough or batter isn't too liquid. Or you may need to compensate with additional stabilizers.

Leaveners: Yeast and chemical leaveners like baking soda and baking powder enable baked items to rise in the oven, developing their final crumb structure. Each

UNIQUE PROPERTIES OF EGGS YOU SHOULD KNOW

EGGS CONTAIN AMYLASE. Egg yolks contain an enzyme called amylase that digests starch molecules. For many egg preparations, this enzyme doesn't play a remarkable role, but it can cause a problem for custards that are thickened with starch, such as pastry cream. The enzyme itself is resistant to heat, so it's important that starch-thickened custards come to a boil, or the enzyme will live on, slowly consuming the starch until your formerly thick custard is runny!

EGGS HAVE LEAVENING ABILITY. Eggs contribute to leavening when aerated through mechanical or physical leavening. Whole eggs, egg whites, and egg yolks can all be whipped (sometimes with a sweetener) to create volume. Air bubbles form during the whipping process, and these bubbles eventually create a foam. How exactly are egg foams made? At the beginning of whipping, the whisk breaks up the eggs/whites/yolks, causing the protein strands to begin to loosen. As the proteins are agitated further, they begin to form bonds with one another, creating long, continuous strands with large bubbles, which increase the volume of the eggs. However, if the protein strands are overbeaten, they can be shaken apart from the water present in the mixing bowl (from the eggs themselves, other ingredients, or both!), and

this separation can lead to a dry, grainy, or clumpy foam. Egg whites can expand to up to eight times their original volume. Whole eggs and yolks are usually beaten with sugar (they won't expand much on their own without the granules to assist), and while they expand significantly less, they create slightly more stable foams.

Egg whites are whipped (with or without sugar) to different stages, described as "peaks" (the same term is used for whipped cream). To determine which peak you have, dip your whisk into the bowl of whites (or cream) and then remove it: Soft peaks will have only a little structure and fall over completely into a soft mass when you release the whisk. Medium peaks are sturdier but are still somewhat soft looking—they will hold a curlicue shape. Stiff peaks will stand straight up and are quite strong.

UNIQUE PROPERTIES OF SUGAR YOU SHOULD KNOW

SUGAR IS HYGROSCOPIC. Sugar and other sweeteners have "hygroscopic" properties, which means they draw moisture out of other ingredients or sources. This characteristic is essential to baking, but it also means that an open package of brown sugar attracts moisture from humid air and can clump. For the same reason, it's best to keep the sugar and yolks separate until the last moment, since yolks are about 50 percent moisture and sugar can make them dry and crumbly.

SUGAR IS PRONE TO CRYSTALLIZATION. This is especially true of granulated sugar (since it's crystalline to begin with), but it's not restricted to it—have you ever seen honey begin to solidify as crystals form in the jar? Crystallization comes from the sweeteners' tendency to bond to other sugars present in whatever mixture it is in. It can occur when a mixture with a large amount of sugar is stirred—the agitation forces the sugar molecules to collide, and they are likely to bond together. It can also occur when a mixture is heavily saturated with sugar. Liquid causes sugar to dissolve, surrounding each molecule and discouraging them from coming in contact with other sugar molecules, which could encourage crystallization. But when the liquid evaporates and the resultant ratio of sugar is higher, crystals can form. Some recipes seek to prevent crystallization (e.g., the sugar syrup used to make buttercream), while others encourage and/or control it (such as fudge, which gains its characteristic texture from crystallization).

When cooking a sugar syrup, stirring before it begins to boil can be helpful, since that can help the mixture to heat evenly and the sugar to dissolve. But once the syrup begins to boil, agitating will encourage it to crystallize, which will harden the sugar before it's done cooking. The exception is a recipe that is formulated to encourage crystallization (like fudge or some types of caramel), where stirring may be called for.

SUGAR CAN BE CARAMELIZED. Caramelization occurs when sugar molecules are heated to a high enough temperature that they melt. Once they've melted, the heat continues to break down the molecules until the syrup begins to darken in color. At first the color is barely discernible, but then it becomes a pale amber, and then a rich golden color; eventually, if cooked long enough, it can turn black. As it cooks, the caramel will become discernibly less sweet and more bitter; it will also begin to acquire other flavors.

of these kinds of leaveners produces different results, depending on the other ingredients in the recipe. Baking soda reacts when combined with an acidic ingredient, creating bubbles inside the dough or batter that cause the baked good to rise in the oven. Baking powder contains the same base, with the addition of an acid to begin the leavening process when the batter is moistened. Double-acting baking powder—which is the most common type of baking powder today—will also leaven the batter or dough again when it hits the heat of the oven. For this reason, many recipes use a combination of baking soda and baking powder; most recipes that use only baking soda also contain an acidic ingredient. Mechanical or physical mixing coaxes ingredients such as sugar, fat, and eggs to become leavening agents by incorporating air into the batter or dough.

Inclusions: This category is a bit random. Inclusions give baked goods more flavor and texture. In many recipes, inclusions are flexible—you can change the amounts and even the type without much thinking (for example, replacing lemon extract with vanilla extract or using nuts in place of chocolate chips). In other recipes, you have to get creative to tweak the inclusions in a way that ensures the recipe still works (adding a swirl of raspberry jam to a cake, or replacing dark chocolate with milk chocolate).

BRINGING INGREDIENTS TO ROOM TEMPERATURE

It's important that most ingredients in a recipe be at room temperature when you begin to mix. This is for a few reasons. Ingredients like butter or coconut oil actually change consistency when they are at room temperature, making them easier to mix. It's also easier to combine ingredients thoroughly if they are all at the same temperature. That's why a batter may seize or separate if you start with soft butter and later add cold eggs or milk.

Milk/buttermilk/cream should be not noticeably cold to the touch. Butter should be soft enough so it can be blended easily, but not gooey or melty. Eggs should be at mean room temperature—ideally 65° to 75°F / 18° to 23°C.

Truth be told, unless I have a big day of baking ahead, I rarely remember to bring dairy products to room temperature before I start the recipe.

My trick for perfectly softened butter? Leave it in its paper wrapper and nuke it in the microwave for 10 seconds, then turn it over on its side and warm it for another 7 seconds. This makes the butter nice and soft, and you've only spent 17 of your valuable seconds. The same trick can be used to take unwanted chill out of liquid dairy products too—just don't overdo it. Better a little too cold than too hot. I have no problem leaving eggs out at room temperature, and I always have a dozen or so out on the counter for baking. But if you prefer, you can put your refrigerated eggs (in the shell) in warm water (around 90°F / 32°C) for 5 minutes.

CHAPTER 1

Cookies
& Bars

My first memories of baking are of making chocolate chip cookies with my mama. Although she was a wonderful cook and baker, the best recipe she had was the one on the bag of chocolate chips. Even using that back of the bag recipe, I learned to make tweaks. I almost always doubled the vanilla, and I regularly threw in way more chocolate chips. And I definitely didn't wait for the cookies to cool completely before eating them. My initial cookie experiments taught me so much about how ingredients and mixing methods work and how a few slight changes can alter a recipe so much—often for the better.

MIXING INFO

Different types of cookies call for different mixing methods, from blending (brownies and tuiles) to creaming (chocolate chip and oatmeal) to variations on foaming (meringues and macarons). But with any method (see page 78 for the basics on mixing), it is essential to mix just enough to incorporate all of the ingredients evenly, without overdoing it.

1. **It's important to scrape down the bowl** as you go. Many cookie recipes have only a few ingredients, and you want to make sure they are uniformly combined. This applies especially to inclusions—you know, the yummy stuff you add at the end: chunks of chocolate, a swirl of caramel, a handful of toasty nuts, and so on. Here are two tips for success when incorporating inclusions:

   * **If you are working with a stiff dough,** lift it out of the bowl and sprinkle half the inclusions into the empty bowl. Then put the dough back in the bowl and sprinkle the remaining inclusions on top. That way, you've started the distribution before you even turn your mixer back on.

   * **For a loose batter,** you may want to toss the inclusions with a small amount of the flour (2 teaspoons per 1 cup inclusions). This will help keep them suspended and evenly distributed in the batter, rather than clumped together at the bottom.

2. **Take care not to overmix the dough.** You want to mix well enough to fully incorporate all the ingredients, but not so much that you overwork the dough.

Cookies are all about tenderness, whether it's a soft and chewy sugar cookie or a crispy, crunchy gingersnap. As with all flour-based baked goods, gluten forms during mixing, and prolonged mixing means longer gluten strands, which, in turn, mean tougher cookies.

TYPES OF COOKIES

DROP COOKIES

Drop cookies are one of the most common types of cookies. Think popular standbys like chocolate chip, oatmeal, and peanut butter. Usually made from creamed batters, they are so named because the dough is scooped and dropped onto baking sheets for baking. They are some of my favorite cookies because of how quickly they can be thrown together.

MY ADVICE: Drop cookies are perfect for dressing up. Consider unusual combinations of inclusions—crumbled pretzels in peanut butter cookie dough or chopped chocolate–covered espresso beans in Flourless Cocoa Cookies (page 30). Or try adding another component entirely—I love making drop cookies into sandwich cookies by adding a scoop of ice cream, a spread of Salted Caramel Sauce (page 54), or a hefty dollop of Dark Chocolate Italian Buttercream (page 149).

CUT-OUT COOKIES

Cut-out cookies are cut from a stiff dough that is rolled out to an even thickness. They can be any shape your little heart desires and are often decorated with icing.

MY ADVICE: Whenever you roll out a dough, it's best to use as little flour as possible. Any flour you throw onto your surface is going to be incorporated into the dough as you roll, and too much flour can make a dough dry and harder to roll out without cracking. Too much flour can also make your finished cookies tough. If you have trouble with your dough sticking, try rolling it out between two sheets of parchment paper or plastic wrap— I don't love doing this, because the sheets often bunch up and leave dents or lines in the dough, but the technique does come in handy for stickier doughs.

Also, if you're using a cookie cutter that has a lot of intricate details (an elaborate snowflake, for instance), I recommend rolling out the dough, transferring it to a baking sheet, and chilling the dough on the baking sheet before cutting out the cookies. Then chill the cut-out dough again before baking, so those details stay sharp.

ICEBOX COOKIES

Icebox cookies are made from a stiff dough that's formed into a log, refrigerated or frozen, and then sliced into rounds. If you keep a log or two in your freezer, you can make freshly baked cookies at the drop of a hat. This is especially great for those times (cough, cough . . . holidays) when you need to make a lot of cookies.

PRO TIP: SCOOPING COOKIE DOUGH

I love cookie scoops. They make my cookies almost perfectly even every time, with minimal effort and no more cleanup than if I'd used the old two-spoon method. The most useful sizes are: #16 / ¼ cup (57 g), #30 / 2 tablespoons (28 g), #60 / 1 tablespoon (14 g). But if you're scoopless, never fear—I provide volume equivalents in every recipe. *My advice if you're scoopless:* Carefully measure out the first mound of dough, then eyeball the others to make them look like that first one. You can also do this with a scale, if you're so inclined.

PRO TIP: MAKESHIFT MOLDS AND STAMPS

No cookie mold or stamp? No problem: Get creative with the stuff you have on hand. Fabric or paper can be used to imprint patterns on cookies. Just be sure the pattern is deep enough to make an imprint. Doilies, for example, can create a gorgeous imprint on the surface of a cookie (made even more fabulous by a brush of glaze after baking). Tiny tart pans or candy molds can also make great cookie molds.

MY ADVICE: I learned a snazzy trick for getting an even log in no time at one of my very first bakery jobs. You need a big piece of parchment and a bench knife (or dough scraper; if you don't have one of these, you can use the blade of a long offset spatula). Position the paper so a long side faces you, plop the dough onto the parchment, and form it into a rough log shape along that long side. (If the dough is very dry, lightly wet your hands to shape it; if the dough is very sticky, flour your hands.) Fold the parchment closest to you over the log. Press the bench knife firmly into the crease made by the paper folded over the log while pulling the parchment taut. Through the magic of pressure, the log will become smooth and even.

SHAPED COOKIES

Shaped cookies are formed in various ways:

Piped cookies (e.g., spritz cookies) are generally made from relatively stiff doughs that will hold their shape when piped and baked. Some doughs used for piped cookies are not stiff but are sturdy enough that they don't lose definition when exposed to heat (e.g., Meringues, page 53).

Molded and stamped cookies include those made from thin batters piped into molds (such as Madeleines, page 60), and from stiffer doughs pressed into molds or shaped with stamps.

Sliced cookies, like biscotti, are baked twice, first as a log of dough, and then sliced and baked again. I love their long shelf life—they're meant to be dry and they don't stale during storage, so you can keep them on hand for coffeetime, anytime.

MY ADVICE: Many of the cookies in this category look super-impressive even though they are beyond easy to make. Buy a nice mold or cookie stamp for your new signature cookie, and you can focus on finishing it in a pretty way (or leave it plain). These cookies are wonderful for finishing touches like a drizzle of, or dunk into, melted chocolate, which turns them into something even more special.

STUFFING DROP COOKIES

There's nothing like a cookie with a surprise inside, which is why I adore stuffing drop cookies with different ingredients. The doughs are firm enough to stuff before baking, and the spreading that occurs in the oven takes care of the rest. To stuff a cookie, scoop a portion of dough onto a prepared baking sheet, make a well in the center with your finger or the handle of a wooden spoon, and place the stuffing inside the cavity. Rather than trying to close the opening, scoop a small amount of additional dough on top and press down lightly to make sure it's sealed. If the dough is firm enough, you can pick the cookie up and roll it gently between your hands to help seal it, then return it to the baking sheet and press down to flatten it slightly.

I like to stuff cookies with mini marshmallows, small squares of chocolate, caramels, sprinkles, chopped candy, nut butters, cream cheese, or even another cookie dough.

SANDWICH COOKIES

Sandwich cookies are a beautiful thing. They can be made with either drop or cut-out cookies, but choose a recipe for a cookie that's on the softer side. Crisp cookies will shatter when bitten into, causing the filling to splooge out the back of the cookie—not good. Be sure to use a filling that can handle the weight of the top cookie. Jam or jelly makes a great filling, but it may need to be boiled down or otherwise thickened, or it may run out the edges when you sandwich it. But

thinner/looser fillings can be used without thickening, as long as they are spread in a very thin layer (think linzer cookies). For more substantial fillings, I often use the same scoop that I used to shape the cookies to fill them.

For the classic look, place the filling in the center of an overturned cookie, place another cookie on top, and apply steady pressure until the filling flows out to the edges. You can stop there or, for a sharp look, continue applying pressure until the filling goes just beyond the edges, then smooth the filling all around the cookie with an offset spatula.

All of these make great sandwich cookie fillings: American Buttercream (page 134), Molasses Cream Cheese Frosting (page 141), Dark Chocolate Italian Buttercream (page 149), or just about any kind of frosting, really; Whipped Ganache (page 132); Caramel Pudding Buttercream (page 152) or dulce de leche (page 206); marshmallow crème (page 63); nut butters; thickened jams/jellies/preserves/marmalade; Lemon Curd Buttercream (page 158); and, of course, ice cream (page 362).

BAR COOKIES

Bar cookies are ten kinds of wonderful. They are easy to make and easy to shape (just pour the batter into the pan), and the batters can be layered to create a ton of amazing flavor combos. The only slightly tricky part is determining doneness. And once they're baked, you can portion them however you wish (i.e., one huge one for now and a bunch of tiny ones for later).

MY ADVICE: A bar cookie with multiple layers is impressive. I start by thinking about flavor, texture, and color and then use one of my favorite recipes to make a whole new, killer recipe.

- **Flavor:** Think about the base first: A layer of salty caramel might make your shortbread bar sing. A topping of tart rhubarb glaze will take those cheesecake bars to a whole new level. When in doubt, take

PRO TIP: HOW TO LINE A BAR COOKIE PAN

Sometimes the hardest part about bar cookies is wondering if they'll come out of the pan cleanly so you can get nice slices. Here's what I do:

- Spray the pan lightly with nonstick spray—make sure to get into the corners. Line it with a sheet of parchment paper, leaving a 1- to 2-inch overhang on two opposite sides of the pan to serve as handles for removing the baked bar.

- Use scissors to make a cut in the parchment in each corner of the pan, cutting all the way down to the bottom of the pan. Press the parchment down to adhere the paper to the spray coating and boom: The cut corners will become flush and overlap at the corners of the pan cleanly. You may have to spray the back of each cut edge so it adheres to the other edge and doesn't droop.

flavor cues from classic combos like turtle, black forest, or German chocolate, and so on.

- **Texture:** You can go two ways: contrasting or melding. If you're starting with a chewy base, like a brownie, you may want to top it with a smooth second layer, then maybe add something for a little crunch. Alternatively, go for three layers that are texturally similar, so that every bite is about the melding of the flavors of the components.

- **Color:** I am a big fan of the contrasting bar cookie: a brown sugar crust topped with bright lemon curd, or a pale blondie sporting a dark chocolate top layer. But they don't necessarily have to be contrasting—chocolate on chocolate on chocolate never hurt anybody, after all!

GLAZING COOKIES OR BARS

In reality, you can glaze almost any cookie, but I especially love to do this with thin cookies (like cut-out cookies), cookies with texture (e.g., molded or stamped cookies), or bar cookies. Cookies must be completely cooled before they are glazed. They can be glazed in any of the following ways:

Drizzle: Use a thin or thick icing (see opposite) for drizzling, depending on what you're going for. The best way to get an even drizzle is to use a pastry bag—I use disposable ones—either with a small opening cut in the tip or fitted with a pastry tip. Arrange the cookies on a piece of parchment paper; you only need to allow a small amount of space between them. Then drizzle with the icing by moving the pastry bag back and forth in a line (either straight or on a diagonal) across the cookies. Generally, the faster you move, the thinner the drizzle, although the size of the opening in the pastry bag or of the tip will also affect this. Then let the cookies sit at room temperature until the glaze sets.

Dunk: Cookies can be dunked in the icing (oh, yeah!). If you use a thin icing, it will probably run down the sides of the cookies. A thicker icing will stay on the surface. Hold each cookie by the base, using your thumb and forefinger, position the cookie over the icing, and then dunk the surface of the cookie. Remove the cookie from the glaze and hold it above the bowl for a few moments to allow the excess to drip off, then turn the cookie over onto a piece of parchment. Let them stand at room temperature until the glaze sets.

Enrobe: Thin icing is best for enrobing a cookie—it will coat the cookie evenly because the excess will run down the sides. Small, thin cookies can be dunked into the glaze. One at a time, drop each cookie into the glaze, top side down, then use a small offset spatula to turn the cookie over and, using the spatula, hold the cookie above the glaze for a few seconds, allowing the excess to drip off. Transfer to a piece of parchment and let stand at room temperature until the glaze is set.

THIN OR THICK GLAZES

Glazes and icings can be made in various consistencies to produce very different results. It's important to match the icing to the task at hand.

THICK: A thick glaze/icing is firm enough to hold its shape when piped, so it should hold a stiff peak after it is mixed. A thick glaze is best for more detailed decor because it's firm and will give you control while you work.

MEDIUM: A medium glaze/icing will be about as thick as buttercream. It should be firm enough to hold its shape when piped, though it may collapse onto itself and/or spread a little. It should hold a peak for a moment, then slowly fold over onto itself but still maintain the approximate shape. Medium-thick glazes/icings are multipurpose and can be piped, drizzled, or spread.

THIN: If you dip a spoon into a thin glaze/icing and hold it above the bowl, the glaze will first form a line on the surface and then be reabsorbed into the rest of the glaze. Thin icing is used for flooding (a technique that entails piping a firm icing around the edge of a cookie and then filling it with a thinner icing to make a smooth, lightly glossy finish) and for enrobing cookies.

Whenever I'm called upon to make something gluten-free, I opt for classics that are naturally sans wheat flour—like Pavlovas (page 274), Macarons (page 44), Macaroons (page 42), and these flourless cocoa delights. These cookies are tender, delicately chewy, and incredibly chocolaty—if a brownie and a cookie had an affair, this would be their love-child. I like to add a sprinkling of flaky Maldon salt, because these are for grown-ups.

Makes 22 cookies

DIFFICULTY: Easy

MAKE AHEAD AND STORAGE: The cookies can be stored airtight for up to 1 week.

Flourless Cocoa Cookies

1. Preheat the oven to 350°F / 175°C with racks in the upper and lower thirds. Line two baking sheets with parchment paper.

2. In a medium bowl, lightly whisk the eggs.

3. Sift together the powdered sugar, cocoa powder, cinnamon, and salt. Add to the eggs, whisking until the mixture forms a smooth batter, about 1 minute. Add the vanilla and chocolate chunks and mix until fully incorporated; switch to a rubber spatula if necessary. The batter will be very thick and sticky.

4. Use a #30 / 2-tablespoon scoop to portion the batter onto the prepared baking sheets—stagger the cookies, leaving about 1½ inches between

them. Sprinkle a little Maldon salt on each cookie.

5. Bake the cookies, rotating the sheets from front to back and top to bottom at the halfway mark, until set around the edges and cracked on top, 10 to 12 minutes. The cookies may look slightly underbaked in the center—that's exactly what you want. Cool the cookies completely on the pans.

170 g / 3 large eggs

340 g / 3 cups powdered sugar

106 g / 1¼ cups unsweetened cocoa powder

1 g / ½ teaspoon ground cinnamon

1 g / ¼ teaspoon fine sea salt

7.5 g / 1½ teaspoons vanilla extract

142 g / 1 cup bittersweet chocolate chunks

Maldon salt, for sprinkling

❋ **WHY IT WORKS**
Like brownies, these cookies get the bulk of their structure from eggs rather than flour. A healthy dose of cocoa powder doesn't provide structure in the same way that flour does, but it helps the batter more closely resemble cookie dough and not spread too much in the oven.

★ **PRO TIP**
Err on the side of underbaking these cookies—they're loaded with chocolate, and just like melted chocolate, they set up as they cool. You can think of baked goods made with substantial amounts of chocolate as a little like steaks: You need to allow for carryover cooking.

These are the chocolate chip cookies I dreamed about as a kid—lightly crisp on the edges, chewy and melty in the center. I have been known to eat them for breakfast—because I was never allowed to eat them as a kid. Here's to adulthood!

Makes 40 cookies

DIFFICULTY: Easy

MAKE AHEAD AND STORAGE: The cookies can be stored airtight for up to 1 week, though they are at their chewiest for the first 2 days. The scooped cookie dough can be frozen on parchment-lined baking sheets until solid, at least 3 hours, and then stored airtight. Bake directly from the freezer, adding 5 to 7 minutes.

Chewy Chocolate Chip Cookies

1. Preheat the oven to 350°F / 175°C, with racks in the upper and lower thirds. Line two baking sheets with parchment paper.

2. In the bowl of a stand mixer fitted with the paddle attachment (or in a large bowl, using a hand mixer), cream the butter and both sugars on medium-low speed until light and fluffy, 4 to 5 minutes.

3. Add the eggs one at a time, mixing on medium speed until each one is fully incorporated. Add the vanilla and mix to combine. Scrape the bowl well.

4. In a medium bowl, whisk together the flour, baking powder, baking soda, and salt. Add to the butter mixture and mix on low speed just until incorporated, 1 to 2 minutes. Add the chocolate chunks and mix to combine. Scrape the bowl well.

5. Use a #30 / 2-tablespoon scoop to portion the cookie dough onto the prepared baking sheets—stagger the cookies, leaving at least 1½ inches between them to allow for spreading.

6. Bake the cookies, rotating the sheets from front to back and top to

227 g / 8 oz unsalted butter, at room temperature

99 g / ½ cup granulated sugar

213 g / 1 cup packed light brown sugar

113 g / 2 large eggs

7.5 g / 1½ teaspoons vanilla extract

331 g / 2¾ cups all-purpose flour

5 g / 1¼ teaspoons baking powder

4.5 g / ¾ teaspoon baking soda

3 g / ¾ teaspoon fine sea salt

283 g / 2 cups semisweet chocolate chunks (see Pro Tip)

bottom at the halfway mark, until golden brown at the edges, 13 to 15 minutes. Transfer to wire racks to cool.

❋ WHY IT WORKS

The key to the chewiness of these cookies is the high ratio of brown sugar, which contributes more moisture than granulated sugar. Also important: The right amounts of butter, for additional moisture as well as richness and tenderness, and flour—enough for structure, but not so much that the cookies become dry and crunchy.

★ PRO TIP

You can use regular chocolate chips if you like, but I prefer a jumble of variously sized chunks in my cookies. Plus, bigger bits stay melty longer.

Moderation be damned! These are the potato chips of the cookie world—meant to be eaten by the handful. They have a heavenly crunchiness and just-right combination of sweetness and chocolatyness. Crumble them into freshly churned ice cream or over a sundae for a whole new kind of delicious.

Makes 40 cookies

DIFFICULTY: Easy

MAKE AHEAD AND STORAGE: The cookies can be stored airtight for up to 1 week. The scooped cookie dough can be frozen on parchment-lined baking sheets until solid, at least 3 hours, and then transferred to an airtight container. Bake directly from the freezer, adding 5 to 7 minutes to the baking time.

Crispy Chocolate Chip Cookies

1. Preheat the oven to 400°F / 205°C, with racks in the upper and lower thirds. Line two baking sheets with parchment paper.

2. In the bowl of a stand mixer fitted with the paddle attachment (or in a large bowl, using a hand mixer), cream the butter, granulated sugar, and brown sugar on medium-low speed until light and fluffy, 4 to 5 minutes.

3. Add the eggs one at a time, mixing on medium speed until each one is fully incorporated before adding the next. Add the vanilla and mix to combine. Scrape the bowl well.

4. In a medium bowl, whisk together the flour, baking powder, baking soda, and salt. Add to the butter mixture and mix on low speed just until incorporated, 1 to 2 minutes. Add the chocolate chunks and mix to combine. Scrape the bowl well.

5. Use a #30 / 2-tablespoon scoop to scoop the dough onto the prepared baking sheets—stagger the cookies, leaving at least 1½ inches between them to allow for spreading.

6. Bake the cookies, rotating the sheets from front to back and top to bottom at the halfway mark, until golden brown at the edges, 10 to 12 minutes. Let cool on the baking sheet.

227 g / 8 oz unsalted butter, at room temperature

248 g / 1¼ cups granulated sugar

53 g / ¼ cup packed light brown sugar

113 g / 2 large eggs

7.5 g / 1½ teaspoons vanilla extract

271 g / 2¼ cups all-purpose flour

4 g / 1 teaspoon baking powder

3 g / ½ teaspoon baking soda

3 g / ¾ teaspoon fine sea salt

248 g / 2 cups semisweet chocolate chunks

❆ WHY IT WORKS

To get the ultimate crispy cookie, you first have to maximize surface area, and a higher ratio of granulated sugar helps with that by changing the ratio of liquefier (i.e., the sugar) to flour. This initiates more spread and eventually browns, creating a crisper cookie. A higher oven temperature also increases the spread and helps make the cookies crisper by drying them out a bit.

★ PRO TIP

To help the cookies stay flat and ensure maximum crispness, bang the baking sheets lightly on the racks when you rotate them.

These cookies will remedy whatever kind of bad day you have had. They're the cookies you eat when you forgot a homework assignment, when your coworkers call in sick on a snow day, or when you're exhausted after moving all your stuff to a new apartment. They're craveable as well as comforting. They also make a great blank canvas: You can add up to 1½ cups of inclusions—some of my favorites are chocolate chunks, dried fruit, coarsely chopped nuts, and/or candied ginger.

Makes 18 large cookies

DIFFICULTY: Easy

MAKE AHEAD AND STORAGE: The cookies can be stored in an airtight container for up to 1 week.

Chewy Oatmeal Cookies

1. Preheat the oven to 350°F/ 175°C, with racks in the upper and lower thirds. Line two baking sheets with parchment paper.

2. In the bowl of a stand mixer fitted with the paddle attachment (or in a large bowl, using a hand mixer), cream the butter and sugars on medium-low speed until light and fluffy, 4 to 5 minutes.

3. Add the eggs one at a time, mixing on medium speed until each one is fully incorporated. Add the vanilla and mix to combine. Scrape the bowl well.

4. In a medium bowl, whisk together the flour, baking soda, baking powder, salt, and cinnamon. Add to the butter mixture and mix on low speed just until incorporated, 1 to 2 minutes.

Add the oats and mix on low speed to combine, 30 seconds to 1 minute. Scrape the bowl well.

5. Use a #16 / ¼-cup scoop to portion the cookie dough onto the prepared baking sheets—stagger the cookies, leaving 1½ inches between them to allow for spreading.

6. Bake the cookies, rotating the sheets from front to back and top to bottom at the halfway mark, until evenly golden brown, 14 to 16 minutes. Transfer the cookies to wire racks to cool.

★ **PRO TIP**
To help keep the cookies flat, gently bang the baking sheets on the oven racks when you rotate them.

227 g / 8 oz unsalted butter, at room temperature

213 g / 1 cup packed brown sugar

66 g / ⅓ cup granulated sugar

113 g / 2 large eggs

5 g / 1 teaspoon vanilla extract

210 g / 1¾ cups all-purpose flour

6 g / 1 teaspoon baking soda

2 g / ½ teaspoon baking powder

4 g / 1 teaspoon fine sea salt

2 g / 1 teaspoon ground cinnamon

199 g / 2 cups old-fashioned oats

❋ **WHY IT WORKS**
This cookie's chewy perfection relies on a just-right combo of moisture, spread, and rise: Brown sugar contributes moisture, granulated sugar and butter promote spread, and baking powder and baking soda give a little lift.

I'm a sucker for a good sandwich cookie—because, really, it's an excuse to have two cookies! Plus, there's the tasty filling inside. These little lime cookies are a great combo: a tender, sandy sablé cookie paired with a light, creamy white chocolate–cream cheese filling. Normally sablé dough can be a little tricky to work with, but I've tweaked the recipe to make these more like easy icebox cookies. They're great with any citrus zest, but lime is my favorite.

Makes 20 sandwich cookies

DIFFICULTY: Easy

MAKE AHEAD AND STORAGE: The cookies can be stored in an airtight container for up to 3 days.

Lime Sablé Sandwiches

1. Have at hand a piece of parchment paper roughly the size of a baking sheet and a bench knife (dough scraper) or offset spatula.

2. **Make the sablés:** In the bowl of a stand mixer fitted with the paddle attachment (or in a large bowl, using a hand mixer), cream the butter, cream cheese, granulated sugar, and lime zest on medium-low speed until light and fluffy, 4 to 5 minutes.

3. Add the egg yolks one at a time, mixing on medium speed until each one is incorporated before adding the next. Add the vanilla and mix well. Scrape the bowl well. Add the flour and salt and mix just until incorporated, 1 to 2 minutes.

4. Turn the dough out onto the parchment and form it into a rough log along one long side of the paper (see page 24). Use the paper and bench knife to help form the dough into a rounded log shape—about 1½ inches in diameter. Unwrap the log and see how it looks—repeat the process if needed. Transfer the dough to the freezer and freeze for 20 to 30 minutes, until nicely chilled.

5. Preheat the oven to 350°F / 175°C, with racks in the upper and lower thirds. Line two baking sheets with parchment paper.

6. Use a sharp knife to cut the cookie dough into ¼-inch / 6-mm-thick slices (see Pro Tip). Transfer the slices to the prepared baking sheets—stagger them, leaving ½ inch between them (they won't spread much).

⟶

LIME SABLÉS

113 g / 4 oz / 8 tablespoons unsalted butter, at room temperature

28 g / 2 tablespoons cream cheese, at room temperature

112 g / ½ cup plus 1 tablespoon granulated sugar

4 g / 2 teaspoons grated lime zest

54 g / 2 large egg yolks

2.5 g / ½ teaspoon vanilla extract

241 g / 2 cups all-purpose flour

1 gram / ¼ teaspoon fine sea salt

FILLING

198 g / ¾ cup plus 2 tablespoons cream cheese, at room temperature

43 g / 1.5 oz / 3 tablespoons unsalted butter, at room temperature

28 g / ¼ cup powdered sugar

2 g / 1 teaspoon grated lime zest

113 g / 4 oz white chocolate, chopped, melted, and cooled slightly

7. Bake the cookies, rotating the sheets from front to back and top to bottom at the halfway mark, until the surface appears set and they are evenly golden brown on the bottom (they won't color on top, so use a spatula to flip a cookie over and check), 13 to 15 minutes. Cool the cookies completely on the baking sheets.

8. Make the filling: In the bowl of a stand mixer fitted with the paddle attachment (or in a large bowl, using a hand mixer), cream together the cream cheese, butter, powdered sugar, and lime zest on medium-low speed until light and fluffy, 4 to 5 minutes.

9. On low speed, beat the cooled melted white chocolate into the cream cheese mixture until well combined. Transfer the mixture to a disposable pastry bag and cut a ¼-inch opening at the tip.

10. Turn half the sablés over. Pipe about 1 tablespoon of filling onto the center of each overturned cookie. Place the remaining cookies on top of the filled cookies to create sandwiches, pressing down gently to help the filling flood to the edges.

❋ **WHY IT WORKS**

Sablés get their sandy texture (*sablé* being the French word for "sand") from a combination of properly creamed butter and sugar and egg yolks. Get it right, and they are tender and crumbly, but not so fragile that they fall apart.

★ **PRO TIP**

When it comes to sandwich cookies, it's ideal for the cookies to be the same size and "match up." The icebox cookie method ensures you'll end up with uniform shapes, but it's important to take care when cutting the cookies that they are the same thickness. I cut the first one carefully and place it on my cutting board to use as a visual guide. You can even hold it up against the log and make score marks where you want to cut. That takes care of the hard part—then all you have to do is slice!

If there's one cookie recipe to have in your back pocket, this is it. This shortbread is so easy and so good, and it only has five ingredients. You can make the dough into various shapes by rolling and cutting it, but I prefer classic (and super-simple) rounds cut into wedges. Feel free to add different flavorings to the dough, like grated lemon zest or cinnamon (2 g / 1 teaspoon), or dunk the finished cookies in 6 g / 2 tablespoons melted chocolate.

Makes 16 cookies

DIFFICULTY: Easy

MAKE AHEAD AND STORAGE: The cookies can be stored airtight for up to 1 week.

Brown Sugar Shortbread

1. Preheat the oven to 350°F/ 175°C. Line a baking sheet with parchment paper. If you want to make yourself a guide, use a 6-inch round cake pan or bowl to trace two circles onto the parchment, then turn the parchment over (so the ink won't touch the dough). Or just wing it.

2. In the bowl of a stand mixer fitted with the paddle attachment (or in a large bowl, using a hand mixer), cream the butter and brown sugar on medium-low speed until light and fluffy, 4 to 5 minutes.

3. Add the vanilla and mix on low speed to combine. Scrape the bowl well. Add the flour and salt and mix on low speed just until incorporated, 1 to 2 minutes.

4. Divide the dough into 2 equal portions (about 306 g each) and shape into disks. Place one disk on one half of the prepared baking sheet and use your hands to flatten the dough into a 6-inch round. Repeat with the second disk, leaving ½ inch of space between the rounds. If using, brush a coat of egg wash onto the surface of each round.

5. Use a sharp knife to score each round gently into 8 wedges—press down just enough to barely cut into the dough, to a depth of about ¼ inch. Bake until the edges of the shortbread are just beginning to turn golden and the surface appears set, 12 to 14 minutes.

227 g / 8 oz unsalted butter, at room temperature (see Pro Tip)

106 g / ½ cup packed light brown sugar

5 g / 1 teaspoon vanilla extract

301 g / 2½ cups all-purpose flour

3 g / ¾ teaspoon fine sea salt

Egg Wash (page 168; optional—see Why It Works)

6. Cool the shortbread completely on the baking sheet, then cut along the score lines into wedges.

✳ WHY IT WORKS

This recipe is all about ratios. The right amount of butter for flavor, flour for structure, and sugar for moisture and tenderness, as well as for sweetness, yield a perfectly crumbly cookie. I like to brush the shortbread with egg wash to give it a lightly golden, crackly look. If you leave it plain, the cookies will have a pale, smooth surface. Both versions are pretty and delicious, so do as you please!

★ PRO TIP

Now is the time to use the fancy butter if you can—with so few ingredients, the rich flavor of higher-fat Irish or European butter makes for truly extraordinary shortbread.

PRO TIP: HOW TO KEEP YOUR BROWN SUGAR SOFT

Until I discovered this trick, when I dug into the brown sugar jar, I often encountered a hard, unscoopable mass. But guess what: Throw one or two marshmallows into the container, and they'll prevent the sugar from drying out. And since marshmallows are shelf stable, you don't have to worry about replacing them.

I inherited a deep love of coconut from my mother, who agrees with me that macaroons are coconut's gift to the cookie world. And since they're so easy, why not add a little flavor twist? Peach jam lends sweetness, bright flavor, and a lovely golden hue. I like to use unsweetened coconut so I have control over the sweetness (and I like its texture better too), but if you can only find the sweetened stuff, just reduce the sugar by half and everything will still work A-OK.

Makes 20 cookies

DIFFICULTY: Easy

MAKE AHEAD AND STORAGE: These macaroons are best eaten within 1 day. Store loosely covered with plastic wrap at room temperature—if you put them in an airtight container, the crispy exteriors will soften.

Peachy Coconut Macaroons

1. Preheat the oven to 350°F / 175°C, with a rack in the upper third. Line two baking sheets with parchment paper.

2. In a large bowl, whisk the egg whites and sugar until well combined and lightly frothy. Add the vanilla and salt and whisk well to combine. Fold in the coconut until it's well coated. Fold in the peach jam until well incorporated.

3. Use a #16 / ¼-cup scoop or two spoons to portion the dough onto the prepared baking sheets. The cookies won't spread, but leave about ½ inch between them so the oven air can circulate and brown the surfaces evenly.

4. Bake the macaroons one sheet at a time (if baked too close to the bottom of the oven, their undersides will overbrown), rotating the sheet from front to back at the halfway mark, until golden around the edges, 20 to 22 minutes. Cool on the baking sheet, then peel the parchment away from the baked cookies.

❋ **WHY IT WORKS**
The protein in egg whites coagulates when heated in the oven, which allows the sweet coconut mixture to set into a delightful combo of crisp on the outside, soft and chewy on the inside. That protein is also responsible for the cookie's structure, holding it together without any flour.

119 g / 4 large egg whites

99 g / ½ cup granulated sugar

2.5 g / ½ teaspoon vanilla extract

1 g / ¼ teaspoon fine sea salt

255 g / 3 cups unsweetened shredded coconut (see headnote)

170 g / ½ cup peach jam or preserves

Variation

When I first started pastry school, the in-house bakery sold huge coconut macaroons that were the size of softballs, and I just loved them. If you find yourself in a "big macaroon" mood, this recipe makes 10 if you portion them out using a #16 / ¼-cup scoop. Increase the baking time to 24 to 26 minutes.

Nothing is prettier, more decadent, or more triumphant than French macarons you've made yourself. You can do it—I swear! Macarons require a fair amount of time and care, but they are definitely not unattainable. It is important to fold the batter just enough, so you don't deflate the whites too much.

Note that the piped macarons need to rest for 1½ to 2 hours before baking, and the finished macarons are best after being refrigerated overnight.

Makes 24 sandwich cookies

DIFFICULTY: Hard

MAKE AHEAD AND STORAGE: Ideally, macarons should be made at least 1 day ahead; they can be refrigerated for up to 4 days.

Double Chocolate Macarons

1. Line two baking sheets with parchment paper. You can pipe the macarons free-form, but it's easier if you give yourself a guide; see Pro Tip. Fit a disposable pastry bag with a #803 plain tip (see page 93).

2. Make the shells: Sift the almond flour through a fine strainer into a large bowl; discard any large pieces that remain behind in the strainer. Sift the powdered sugar, cocoa powder, and salt into the bowl.

3. In the bowl of a stand mixer fitted with the whisk attachment (or in a large bowl, using a hand mixer), whip the egg whites on medium speed until lightly foamy. Raise the mixer speed

to high and gradually add the granulated sugar in a thin stream, then continue whipping until the meringue holds medium peaks, 5 to 7 minutes. Add the vanilla and mix to combine, 30 seconds.

4. Gently fold the almond mixture into the meringue, using as few folds as possible to prevent the batter from deflating. The goal is to end up with a batter that no longer holds peaks but still maintains its shape, so it forms and holds nicely domed mounds when piped.

5. Gently transfer half the batter to the pastry bag (it's easier to pipe when the bag isn't totally full). Pipe

SHELLS

142 g / 1⅓ cups fine almond flour (such as Bob's Red Mill)

198 g / 1¾ cups powdered sugar

28 g / ⅓ cup unsweetened cocoa powder (dark, if you can get it)

2 g / ½ teaspoon fine sea salt

119 g / 4 large egg whites

66 g / ⅓ cup granulated sugar

2.5 g / ½ teaspoon vanilla extract

FILLING

113 g / 4 oz bittersweet chocolate, chopped

120 g / ½ cup heavy cream

28 g / 1 oz / 2 tablespoons unsalted butter, at room temperature

the batter into 24 mounds spaced about 1 inch apart on one of the prepared baking sheets (see Pro Tip). You're aiming for mounds about 1½ inches wide—keep in mind that the batter will spread slightly once you lift the bag away, so ease off the pressure a few moments before reaching the full width. Repeat with the remaining batter on the second sheet.

6. Let the piped macarons stand at room temperature for 1½ to 2 hours, until a skin forms on the surface and the macarons are no longer sticky to the touch. The wait is really worth it—this rest helps your macarons form beautiful "feet"! Toward the end of the resting time, preheat the oven to 300°F / 150°C, with a rack in the middle of the oven. (I bake these in batches—one baking sheet at a time—because they are so finicky.)

7. Bake the macarons undisturbed (don't turn the baking sheet) until they have risen, forming a foot at the base, and the surface of the cookies is dry and set, 17 to 20 minutes. Repeat with the remaining sheet of macarons. Cool the macarons completely on the baking sheets.

8. Meanwhile, make the filling: Place the chocolate in a medium heatproof bowl. In a small saucepan, bring the cream to a simmer over medium heat. Pour the hot cream over the chocolate and let stand for 15 to 20 seconds.

9. Add the butter to the chocolate mixture and use a silicone spatula to cut vertically down into the center of the bowl, and then, beginning with a small circular motion, stir the ganache, gradually widening the circles until it is smooth. Let cool slightly, to a pipeable consistency, then transfer the ganache to a disposable pastry bag and cut a small opening in the tip.

10. Gently release the macarons from the parchment, using a small offset spatula or your fingers, and turn half of them over. Pipe about 10 g / 2 teaspoons of the ganache onto the center of each overturned macaron: Hold the pastry bag straight down over the center of each cookie and let the ganache run out until it nearly reaches the edges. Top the ganache-filled cookies with the remaining macarons, pressing down gently to "flood" the filling nearly to the edges.

11. Refrigerate the macarons for at least 2 hours, preferably overnight, before serving. Serve straight from the refrigerator, unless you prefer your macarons a bit softer—in which case, let them stand at room temperature for 10 to 15 minutes before serving.

❋ **WHY IT WORKS**

Properly whipped egg whites are essential to macaron success. They leaven the cookies, creating the signature "foot," the little frill around the bottom edge, in the oven. They also provide most of the structural integrity (with help from the almond flour—in lieu of regular flour—in binding the batter). And they contribute that gorgeous sheen and result in a totally smooth surface.

★ **PRO TIP**

To give yourself a guide for piping the batter onto the parchment, use a thick marker and a 1½-inch round cutter to trace 24 circles onto each sheet of parchment—stagger the circles, leaving 1 inch between them; the batter won't spread much. Then turn the parchment over so the ink doesn't touch the batter.

Variations

Macaron S'mores: Before sandwiching the macarons, top the ganache on each one with a toasted marshmallow (use a kitchen torch to toast the marshmallows one at a time, or toast them over a gas flame).

Vanilla Macarons: Omit the cocoa powder and add an additional 28 g / ¼ cup powdered sugar. These macarons can be tinted any color—add a few drops of food coloring to the meringue at the end of step 3. They can be filled with any flavor of buttercream, such as American Buttercream (page 134) or Lemon Curd Buttercream (page 158), jam, Fruit Curd (page 339), Salted Caramel Sauce (page 54), or a combo.

If you want to make different flavors or colors, use the vanilla variation as a base.

Peanut butter and jelly is still one of my favorite combos, and I bake it into cakes, pies, or pastries regularly. This whoopie pie recipe is my ode to a PB & J: The bread is cake and the peanut butter is blended into a marshmallow crème. The jam hidden inside is the perfect surprise when you bite into it!

Makes 16 whoopie pies

DIFFICULTY: Medium

MAKE AHEAD AND STORAGE: Whoopie pies are best within 2 days, but they will keep up to 4 days. Store in a single layer airtight at room temperature.

PB & J Whoopie Pies

1. Preheat the oven to 350°F / 175°C, with racks in the upper and lower thirds. Line two baking sheets with parchment paper.

2. Make the cakes: In the bowl of a stand mixer fitted with the paddle attachment (or in a large bowl, using a hand mixer), cream the butter, brown sugar, and granulated sugar on medium-low speed until light and fluffy, 4 to 5 minutes.

3. Add the egg and mix until well incorporated, 1 to 2 minutes. Scrape the bowl well. Beat in the vanilla, about 30 seconds.

4. In a medium bowl, whisk together the flours, baking powder, baking soda, and salt. Add one third of the flour mixture to the wet ingredients, mixing on low speed just until incorporated, about 1 minute. Add 120 g / ½ cup of the buttermilk and mix on low speed until fully incorporated, about 1 minute. Repeat, alternating between the flour mixture and the remaining buttermilk, until the ingredients are uniformly incorporated and the batter is smooth.

5. Use a #30 / 2-tablespoon scoop to portion the batter onto prepared baking sheets—stagger the cakes about 2 inches apart. Bake the cakes, rotating the sheets from front to back and top to bottom at the halfway mark, until lightly golden at the edges and the centers spring back lightly when touched, 12 to 15 minutes. Cool the cakes completely on the baking sheets.

6. Make the marshmallow crème: If you have a stand mixer with two bowls to go with it, fit the mixer with the whisk attachment, combine the butter, peanut butter, vanilla, and salt in one of the bowls, and mix on

CAKES

113 g / 4 oz / 8 tablespoons unsalted butter, at room temperature

213 g / 1 cup packed light brown sugar

99 g / ½ cup granulated sugar

57 g / 1 large egg

5 g / 1 teaspoon vanilla extract

241 g / 2 cups all-purpose flour

96 g / 1 cup whole wheat pastry flour

6 g / 2½ teaspoons baking powder

4.5 g / ¾ teaspoon baking soda

3 g / ¾ teaspoon fine sea salt

240 g / 1 cup buttermilk

⟶

medium speed until smooth and well combined; remove the bowl from the mixer stand. Or use a hand mixer or a spatula or wooden spoon to blend the mixture in a large bowl. Set aside.

7. In a small saucepan, combine the granulated sugar, corn syrup, and water and bring to a boil over medium heat. Attach a candy thermometer to the side of the pan. As the mixture heats, you can stir to help the sugar dissolve, but stop stirring as soon as it comes to a boil. Continue cooking the sugar syrup, without stirring, until the thermometer reads 240°F / 115°C.

8. While the syrup cooks, whip the egg whites on low speed in the bowl of a stand mixer fitted with the whisk attachment (or in a large bowl, using a hand mixer) until lightly foamy, 1 to 2 minutes.

9. When the syrup reaches 235°F / 113°C, raise the mixer speed to high—the idea is to have the whites at soft peaks when it's time to add the syrup. Cook the syrup until it reaches 240°F / 115°C.

10. With the mixer running, gradually add the syrup to the egg whites in a slow stream, then continue whipping until the meringue is thick and glossy and holds medium peaks, 5 to 7 minutes.

11. Temper (lighten) the peanut butter mixture by adding about one quarter of the meringue to it and folding thoroughly to combine (see page 147 for more about tempering). Then add the remaining meringue in three batches, folding very gently just until evenly incorporated.

12. Assemble the whoopie pies: Gently transfer the crème to a disposable pastry bag fitted with a large plain tip (such as #803; see page 93), or just snip a ½-inch opening at the tip of the bag after filling it. Put the jam in another pastry bag and snip a ¼-inch opening at the tip (you can also use a #60 / 1-tablespoon scoop or a tablespoon measure for the jam).

13. The cakes should all be roughly the same shape/size, but if you like, you can go through and pair each one up with its best match. Turn half of the cakes over. Pipe a thick ring of peanut butter crème around the edge of each overturned cake, about ¼ inch from the edge. Pipe/scoop about 8.5 g / 1 heaping tablespoon of jam into the center of each peanut butter ring, then top with the plain cakes. Press gently to "flood" the crème out to the edges.

PEANUT BUTTER
MARSHMALLOW CRÈME

227 g / 8 oz unsalted butter, at room temperature

102 g / 1 cup smooth peanut butter

7.5 g / 1½ teaspoons vanilla extract

2 g / ½ teaspoon fine sea salt

99 g / ½ cup granulated sugar

78 g / ¼ cup light corn syrup

45 g / 3 tablespoons water

170 g / 3 large egg whites

255 g / ¾ cup raspberry jam

❄ WHY IT WORKS

Despite their adorable name, whoopie pies are actually little cakes. The right amount of baking powder helps the batter rise in the oven before it spreads too much, resulting in soft cookie-like cakes. A light, airy filling (hello, marshmallow crème) is the perfect complement, providing moisture but still substantial enough to bite through.

★ PRO TIP

Surrounding a runny filling (like jam, jelly, or curd) with a piped ring of frosting helps contain it, so there's no worry that the filling will spill out the sides.

These little-known Italian cookies are the kind of hidden-gem recipe I'd like to spend my life discovering in all corners of the world. They have a wonderfully tender dough with a creamy, lemon-scented filling hiding inside. The method looks more complicated than it really is. After you roll out the dough, you cut out circles with two different cutters—a slightly smaller one for the bases and a larger one for the tops that cover the little mounds of custard.

Makes 24 cookies

DIFFICULTY: Hard

MAKE AHEAD AND STORAGE: Both the dough and the custard can be made up to 3 days ahead. Although the cookies are best the day they are made—and are amazing while still slightly warm—they can be stored airtight at room temperature for up to 3 days.

Genovesi *(Italian Custard Cookies)*

1. **Make the custard:** In a medium saucepan, combine the milk, 50 g / ¼ cup of the granulated sugar, and the lemon zest. Scrape the seeds from the vanilla bean and add the seeds and pod to the pan. Bring the milk to a simmer over medium heat.

2. Meanwhile, combine the remaining 49 g / ¼ cup granulated sugar and the cornstarch in a heatproof bowl and whisk to blend. Add the egg yolks and mix well to combine.

3. As soon as the milk begins to bubble, pour it in a slow, steady stream into the egg yolk mixture, whisking constantly. Return the custard mixture to the pan and cook over low heat, whisking constantly, until it comes to a first boil (a single large bubble comes up to the surface in the center), 3 to 5 minutes. The custard will be thick, and it will continue to thicken as it cools.

4. Transfer the custard to a heatproof bowl and cover with plastic wrap, pressing the wrap against the surface of the custard (this will prevent a skin from forming). Refrigerate until thoroughly chilled, at least 1 hour, or up to overnight.

5. **Make the dough:** In a large bowl, whisk together the semolina flour, all-purpose flour, granulated sugar, and salt. Add the butter cubes and toss to coat, then use a pastry blender or two knives to cut the butter into the flour until it is well incorporated; some of the butter will combine with

CUSTARD FILLING

454 g / 2 cups whole milk

99 g / ½ cup granulated sugar

12 g / 2 tablespoons grated lemon zest

½ vanilla bean, split lengthwise

28 g / ¼ cup cornstarch

54 g / 2 large egg yolks

COOKIE DOUGH

244 g / 1½ cups semolina flour

181 g / 1½ cups all-purpose flour

198 g / 1 cup granulated sugar

2 g / ½ teaspoon fine sea salt

170 g / 6 oz / 12 tablespoons cold unsalted butter, cubed

54 g / 2 large egg yolks

60 g / ¼ cup heavy cream

6 g / 1 tablespoon grated lemon zest

Powdered sugar, for dusting

the flour, and a few pieces should be roughly the size of peas, but no larger.

6. In a small bowl, whisk together the eggs, cream, and lemon zest. Make a well in the center of the flour mixture, pour in the egg mixture, and use a silicone spatula or your hands to mix until a smooth dough forms. The dough shouldn't be sticky.

7. Turn the dough out and divide it into 2 equal pieces. Form each into a disk about ½ inch thick, wrap tightly in plastic wrap, and refrigerate for at least 3 hours or up to overnight. (The colder the dough is, the easier it is to work with, so don't skimp on chill time.)

8. Preheat the oven to 350°F / 175°C, with racks in the upper and lower thirds. Line two baking sheets with parchment paper.

9. On a lightly floured surface, roll one disk of dough out to ¼ inch / 6 mm thick. Use a 3¼-inch round cutter to cut out 12 cookie bases. Transfer 6 of the bases to each of the prepared baking sheets—stagger them, leaving about ½ inch between them.

10. Flour the work surface again. Roll out the second disk of dough to ¼ inch / 6 mm thick. Use a 3½-inch round cutter to cut out 12 cookie tops. Leave the cookie tops on the work surface while you pipe the filling onto the bases.

11. Remove the vanilla pod from the chilled custard and discard it or use for Vanilla Sugar (page 97). Transfer the custard to a disposable pastry bag and cut a ½-inch opening in the tip. Pipe 2 tablespoons of the filling onto each base in a rounded mound, leaving about a ⅛-inch border around the edges. Lightly brush the edges of each base with water. Top each base with one of the larger dough rounds, gently pressing the edges together to seal, carefully working around the filling (as if you were making ravioli) and trying to remove any air pockets without squeezing out any of the custard.

12. Use a 3¼-inch scalloped or plain round cutter to cut away the excess dough and help seal the cookie edges. Discard the excess dough.

13. Bake the cookies, rotating the sheets from front to back and top to bottom at the halfway mark, until they are lightly brown at the edges, 17 to 20 minutes. Let the cookies cool on the baking sheets for 15 to 20 minutes. When they are nearly at room temperature but still warm, dust the tops with enough powdered sugar to coat the surface.

✳ **WHY IT WORKS**
Semolina flour adds a subtle texture to the dough while keeping it tender. If the cookies are properly sealed, the custard stays trapped inside, where it softens just a touch, but not enough to ooze or make a mess when you bite into a cookie.

★ **PRO TIPS**
These cookies are a bit of a project, but both the components can be made ahead. I make the custard and dough the day before I plan to make the cookies, and then the shaping and baking doesn't seem like such a to-do.

When you make the custard, you want to bring it to a boil, but keep the heat low to reduce the chance of scorching and clumps while thickening it properly.

While I do enjoy a plain meringue cookie, I like them better swirled with caramel. I love how that touch of extra richness and hint of bitterness from the caramel complements the sweetness of the meringue. This is great example of putting a twist on a recipe—take a base recipe, then add other flavors and textures.

The sauce makes more than you will need for this recipe, which is intentional—it's great to have on hand. See Pro Tip for ideas for the extra sauce.

Makes 24 cookies (made with a #16 / ¼-cup scoop)

DIFFICULTY: Medium

MAKE AHEAD AND STORAGE: The caramel sauce can be refrigerated, covered, for up to 2 weeks. The cookies are best eaten the same day, but they can be stored, uncovered, at room temperature for up to 2 days if the weather is dry (humid weather will make them deteriorate).

Salted Caramel–Swirled Meringues

1. Preheat the oven to 325°F / 162°C. Line two baking sheets with parchment paper.

2. In the bowl of a stand mixer fitted with the whisk attachment (or in a large bowl, using a hand mixer), whip the egg whites and cream of tartar on medium speed until lightly foamy. Raise the mixer speed to high and add the sugar in a slow, steady stream. Continue whipping until the meringue holds medium peaks, 5 to 7 minutes. Add the vanilla and salt and mix to combine, about 1 minute.

3. Gently scoop the meringue onto the prepared baking sheets using a #16 / ¼-cup scoop or two spoons to create ¼-cup dollops, leaving 1½ inches between each. Use a small offset spatula to slightly flatten the mounds, keeping them circular.

4. Drizzle 2 teaspoons of the caramel sauce over each meringue (you can transfer the caramel to a disposable pastry bag to do this, or just use a spoon), then use the tip of a paring knife to gently swirl them together, keeping the swirl to one or two wide strokes (the more you swirl, the more likely the meringues will deflate).

119 g / 4 large egg whites

1 g / ¼ teaspoon cream of tartar

198 g / 1 cup granulated sugar

2.5 g / ½ teaspoon vanilla extract

1 g / ¼ teaspoon fine sea salt

266 g / 1 cup Salted Caramel Sauce (recipe follows), at room temperature

⟶

5. Transfer the meringues to the oven, lower the oven temperature to 250°F / 121°C, and bake until the meringues are very dry to the touch (the caramel will melt slightly into the cookies). How long this takes will depend on how dry the weather is—anywhere from 45 to 90 minutes. When the meringues are dry, turn off the oven and leave the sheets in the oven until the cookies and sheets cool completely.

❋ **WHY IT WORKS**

Fat will prevent meringue from achieving and maintaining its full volume, so additions like caramel are normally out of the question. But if you introduce the caramel at the very end, just before baking, everything is copacetic. A low oven temperature is key to obtaining meringue's dry-crisp texture; as a bonus, it also ensures that the caramel won't melt completely and ooze out of the cookies.

★ **PRO TIP**

The caramel sauce is very thick, which makes it a great addition for baking: Swirl it into things like these cookies, use it to flavor frostings and custards, or spread it on top of brownies or between layer cakes. To loosen the sauce to use it for glazing cakes or pastries or drizzling over ice cream, thin it with an additional 4 oz / ½ cup heavy cream.

Salted Caramel Sauce

1. Combine the sugar, corn syrup, and water in a medium saucepan. If using a vanilla bean, scrape the seeds and add the seeds and pod to the pan. Bring to a boil over medium-high heat. You can stir the mixture before it boils to help dissolve the sugar, but stop stirring the moment it starts. Boil the syrup until it's a medium amber color. Once it starts to color, tilt the pan occasionally—it's easier to see the true color of the caramel when you're looking at less of it (or it may seem darker than it really is). As soon as it's close to medium amber, turn off the heat—the caramel will retain some heat, so it's good to allow for carryover cooking.

2. Add the butter to the caramel and stir gently to combine. Stir in the cream (be careful—the caramel may bubble up and steam a lot! Just keep stirring and it will die down). The sauce should be smooth and creamy. If it seizes up and you see chunks of caramel that haven't fully dissolved in the sauce, return the pan to low heat and heat, stirring occasionally, until the sauce is smooth. Stir in the salt (and vanilla, if using). Remove from the heat and let cool to room temperature.

298 g / 1½ cups granulated sugar

81 g / ¼ cup corn syrup

61 g / ¼ cup water

½ vanilla bean, split lengthwise, or 5 g / 1 teaspoon vanilla extract

113 g / 4 oz unsalted butter, cut into cubes, at room temperature

121 g / ½ cup heavy cream

3 g / ¾ teaspoon fine sea salt

Makes 30 to 35 small cookies

DIFFICULTY: Easy

MAKE AHEAD AND STORAGE: The pizzelle, dipped or undipped, can be stored airtight at room temperature for up to 3 days. Any longer, and they tend to lose their crispness, especially in humid weather. You may be tempted to refrigerate them if you coat them with chocolate, but the fridge will rob the cookies of their crispness.

Pizzelle are wonderful, crisp cookies that are incredibly easy to make, but their embossed patterns make them look impressive. The downside: You need a special piece of equipment to create them—a pizzelle iron (see Resources, page 369). These are intensely chocolaty, and my favorite way to serve them is dipped in melted chocolate. You can also use them to make sandwich cookies, cake decorations, and even killer ice cream cones (see Pro Tips).

Chocolate Pizzelle

1. Sift together the flour, cocoa powder, baking powder, and salt into a medium bowl.

2. In another medium bowl, whisk the eggs, sugar, melted butter, and vanilla well to combine. Add to the flour mixture, whisking well to combine. The batter should be thick, but smooth.

3. Preheat a pizzelle iron until hot (sprinkle a little water on it, and if it sizzles, it's ready). Lightly coat the surface with nonstick spray or vegetable oil. Use a large spoon or small ladle to place a mound of batter in the center of each mold, then close the iron and cook until steam comes out of it and the cookies are baked through, 45 seconds to 1 minute. Use tongs to remove the cookies from the iron to a cooling rack, and repeat with the remaining batter. Let cool completely.

4. If dipping the pizzelle in chocolate, line your work surface with parchment or wax paper. Transfer the melted chocolate to a wide shallow dish. With your hands, lay the cookies, one or two at a time, flat in the chocolate so that the bottom side gets coated and the top remains bare. Then use a small pair of tongs to lift the cookies out of the chocolate, shake off the excess, and lay undipped side down on the parchment. Let the chocolate set until firm and shiny, at least 5 minutes.

120 g / 1 cup all-purpose flour

43 g / ½ cup unsweetened cocoa powder (dark, if you can get it)

4 g / 1 teaspoon baking powder

2 g / ½ teaspoon salt

170 g / 3 large eggs

198 g / 1 cup granulated sugar

113 g / 4 oz / 8 tablespoons unsalted butter, melted

5 g / 1 teaspoon vanilla extract

284 g / 10 oz bittersweet chocolate (up to 70% cacao), chopped and melted, for dipping (optional)

❉ WHY IT WORKS

This recipe works much in the same way recipes for waffles do—the batter is thin and contains a high ratio of fat. That, combined with direct high heat from both sides, ensures even browning and a crisp texture.

★ PRO TIPS

Pizzelle are malleable when warm, which means they can be formed into shapes like cones, bowls, or even sweet taco shells. The tricky part is handling them when they are still hot; wearing disposable gloves helps if your hands are sensitive. You can buy molds for shaping pizzelle or just use whatever you've got on hand. The top of a wine bottle or the end of a tapered rolling pin makes a good cone guide. You can also drape warm pizzelle over upturned small bowls or press them into the cavities of muffin pans. Or just use your fingers and hold each cookie in place until it cools.

If you want to get really snazzy, ladle melted chocolate into a pizzelle cone/bowl, then invert to pour the excess chocolate back into the bowl of chocolate. Let set before filling with custard or ice cream.

Variation

Vanilla Pizzelle: Replace the cocoa powder with an additional 60 g / ½ cup all-purpose flour and add the seeds from ½ vanilla bean along with the vanilla extract.

One of my best buds only eats waffles when she's very happy. ("We need waffles—I got the job!" or, "It's so nice out today, we should get waffles.") So I created this recipe for her—and for anyone else looking for a little happy in their day; it's super-fast and easy. If you want to get fancy, you can make a few different fruit glazes to tint your cookies with different colors and flavors.

Makes 55 small cookies

DIFFICULTY: Easy

MAKE AHEAD AND STORAGE: The glazed cookies will keep airtight for up to 3 days. The glaze keeps them from going stale at first, but it begins to break down after a few days.

Glazed Waffle Cookies

1. Preheat your waffle iron according to the manufacturer's instructions. Lightly grease the iron with nonstick spray. Keep the spray handy and occasionally reapply it between batches.

2. **Meanwhile, make the cookie batter:** In a medium bowl, whisk together the butter and both sugars. Add the eggs one at a time, beating well to incorporate each one. Beat in the vanilla.

3. In another medium bowl, whisk together the flour, baking soda, and salt. Gently fold into the butter mixture, mixing just until fully incorporated.

4. Working in batches, use a #60 / 1-tablespoon scoop or spoon to place 1-tablespoon mounds of batter onto the center of the preheated waffle iron, then close the iron. Bake the cookies until golden on both sides and cooked through, 1 to 2 minutes. Remove the cookies from the iron and transfer to a wire rack to cool. Repeat with the remaining batter. Cool completely.

5. **Make the glaze:** Combine the berries, sugar, lemon zest, and lemon juice in a medium saucepan; bring the mixture to a simmer and cook over medium heat until the berries break down, 10 to 12 minutes. Use a potato masher or the back of a wooden spoon to crush the berries. When the berries are very soft and have released their juices, strain the juices through a strainer set over a medium bowl and let cool to room temperature.

COOKIES

113 g / 4 oz / 8 tablespoons unsalted butter, melted

99 g / ½ cup granulated sugar

53 g / ¼ cup packed light brown sugar

113 g / 2 large eggs

5 g / 1 teaspoon vanilla extract

120 g / 1 cup all-purpose flour

3 g / ½ teaspoon baking soda

2 g / ½ teaspoon fine sea salt

GLAZE

120 g / ¾ cup fresh berries (blueberries, raspberries, or blackberries, or a combination)

25 g / 2 tablespoons granulated sugar

Grated zest and juice of 1 lemon

228 g / 2 cups powdered sugar

6. Add the powdered sugar to the juice and whisk until a smooth glaze forms.

7. One at a time, dunk the cooled cookies into the glaze, shake off the excess glaze (glaze that pools in the nooks and crannies won't set very well), and invert the cookies onto a wire rack—the glaze will set in 10 to 15 minutes.

❋ **WHY IT WORKS**

A waffle iron applies direct, even high heat to the batter. The result is a cookie with all the same pros as great waffles—crisp on the outside and slightly soft inside—but just cookie-er.

★ **PRO TIP**

The glaze recipe makes more than you need, but it's great to have on hand— lovely on scones, muffins, doughnuts, cupcakes, or sugar cookies. Store extra glaze in an airtight container in the refrigerator for up to 2 weeks. Bring to room temperature and stir before using again. If it dries out, thin it with water, milk, or cream.

I love a fresh, buttery madeleine. While it is true that the best madeleines are found in the pâtisseries of Paris, these are an excellent homemade version if you find yourself elsewhere in the world. Many recipes call for chilling the batter, but you can skip that step if you are pressed for time. If you do chill it, though, the madeleines rise a little higher and bake up a little lighter. I add rosemary and lemon zest to mine because I love the taste and the way they make the cookies smell (especially during baking).

Makes 32 madeleines

DIFFICULTY: Easy

MAKE AHEAD AND STORAGE: Madeleines are best served straight out of the oven, and they are still good when eaten within 1 day of baking. You can store them airtight for up to 3 days, but they won't be quite the same.

Lemon–Rosemary Madeleines

1. Preheat the oven to 375°F / 190°C, with a rack in the upper third. Grease and flour two 16-cavity madeleine pans (see Pro Tip).

2. In the bowl of a stand mixer fitted with the whisk attachment (or in a large bowl, using a hand mixer), whisk the eggs and sugar on low speed until combined and lightly frothy, 1 to 2 minutes. Add the extracts and lemon zest and whisk well to combine, about 30 seconds.

3. Add the flour, baking powder, and salt and mix just until incorporated, 1 to 2 minutes. With the mixer on low, add the butter in a slow, steady stream, mixing until it is fully incorporated, 1 to 2 minutes. Scrape the bowl well, then fold in the rosemary. (You can chill the batter, covered with plastic wrap, at this point. One hour is good. Overnight works too— madeleines for breakfast!)

4. Using a #30 / 2-tablespoon scoop or spoon, fill the prepared molds with the batter. Don't spread the batter around at all—it will level out on its own as it bakes.

5. Bake until the madeleines are puffed with a small mound in the center and the edges are lightly golden, 9 to 10 minutes. Do not overbake, or the cookies will be dry. Cool the madeleines in the pans for 5 minutes, then unmold.

170 g / 3 large eggs

198 g / 1 cup granulated sugar

5 g / 1 teaspoon vanilla extract

1 g / ¼ teaspoon almond extract

2 g / 1 teaspoon grated lemon zest

181 g / 1½ cups all-purpose flour

2 g / ½ teaspoon baking powder

2 g / ½ teaspoon fine sea salt

142 g / 5 oz / 10 tablespoons unsalted butter, melted

2 g / 2 teaspoons chopped fresh rosemary

Powdered sugar, for dusting

6. Dust the warm madeleines with powdered sugar. The quicker you eat them, the better.

❄ **WHY IT WORKS**

The mold is the key to madeleines' lovely shell shape. A relatively high ratio of butter, sugar, and eggs to flour means the batter will rise, resulting in a cookie that's more cakelike and oh-so-pretty.

★ **PRO TIP**

The cavities of my madeleine pans are 3¼ by 1½ inches. If the wells in your pans are larger, you may need to use slightly more batter for each cake and increase the baking time—or the opposite if your pans are smaller.

Layering flavors and textures makes for a very special cookie. And these "'shmallow" grahams are exactly that—they are gorgeous to behold, and, when you bite into one, the fluffy white marshmallow is beautifully flecked with vanilla beans. I also love that they look beautiful whether they are carefully done or a little messy.

Makes about 55 cookies

DIFFICULTY: Hard

MAKE AHEAD AND STORAGE: The cookies can be refrigerated in a single layer airtight for up to 4 days, but they are really best within 1 to 2 days, as the glaze can bloom or weep when stored longer.

Chocolate-Glazed 'Shmallow Grahams

1. Make the chocolate glaze: Combine the chopped chocolate and coconut oil in a medium heatproof bowl and place over a medium saucepan of barely simmering water (with the bowl not touching the water). Heat, stirring occasionally, until the mixture is fully melted and combined. Remove from the heat and let cool to room temperature.

2. Preheat the oven to 325°F / 162°C, with racks in the upper and lower thirds. Line three baking sheets with parchment paper.

3. Make the graham crackers: Sift the graham flour, all-purpose flour, cocoa powder, powdered sugar, and baking powder into a food processor. Pulse a few times to combine. Add the butter and pulse until the mixture resembles coarse meal, 1 to 2 minutes. Add the milk 1 tablespoon at a time, pulsing just until the dough forms a ball around the blade. The dough should be smooth and only lightly sticky.

4. Turn the dough out and divide in half (about 275 g each). Form each piece into a rectangle about 1 inch thick.

5. Flour a work surface well and flour the dough on both sides. Roll one rectangle of the dough out to a ¼-inch thickness; it is prone to sticking, so be sure to rotate it every few rolls and keep the surface floured. Using a 2-inch round cutter, cut the dough into circles. Use a small offset spatula to transfer the circles to one

CHOCOLATE GLAZE

227 g / 8 oz semisweet chocolate, chopped

100 g / ½ cup coconut oil

CHOCOLATE GRAHAM CRACKERS

149 g / 1 cup graham flour

60 g / ½ cup all-purpose flour

28 g / ⅓ cup unsweetened cocoa powder

113 g / 1 cup powdered sugar

4 g / 1 teaspoon baking powder

113 g / 4 oz / 8 tablespoons cold unsalted butter, cut into cubes

28 g / 2 tablespoons whole milk

⟶

of the prepared baking sheets— stagger the crackers, leaving about ½ inch between them. Reserve the dough scraps. Roll and cut the other rectangle of dough. Then gather the scraps together, roll the dough once more, and cut out more circles as needed to reach a total of about 55. Prick the surface of each cracker a few times with a fork.

6. Bake the crackers, rotating the sheets from front to back and top to bottom at the halfway mark, until they are dry on the surface and appear set, 14 to 16 minutes. Transfer the baking sheets to wire racks and let the graham crackers cool completely. Repeat with the remaining baking sheet.

7. Make the marshmallow crème: Measure 81 g / ⅓ cup of the water into a small heatproof bowl. Sprinkle the gelatin over the water and let bloom (soften) for about 5 minutes.

8. Lightly coat a silicone spatula with nonstick spray. Fit a disposable pastry bag with a #803 plain tip (you can just cut a ½-inch opening in the tip of the bag, but using the tip is a little easier and produces sexier curves). Lightly coat the inside of the bag and tip as best you can with nonstick spray.

9. Combine the sugar, corn syrup, and the remaining 80 g / ⅓ cup water in a medium saucepan. Scrape the seeds from the vanilla bean and add the seeds and pod to the pan. Bring the mixture to a boil over medium-high heat; you can stir the mixture before it comes to a boil to help dissolve the sugar, but stop stirring the moment it starts to boil. Attach a candy thermometer to the side of the pan (or have an instant-read thermometer ready). Continue to boil until the sugar syrup reaches 240°F / 115°C on the thermometer.

10. Meanwhile, in the bowl of a stand mixer fitted with the whisk attachment (or in a large bowl, using a hand mixer), beat the egg whites on low speed until lightly frothy.

11. Melt the gelatin in the microwave, about 30 seconds, or by setting the bowl in a shallow dish of hot water.

12. When the sugar syrup reaches 240°F / 115°C, carefully remove the vanilla bean with tongs and discard. Increase the mixer speed to medium-high and add the syrup to the egg whites in a slow, steady stream, then pour in the melted gelatin. Continue whipping on high speed until the marshmallow crème is bright white

MARSHMALLOW CRÈME

161 g / ⅔ cup cool water

15 g / 1 tablespoon powdered gelatin

198 g / 1 cup granulated sugar

156 g / ½ cup corn syrup

1 vanilla bean, split lengthwise

60 g / 2 large egg whites

and fluffy and holds medium peaks, 4 to 5 minutes.

13. Finish the cookies: Use the greased spatula to transfer some of the marshmallow crème to the pastry bag, filling it about halfway. Working quickly and using a spiral motion, pipe a mound about 2 to 2½ inches high onto each cookie, releasing the pressure and lifting up the bag to finish each with a point or even a little curlicue. It's important to work quickly so the gelatin doesn't firm up too much (it will begin to set as it cools). Let the marshmallow topping set at room temperature for 5 to 10 minutes.

14. Check on the chocolate glaze: It should be cool but still fluid; if it has set up, rewarm very gently (10-second intervals over the pan of hot water or 10-second bursts in the microwave). The chocolate should be fluid but not at all warm.

15. Spoon the glaze over the cookies to coat them. Let the cookies stand (at room temperature or in the refrigerator) until the chocolate is firm, about 30 minutes to 1 hour.

❋ **WHY IT WORKS**
Marshmallow crème can be made without egg whites, but adding them makes this recipe easier to work with; traditional marshmallow crème can be tricky to pipe. Even so, it pays to follow the same rules I do when I work with regular marshmallow: Coat everything with nonstick spray to help ease the process and minimize cleanup.

★ **PRO TIP**
For this recipe, the graham crackers are on the thick side. To make more traditional, thinner graham crackers, transfer the rolled-out dough to two parchment-lined baking sheets and prick with a fork all over. Bake the dough as sheets, rotating the baking sheets from front to back and top to bottom at the halfway mark, until the surface is noticeably dry and set— you'll need to increase baking time by up to 5 minutes. When the grahams are fully baked, remove them from the oven and, while they are still warm, use a pastry wheel or knife to cut them into squares of whatever size you like.

Blondies are the butterscotchiest of bar cookies, but I wanted them even butterscotchier! A drizzle of homemade butterscotch sauce kicks their flavor up to the next level.

Makes 16 blondies

DIFFICULTY: Easy

MAKE AHEAD AND STORAGE: The blondies can be stored airtight for up to 5 days. The sauce makes more than you need; it keeps covered, refrigerated, for up to 2 weeks.

Butterscotch Blondies

1. Preheat the oven to 350°F / 175°C. Lightly grease a 9-inch square baking pan and line it with parchment paper, leaving a 1-inch overhang on two opposite sides (see page 27). Lightly grease the parchment.

2. In the bowl of a stand mixer fitted with the paddle attachment (or in a large bowl, using a hand mixer), cream the butter, brown sugar, and granulated sugar on medium-low speed until light and fluffy, 4 to 5 minutes.

3. Add the eggs one at a time, mixing on medium speed until each one is fully incorporated. Add the vanilla and mix to combine.

4. Add the flour, baking powder, and salt and mix on low speed just until fully incorporated—do not overmix. Pour the batter into the prepared pan and spread into an even layer.

5. Transfer the butterscotch sauce to a disposable pastry bag and snip a small (about ¼-inch) opening at the tip. Drizzle the butterscotch randomly over the blondies—it will spread in the oven, so don't bother making pretty designs. I like loopy drizzles best.

6. Bake the blondies until a toothpick inserted in the center comes out with a few moist crumbs attached, 30 to 33 minutes. Cool completely in the pan.

7. Use the parchment overhang as handles to lift the blondie slab out of the pan, then cut it into 16 equal pieces.

170 g / 6 oz / 12 tablespoons unsalted butter, at room temperature

212 g / 1 cup packed light brown sugar

99 g / ½ cup granulated sugar

113 g / 2 large eggs

15 g / 1 tablespoon vanilla extract

151 g / 1¼ cups all-purpose flour

4.5 g / ¾ teaspoon baking powder

1 g / ¼ teaspoon fine sea salt

92 g / ⅓ cup Brown-Butter Butterscotch Sauce (recipe follows), at room temperature

⟶

Brown-Butter Butterscotch Sauce

1. In a medium saucepan, melt the butter over medium heat. Reduce the heat to low and cook, stirring occasionally, until the milk solids in the butter are visibly golden brown and exude a nutty aroma, 8 to 10 minutes.

2. Add the brown sugar and heavy cream and bring the mixture to a simmer over medium heat, stirring occasionally, then reduce the heat to low and continue simmering, without stirring, for 4 minutes.

3. Remove the pan from the heat and stir in the vanilla, salt, and cinnamon. Transfer the sauce to a heatproof jar and let cool.

85 g / 3 oz / 6 tablespoons unsalted butter

266 g / 1¼ cups packed dark brown sugar

104 g / ⅓ cup plus 2 tablespoons heavy cream

5 g / 1 teaspoon vanilla extract

2 to 4 g / ½ to 1 teaspoon fine sea salt (depending on how salty you want it)

Pinch of ground cinnamon

Variation

Regular Blondies: Just skip the sauce. Leave the blondies plain or add mix-ins—170 g / 6 oz chopped chocolate or 99 g / 1 cup chopped toasted nuts. Or both!

❊ **WHY IT WORKS**

I like my blondies gooey, like brownies, but brownies contain large quantities of chocolate to help them achieve that consistency. Here the butterscotch sauce lends moisture and fat that are absorbed by the batter while it bakes, resulting in soft, chewy blondies with an extra boost of butterscotch flavor.

★ **PRO TIPS**

It's best to use a pastry bag to drizzle on the butterscotch, because you want to distribute it fairly evenly and it's a thick sauce that would fall in big glops from a spoon and won't schmear well on top of the slippery batter.

Leftover sauce is killer on ice cream or mixed into frostings. Add some powdered sugar to it when it's slightly warm, and you can use it as a glaze.

In a past life, these brownies were fudge; they've just been reincarnated into the richest, densest, chocolatiest bar cookie ever. Talk about hitting the mark—not only are they lusciously soft without being overly gooey, they've also got that really good crackly-top thing going on.

Makes 16 brownies

DIFFICULTY: Easy

MAKE AHEAD AND STORAGE: The brownies can be stored airtight for up to 1 week. They stay fresh for a long time (my boyfriend says they're even better after a day or two).

Fudgy Brownies

1. Preheat the oven to 350°F / 175°C. Lightly grease a 9-inch square pan and line it with parchment paper, leaving at least 1 to 2 inches of overhang on two opposite sides (see page 27). Lightly grease the parchment.

2. In a medium heatproof bowl, combine the butter, oil, and chocolate. Set the bowl over a medium saucepan of simmering water (with the bowl not touching the water) and heat, stirring occasionally, until the mixture is fully melted and combined. Remove from the heat and let cool slightly.

3. Add both sugars to the chocolate mixture and beat well with a silicone spatula to combine. Gradually add the eggs, mixing until fully incorporated. Beat in the vanilla.

4. Add the flour and salt and mix well with the spatula to combine, about 1 minute; the batter should be evenly smooth and thick. Make sure that there are no flour pockets, but do not overmix.

5. Pour the batter into the prepared pan and bake until a toothpick inserted in the center comes out with a few moist, clumpy crumbs attached, 20 to 23 minutes, turning the pan around halfway through the baking time.

6. These super-fudgy brownies don't cut well unless they are completely cool. Cool the brownies in the pan, then use the parchment overhang as handles to lift the slab out of the pan and cut it into 16 equal pieces. But if you don't care about them being pretty, don't wait—just go to town!

57 g / 2 oz / 4 tablespoons unsalted butter, at room temperature

50 g / ¼ cup neutral oil (such as vegetable, canola, or peanut; see Pro Tip)

227 g / 8 oz bittersweet chocolate (preferably 70 to 80% cacao), chopped

106 g / ½ cup packed brown sugar

99 g / ½ cup granulated sugar

170 g / 3 large eggs, lightly whisked

10 g / 2 teaspoons vanilla extract

69 g / ⅔ cup all-purpose flour

2 g / ½ teaspoon fine sea salt

Variations

Cream Cheese Swirl: In a small bowl, beat 151 g / ⅔ cup room-temperature cream cheese, 50 g / ¼ cup granulated sugar, 57 g / 1 large egg, and 5 g / 1 teaspoon vanilla extract to combine thoroughly. Dollop the mixture all over the surface of the batter and use a paring knife to swirl the two mixtures together, then bake as directed.

Peanut Butter Swirl: In a small bowl, beat 43 g / 3 tablespoons unsalted butter, melted, 135 g / ½ cup creamy peanut butter, 38 g / ⅓ cup powdered sugar, and 5 g / 1 teaspoon vanilla extract to combine thoroughly. Dollop the mixture all over the surface of the batter and use a paring knife to swirl the two mixtures together, then bake as directed.

Salted Caramel Swirl: Dollop 92 g / ⅓ cup Salted Caramel Sauce (page 54) all over the surface of the batter and use a paring knife to swirl the two mixtures together. Bake as directed.

❊ **WHY IT WORKS**

This recipe is another lesson in delicate baking balance. There's butter for flavor and oil for tenderness. The brown sugar lends some moisture and the slightest chew, while the granulated sugar is largely responsible for the crackly top I love so much. The eggs provide the bulk of the structure, which is why the brownies are so fudgy—you need just enough flour to hold things together. Chocolate is the star here.

★ **PRO TIP**

If you're skeeved out by vegetable, canola, or peanut oil, you can substitute almost any oil. Olive oil is good, but I'd steer clear of extra-virgin because its flavor can be too pronounced. Coconut oil is one of my favorite neutral options.

A lack of cocoa flavor has always been one of my complaints about cakey brownies, but these are seriously chocolaty. And they stand up even better than fudgy brownies to swirls and inclusions like chopped nuts, dried fruit, or chocolate chunks. So, to each their own brownie—but cakey lovers, I am now on your side, at least sometimes.

Makes 16 brownies

DIFFICULTY: Easy

MAKE AHEAD AND STORAGE: The brownies can be stored airtight for up to 5 days.

Cakey Brownies

1. Preheat the oven to 350°F / 175°C. Lightly grease a 9-inch square pan and line it with parchment paper, leaving at least 1 to 2 inches of overhang on two opposite sides (see page 27). Lightly grease the parchment.

2. In a medium heatproof bowl, combine the butter, oil, and cocoa powder. Place over a medium pot of simmering water (with the bowl not touching the water) and heat, stirring occasionally, until the mixture is fully melted and combined. Remove from the heat and let cool slightly.

3. Add the sugar to the cocoa mixture and whisk to combine. Add the eggs one at a time, whisking until each one is fully incorporated before adding the next. Whisk in the vanilla.

4. In another medium bowl, whisk together the flour, baking powder, and salt. Add to the cocoa mixture and stir well to ensure there are no flour pockets, but do not overmix. Switch from the whisk to a silicone spatula if you need to.

5. Pour the batter into the prepared pan and bake until a toothpick inserted in the center comes out with a few moist crumbs attached, 25 to 27 minutes, turning the pan around halfway through the baking time. Cool the brownies completely.

6. Use the parchment overhang as handles to lift the slab out of the pan, then cut it into 16 equal pieces.

113 g / 4 oz / 8 tablespoons unsalted butter, at room temperature

57 g / ¼ cup vegetable oil (such as vegetable, canola, or peanut; see Pro Tip, page 69)

43 g / ½ cup unsweetened cocoa powder (dark, if you can get it)

298 g / 1½ cups granulated sugar

170 g / 3 large eggs

10 g / 2 teaspoons vanilla extract

120 g / 1¼ cups all-purpose flour

3 g / ¾ teaspoon baking powder

2 g / ½ teaspoon fine sea salt

❋ WHY IT WORKS

This recipe is all about balance. The butter is there for flavor, but a small amount of oil keeps the brownies chewy. Using cocoa powder rather than chocolate adds flavor without adding moisture, which gives more control over the end result. Cakey brownies use more flour for structure than fudgy ones do—it helps support the rise from the baking powder and gives the finished brownies a more cakelike crumb—and using cocoa powder in this recipe also aids in creating the ideal cakey texture.

★ PRO TIP

When it comes to brownies, it's always best to err on the side of underbaking. When the edges begin to pull away from the pan, it's a sign you don't want those brownies in the oven much longer—time to do that toothpick check!

No joke—I once dreamed about a chocolaty but delectably crisp crust, a layer of raspberries, and a creamy filling holding it all together. In the morning, I set about turning my dream into reality. These are cheesecake bars at heart, but the crunch makes them really special. If you can't find cocoa nibs, you can sub a quarter cup of your favorite chopped nut, or just omit them—the bars will still be dreamy.

Raspberry-Ripple Crunch Bars

Makes 14 bars

DIFFICULTY: Medium

MAKE AHEAD AND STORAGE: The bars can be refrigerated in a single layer airtight for up to 3 days.

1. Preheat the oven to 325°F / 162°C. Lightly grease a 9-by-13-inch baking pan and line it with parchment paper, leaving 1 inch of overhang on the two long sides (see page 27). Lightly grease the parchment.

2. Make the crust: Sift the powdered sugar and cocoa powder into a large bowl. Add the Rice Krispies and stir to combine. Add the melted butter and mix until the mixture is evenly moistened.

3. Press the mixture into the prepared pan in an even layer. Pour the melted chocolate over the crust and use a small offset spatula to spread it into an even layer.

4. Arrange the raspberries in rows across the crust—you don't need to be precise, but placing the berries in rows means you can see them in cross section when you cut the bars, which is pretty cool. I do 9 or 10 rows of 6 or so berries each. (If you don't care, just scatter them—still delish!) Sprinkle the cocoa nibs evenly over the berries.

5. Make the custard filling: In a food processor, combine the cream cheese and granulated sugar. With the machine running, add the eggs one at a time, processing until well combined. Scrape the bowl well, then add the vanilla and process to combine.

6. Pour the custard over the crust—it should flow into an even layer, but

CRUST

113 g / 1 cup powdered sugar

43 g / ½ cup unsweetened cocoa powder

113 g / 4 cups Rice Krispies

141 g / 5 oz / 10 tablespoons unsalted butter, melted

170 g / 6 oz bittersweet chocolate (up to 70% cacao), chopped, melted, and cooled slightly

198 g / 2 cups fresh raspberries

14 g / 2 tablespoons cocoa nibs (see headnote)

CUSTARD FILLING

680 g / 3 cups cream cheese, at room temperature

198 g / 1 cup granulated sugar

284 g / 5 large eggs

10 g / 2 teaspoons vanilla extract

⟶

you can use a small offset spatula to coax it into the edges if needed. Bake until the custard is set and lightly golden at the edges but still slightly jiggly in the center, 45 to 50 minutes. Let cool to room temperature, then refrigerate for at least 2 hours.

7. When the custard is thoroughly chilled, drizzle on the melted chocolate for the topping. Refrigerate for 5 minutes, or until the chocolate sets.

8. Use the parchment overhang as handles to lift the slab out of the pan. I like to trim away the edges for clean cuts (snack time!), but you don't have to. Cut into 14 bars—1 lengthwise cut and 6 crosswise cuts. Keep refrigerated until ready to serve.

9. Just before serving, finish each bar with a few raspberries and a sprinkling of cocoa nibs.

Above: Raspberry-Ripple Crunch Bars and Coconut Tres Leches Bars (page 74)

❊ WHY IT WORKS

These bars take a cue from their close cousin, cheesecake: The filling is a custard, gaining most of its structure from eggs instead of flour. Like cheesecake, determining doneness can be tricky—you don't want to overbake the custard (which could make it tough), but if it's underbaked, it can be difficult to slice. Err on the side of overdoing it.

★ PRO TIP

The colder the slab, the better it will slice into bars. Two hours is sufficient, but if you've got time, just let it hang out in the fridge for as long as overnight. If you're in a hurry, though, cut it into small squares (about 2 by 2 inches) instead of rectangles and maybe drop a dollop of whipped cream on top.

TOPPING

113 g / 4 oz bittersweet chocolate (up to 70% cacao), chopped, melted

99 g / 1 cup fresh raspberries

7 g / 1 tablespoon cocoa nibs

These bars boast a coconut shortbready crust and a custard filling made with—you guessed it—three milks: sweetened condensed, evaporated, and coconut. I like to finish them with a layer of whipped cream and more coconut, but you can omit that if you prefer. The photo is on page 73.

Makes 16 bars

DIFFICULTY: Medium

MAKE AHEAD AND STORAGE: The plain bars can be refrigerated for up to 4 days. Once you top with the whipped cream, the bars need to be served within 1 day, though they are best when the topping is added just before serving.

Coconut Tres Leches Bars

1. Preheat the oven to 375°F / 190°C. Lightly grease a 9-inch square baking pan and line it with parchment paper, leaving 1 inch of overhang on two opposite sides (see page 27). Lightly grease the parchment.

2. **Make the crust:** In the bowl of a stand mixer fitted with the paddle attachment (or in a large bowl, using a hand mixer), cream the butter and granulated sugar on medium-low speed until light and fluffy, 4 to 5 minutes.

3. Add the salt and vanilla and mix to combine, 1 minute more. Add the flour and coconut and mix on low speed until thoroughly combined, 1 to 2 minutes.

4. Turn the dough out into the prepared pan and press it into an even layer—make sure you get into the corners. Bake until the edges of the crust start to turn golden brown, 15 to 17 minutes. Remove the pan from the oven and let the crust cool while you make the filling. Turn the oven temperature down to 325°F / 162°C.

5. **Make the filling:** In a small bowl, whisk together the sugar and cornstarch. In a medium bowl, whisk together the condensed milk, evaporated milk, coconut milk, eggs, and vanilla until smooth. Add the sugar mixture and whisk until fully combined.

CRUST

170 g / 6 oz / 12 tablespoons unsalted butter

99 g / ½ cup granulated sugar

2 g / ½ teaspoon salt

2.5 g / ½ teaspoon vanilla extract

151 g / 1¼ cups all-purpose flour

64 g / ¾ cup unsweetened shredded coconut, toasted and cooled (see Pro Tips)

FILLING

199 g / 1 cup granulated sugar

7 g / 1 tablespoon cornstarch

278 g / 1 cup sweetened condensed milk

241 g / 1 cup evaporated milk

234 g / 1 cup coconut milk

227 g / 4 large eggs

5 g / 1 teaspoon vanilla extract

⟶

6. Pour the custard over the crust and transfer the pan to the oven. Bake until the custard is set, 1 hour to 1 hour 15 minutes. The edges will look firm, but there still might be a little jiggle in the center—that's OK! It will continue to set while it cools. Let cool to room temperature, then refrigerate for about an hour before cutting into bars, for cleaner slices.

7. **If desired, make the optional topping:** Just before serving, combine the cream, powdered sugar, and vanilla in the bowl of a stand mixer fitted with the whisk attachment (or combine in a medium bowl, using a hand mixer) and whip to medium peaks. Spread the whipped cream evenly over the bars. Garnish with the toasted coconut.

8. Use the parchment overhang to carefully remove the bars from the pan and slice into 16 squares. Refrigerate until ready to serve.

❆ WHY IT WORKS

These bars are made in much the same way as a custard pie (like pecan): The custard is totally liquid when you mix it and slowly sets up in the oven. A slow, steady baking time is necessary to achieve a smooth, silky custard. Parbaking the crust helps it keep a nice, crumbly texture instead of becoming soggy.

★ PRO TIPS

To toast the coconut, spread it on a baking sheet. Toast at 350°F / 175°C until evenly golden, 3 to 4 minutes. You can also do this in a large pan over medium-low heat on the stovetop.

You don't want to lose any of that precious custard en route to the oven, so when you're ready to bake, place the pan on a baking sheet for easier transport.

TOPPING (OPTIONAL)

121 g / ½ cup heavy cream

21 g / 3 tablespoons powdered sugar

2.5 g / ½ teaspoon vanilla extract

21 g / ¼ cup unsweetened shredded coconut, toasted and cooled

CHAPTER 2

Cakes

I was sixteen when I first decided I wanted to be a baker. In an effort to convince my family that I should go to culinary school, I embarked on a series of recipe tests—mostly disastrous—after school and on weekends. I baked cake after cake and made batch after batch of frosting. My niece Maisy, who was about two years old, began to associate my presence in the house with cake. "Hi, Ewin, where's the cake?" she would say, with her tiny arms wrapped around my legs. At that age, her *d*'s sounded a lot like *g*'s, so when I gave her a taste, she'd say, "Mmmm . . . golicious . . ."

Whether you're two or ninety-two, there's a cake for every occasion and mood, from simple throw-everything-together-in-a-single-bowl recipes for lazy weekends and busy weeknights to towering masterpieces with lots of pretty finishes for special occasions. Whatever kind of day you're having, there's a perfect cake to make. This chapter is full of them—and they're all golicious.

HOW TO PREPARE CAKE PANS

Cake pans are usually greased or greased and floured. Greasing and flouring helps prevent delicate cakes, like sponge cakes, from sticking, but just greasing will work for most simpler cakes. There are exceptions—angel food cake, for example, needs an ungreased pan so that the meringue-based batter has a surface to cling to as it rises in the oven.

You can grease a pan with a thin coating of softened butter, a neutral oil (I usually use a paper towel to apply the oil evenly), or non-stick spray. I love Baker's Joy, which is a spray that also has flour in it, but if you don't have it and need a floured pan, just add a few tablespoons of flour to the greased pan and tap it around until it's fully coated, then tap out any excess. There are other instances, such as for upside-down cakes, when it's especially important that the pan be greased with a flavorful fat (usually butter), which caramelizes in the base of the pan, eventually making a topping for fruit. Don't skimp in these situations—it's worth it!

MIXING INFO

The main methods for mixing cake batter are:

Blending: The easiest. The liquid ingredients are combined and then the dry ingredients are mixed in.

Creaming: One of the most common methods. Room-temperature fat (usually butter) is beaten with sugar until the mixture is aerated. The eggs are added gradually, followed by the dry ingredients and the liquid ingredients, if any.

Foaming: Eggs and sugar are whipped to full volume, then the other ingredients are folded into this base. Whole eggs may be used, but sometimes the eggs are separated and the whites and yolks whipped separately. There are several variatons of the foaming method, according to how you whip up the eggs:

- **Cold Foaming Method:** Eggs and sugar are whipped together, without being heated.

- **Warm Foaming Method:** The eggs and sugar are warmed in a bowl over a water bath until the sugar is dissolved and the mixture is slightly warm (around 110°F / 43°C) before it is whipped.

- **Chiffon:** The eggs are separated and the yolks are incorporated into the base of the batter. Then the egg whites are whipped with sugar and gently folded into the batter.

- **Separation Foaming:** The eggs are separated and the yolks are whipped with a portion of the sugar. The other ingredients are folded into the yolk mixture, and then the whites are whipped with the remaining sugar and folded into the batter.

Hi-Ratio: Common in large-scale production bakeries, this method uses a higher proportion of sugar and eggs to flour. The fat is blended with the dry ingredients, including sugar, first, and then the liquid ingredients, including eggs, are added gradually.

Combination: Part creaming method, part foaming method. The fat is creamed with a portion of the sugar and whole eggs and/or yolks are beaten in, just as in the creaming method. Then the egg whites are whipped with the remaining sugar to stiff peaks and folded into the creamed mixture. Finally the dry ingredients are folded in.

Regardless of the method, keep these tips in mind:

Ingredient preparation: Many recipes call for the dry ingredients to be sifted together. Sifting breaks up any lumps and helps combine these ingredients, and I recommend it. But if you don't have a sifter or sieve (or you feel like skipping a step), whisking the ingredients produces pretty similar results.

Mixing the batter: It's important to scrape down the sides of the bowl as you work and to mix until the ingredients are well combined. If the batter isn't homogeneous, the cake may bake unevenly—doming excessively or falling during or after baking. But while you want to mix thoroughly, it's also super-important not to overmix the batter. Overmixing leads to excess gluten formation, which can make cakes tough. It can also stunt the batter's rise, or make it rise unevenly.

FOR EVEN LAYERS, TURN TO A SCALE

As I always tell people, it's worth having a scale if you like baking. It's definitely the most accurate way to measure ingredients, but for me, it's valuable beyond that. I use my scale to help me make baked goods of uniform sizes. I weigh portions of brioche dough, for example, so that each pastry will come out about the same, and I always, always weigh my cake batter. It's the best way to ensure that your layers will come out evenly, because each pan has the same amount of batter. (I have included approximate weights of batter for each layer in the recipes.) Do you have to weigh your batter? Of course not. Are you fine eyeballing it if you don't have a scale? Totally. But if you love baking, I encourage you to get a scale; you can get a decent one for only about $25. You'll find yourself using it all the time.

HOW TO ADJUST RECIPES FOR DIFFERENT CAKE PANS

My huge collection of cake pans qualifies me as a borderline hoarder, but I know not all bakers share my penchant for pans. If you want to adjust a recipe that was designed for a certain size pan for use with another one, you just need to do a little math. First, using the chart to the right, determine the surface area of the cake pan called for in the recipe. Then determine the area of the pan you want to use. Remember that using a different pan will also require you to alter the baking time. While it's difficult to predict *exactly* how much time you need to add or subtract (every recipe is different), determine if the pan you're using will make the batter thicker or thinner—this will help you decide which way you need to go (for a thicker level of batter, add time; for thinner, subtract).

Divide the area of the cake pan you want to use by the area of the pan the recipe calls for. For example, if you want to turn a recipe for a 10-inch round pan into one for a 13-by-18-inch pan, the equation would look like this:

$$234 \div 79 = 2.96$$

Then use the number you get to increase or decrease the amounts of each ingredient. You can round the number up or down, or use the exact number. In the preceding example, you could use 2.96 or just round it up to 3 and multiply every ingredient by 3.

SURFACE AREA OF STANDARD CAKE PANS

ROUND PANS	
6-inch	29 square inches
8-inch	50 square inches
9-inch	64 square inches
10-inch	79 square inches
12-inch	113 square inches
14-inch	154 square inches
SQUARE PANS	
8-inch	64 square inches
9-inch	81 square inches
RECTANGULAR PANS	
9-by-13-inch	117 square inches
12-by-17-inch (jelly-roll pan)	219 square inches
13-by-18-inch (half sheet pan)	234 square inches

BROKEN BATTER

If your batter breaks, meaning it separates or looks grainy, it may be because the ingredients were not at the same temperature when you mixed them. Cold butter, for example, won't mix well with the room-temperature sugar, and adding cold milk to room-temperature flour will make your batter lumpy. So when you're making a cake, it's important to take the time to bring refrigerated items (eggs, sour cream, and the like) to room temperature (see page 19).

Another reason a batter can break is that the proportions of the ingredients are out of whack. This is especially likely if you've begun tweaking a recipe or creating your own. If a batter consistently breaks each time you make it, compare the recipe with others of its kind and make sure it's in line with them.

MY ADVICE: Luckily, the solution for fixing a broken batter is the same, regardless of the source of the problem: Just add a small amount of the flour called for (up to one third of the total) and mix gently to combine. The flour will absorb some of the moisture and provide structure, bringing the batter back together. Once the mixture looks smooth, proceed with the recipe as directed.

WHEN AND HOW TO REMOVE AIR POCKETS

Cake batters are prone to form pockets of air, especially where the batter meets the pan and when the pan has grooves, ridges, or other details, as do certain Bundt pans or miniature cake molds. So I usually give cake pans a few solid raps on the countertop before putting them in the oven. I'm not talking gentle taps here—really smack the pan down for the best chance of bursting air bubbles.

However, when you're working with foamed batters (sponge cake, for example), you do not want to do this—any excess movement is likely to deflate the batter. For this reason, foamed batters aren't usually baked in Bundt pans or detailed molds—they're too likely to end up with pockets of air.

CUTTING CAKES INTO LAYERS

A cake turntable is ideal for cutting cakes into layers, but if you don't have one, you can use a cake stand, turning it around with your hands, or a platter, but the stand gives you height, which is helpful. Or, if you have a lazy Susan, you can rig up your own turntable.

Some recipes produce very flat-topped cakes, but if you've got a domed top, you'll want to level the cake: Use a long serrated knife to slice off a thin layer to make a flat surface. The best way to level any cake is to start by scoring it all the way around. Working with the cake as close to eye level as you can, hold the knife blade parallel to the work surface and lightly touch the knife to the side of the cake to mark it with a shallow cut, then carefully rotate the cake and make another score mark that aligns with the first. (If your cake rose above the rim of the pan during baking, you can use the mark from the rim as a guide for where to make the score marks.) Continue until you've scored the cake all the way around. Now you're ready to cut: Touch the knife to the score mark, hold it firmly, and move it toward the center of the cake while you rotate the turntable (or cake stand/platter/lazy Susan). Try not to use a sawing motion, which can make rough-edged cuts. When you've made it all the way through, lift the domed piece off the cake. Then tear off a piece of the domed top and eat it—you've earned it!

Follow this same technique to slice the cake into layers. You can use a ruler to measure the cake before you make the first score mark to help ensure that the layers are even. Once you have a careful score, it's easy!

ALTERNATING LAYERS

Special cakes don't have to look fancy just on the outside—it's also fun to create an effect that is shown off when the cake is sliced. I love to make two flavors of cake and build them into a four- or six-layer cake, alternating the layers. Or, if you have a pale batter, you can divide it and dye it with different food colors. You can also alternate fillings to achieve different effects.

MY ADVICE: While I often recommend baking cakes in advance so that on the day of serving you can focus on assembly, it's usually not advisable to cut the layers ahead of time, because most cakes are prone to drying out. Plus, cut layers are more delicate and are more likely to break or tear. So save the cutting for the day of.

FILLING A CAKE

When I build a layer cake, I start with a flat base from one of the cakes and end with the flat base of the second cake facing up, to better my chances of achieving a polished look. The top layers that I've leveled go in between.

frosting you are using: Use a pastry bag to pipe a ring of frosting around the outer edge of the cake layer, then pipe or scoop the filling into the center of the ring and spread it into an even layer.

⚙ Place another cake layer on top and repeat, aligning the layers as best you can, and press the cake layer down gently. Repeat as necessary, building successive layers of cake and filling until you reach the last layer, placing it flat side up on top.

MY ADVICE: Once the cake is assembled, I refrigerate it for a bit before I begin frosting. This helps the filling firm up, which makes the cake easier to decorate—your carefully built layers can slide if the filling and/or inclusions are slippery. Thirty minutes usually works for me, but you can get away with less chilling time, or none at all; it's just something that helps things go more smoothly.

Begin by placing the first layer on a turntable (or cake stand/platter/lazy Susan).

⚙ If you're using a simple syrup to soak the cake layers, apply it once the layers have been sliced in half. Apply the syrup to each layer as you build the cake.

⚙ Pipe or scoop the filling on top of the bottom layer and spread it evenly all the way to the edges.

⚙ If you're adding inclusions like crushed nuts or candy, sprinkle them evenly on top of the filling.

⚙ If you're using a looser filling, like curd or jam, it's best to first build a sort of retaining wall out of the

MAKE IT PRETTY

There are tons of ways to decorate a cake, from basic to elaborate, but the best cakes are creative—sometimes you can even combine two or three techniques in one showstopper.

BUNDT CAKES

Bundt pans make simple cakes look like a million bucks—and you don't even have to decorate them if you prefer not to. I love to collect Bundt pans, and I'm especially fond of Nordic Ware's Bundts (new and vintage), which always release cleanly. Denser batters, which produce cakes with a tight crumb, are best for Bundts. It's also important to try to remove air pockets (see page 82).

A few of my favorite ways to kick Bundts up a notch: Add a swirl of jam to the batter (see page 98) or use two batters for a marble cake. Or finish the cake with a dusting of sugar or a glaze, either drizzled or dripped (see page 86).

NAKED CAKES

Naked cakes have little to no frosting on the top and outside edges.

* For a casual look, when filling a cake, press down lightly when you put each layer on and let the filling ooze out a bit at the sides. You can leave the top layer plain or pile on a layer of frosting (see page 139).

* For a more polished look, pipe out the filling (see page 89). If you use a plain round tip, you can then use a small offset spatula to apply pressure on just the areas with frosting to smooth and flatten the edges. Alternatively, use a decorative tip, such as a large star tip, to pipe the frosting right at the edge of the cake so that the detail is visible on the finished cake.

CUPCAKES

Cupcakes are pretty cute no matter what you do to them, but I have a few tricks for making them just right. Sometimes I like a domed cupcake with a swirl of frosting on top; other times I like a flat-topped cupcake dunked in ganache or glaze.

* I bake my cupcakes three different ways: in a muffin pan without paper liners; in a pan with liners; or in freestanding thick paper baking cups on a baking sheet (see Resources, page 369). I can't tell you how often people comment on these cups, which have been commonly used by professional bakers but are now available to home cooks as well. Fill your molds or cups three-quarters full—this will result in a rise just above the top edge.

* To frost a cupcake with an offset spatula, place a portion of frosting on top of it, using a scoop that's about the size of the cupcake (like a regular ice cream scoop). If you don't have a scoop, it's totally fine to eyeball it with a spoon.

* To pipe frosting onto cupcakes, fit a pastry bag with a tip. Medium to large tips result in the best cupcake toppers, in my experience. I especially love star tips, which make swirly patterns that are both appealing and a good camouflage for uneven piping or other imperfections. (For more on piping, see page 89.)

1. To give a squareish finish to the frosting, even out the top of the frosting a bit on the top of the cupcake, then hold the spatula flat against the edge and rotate the cupcake to smooth the edges and work some of the frosting upward.

2. To make a swirl of frosting, touch the spatula (or the back of a small spoon) at a 45-degree angle near the edge of the frosting and apply gentle pressure while rotating the cupcake, forming a spiral.

GLAZING, DRIPS, AND DRIZZLES

Whether it fully covers the cake, drips down the sides, or is drizzled everywhere, a glaze is a super-simple way to decorate a cake. Here are a few tips to get those perfect finishes:

Full Glaze: First, you want a cake that's as smooth as possible on the top and sides so the glaze will cover it evenly. This could be a single, dense cake, a layer cake that's been given a crumb coat (see page 87), or a fully chilled mousse cake (see page 160). You want a glaze that's thin enough to pour easily over the cake but thick enough that it will stay in place after the excess drips off. Generally, the glaze should be at room temperature or lightly chilled. The cake itself can be at room temperature or chilled. But remember that if the cake is chilled, the glaze will begin to set relatively quickly, so use a slightly warm glaze or work quickly!

Partial Glaze: Partial glazes are easier to do than their more precise cousin, drip cakes. The definition of the "drip lines," the lines of glaze that will run down the sides, depends on the thickness of the glaze. Thinner glazes will fall in thin lines, usually all the way down to the bottom of the cake; I love their random look. Thicker glazes can be coaxed into falling in lines of various thickness and are generally easier to control. You can go casual and just pour the glaze over the top of the cake and let the drips fall where they may, or you can spoon the glaze onto the surface and encourage it to fall in certain places. My preferred tool for this task is the back of a spoon.

Drips: Drips are best on a very smooth cake, either one that is lightly frosted (see page 85) or fully frosted with a very smooth result. I chill the frosted cake for at least 30 minutes before adding the drips—this helps you control the drippage. Use a glaze, ganache, or icing that is at room temperature or only very slightly warm to the touch. To get long drips, use a warmer glaze—it will drip farther down the cake when you apply it. For shorter drips, use a glaze closer to room temperature—the glaze will stop before it reaches the base, because the cake is cold.

For maximum control with this technique, I use a pastry bag (for more details, see pages 89 to 91). Pour some of the glaze (about one third of the recipe) into a disposable pastry bag (you can also use a heavy-duty zip-top bag) and snip a ⅛- to ¼-inch opening at the tip. Transfer the remaining glaze to a container with a spout. Then pipe on the glaze in a 1-inch band around the top of the cake and let it fall naturally. To get a random drippy effect, squeeze on more glaze in some parts and less in others. Once you've applied drips all the way around, pour a shallow pool of the remaining glaze onto the center of the cake—it will flood outward to combine with the glaze at the edges and become smooth.

Drizzles: Drizzling is easy and is one of my favorite ways to make something plain look great. For more precise drizzles, use a pastry bag; otherwise, just use a spoon. Decide on the angle you want for the drizzle: straight, diagonal, or crisscross. I usually place the cake on a piece of parchment paper and begin the drizzle onto the paper before I make contact with the cake to

get the feel of how quickly the glaze is coming out of the bag. The faster you move, the thinner the drizzles will be. I'm especially fond of using multiple drizzles in contrasting colors (like milk, dark, and white chocolate).

FROSTING TECHNIQUES

✿ An offset spatula is the ideal tool for frosting a cake; 8 inches is my preferred size for decorating standard 8- and 9-inch cakes.

✿ Frosting should resemble mayonnaise in texture: glossy, smooth, and easily spreadable. The firmer your frosting, the more difficult it is to spread, smooth out, and make even. You can soften firm frosting by warming it with a few short bursts in the microwave or with a few minutes in the top of a double boiler. (For piping and other decor techniques, you do want firmer frosting; see pages 89 to 92.)

✿ It's a good idea to start by applying a **crumb coat**—a thin layer of frosting all over the cake that helps trap any loose crumbs or cake dust and "seal" the whole cake together, making smooth sides that are easier to frost later. Then, when you go to apply the final frosting, you don't have to worry about bits of cake getting mixed in and messing up the look. Is it always necessary? No. But if you're going to the effort of making a lovely layer cake, it's worth it for a more finished result. The crumb coat should be very thin; you'll likely see the cake layers through it. Then chill the cake for up to 30 minutes to set the crumb coat before you apply the final layer of frosting.

* **To frost the top of the cake:** Use more frosting than seems necessary—that way, you can get an even coating that will be easy to thin down as you're smoothing it out. Heap a generous amount of frosting in the center of the top of the cake and swoop your offset spatula back and forth to spread the frosting to the edges. If you're using a turntable, you can finish by holding the spatula flat against the top of the cake (with the tip of the spatula in the very center) and quickly turning the turntable around a few times while applying gentle pressure to the spatula. The excess frosting will pile up on the end of the spatula. After a few rotations, stop turning and lift the spatula (and the excess frosting) away.

* **To frost the sides of the cake:** Scoop the frosting onto the end of the spatula and, holding the spatula parallel against the sides, swoop it back and forth to ensure even coverage. Then, again holding the spatula parallel to the side of the cake, move it straight up and down while applying gentle pressure, quickly turning the turntable, to remove the excess frosting. This will leave a "rim" of excess frosting on the top edge of the cake, which you can easily swipe away by holding the spatula flat just above the surface of the cake and giving the turntable another spin. It takes a little practice to get the hang of it, but once you do, it's smooth sailing.

SPATULA FINISHES

Spatula finishes range from easy and effortless to those requiring a skilled hand. For me, these are some of the most attractive finishes for any kind of cake—they show off the texture of the frosting and make the cake extra appealing. The smaller your spatula, the more detailed the effect will be. For more casual, effortless looks, opt for a larger spatula.

Swirly: This is my favorite way to ice a cake—there's nothing more alluring than thick swoops of swirly frosting. You can achieve this look with an offset spatula or just the back of a spoon. I usually frost the cake first, then add more frosting to make the swirls. Apply dollops of frosting and then move your spatula or spoon back and forth to make swoopy waves; this one's all in the wrist. You can do this in an intentional pattern or go random (my fave)!

Lines: You can apply lines/stripes to the sides of a cake for a cool effect. Touch the tip of an offset spatula to the base of the frosted cake and draw it up in a straight line. Apply a little pressure so the frosting you pressed out the sides forms lines on either side of the indentation from the spatula. Repeat all the way around the cake.

Spiral: I love to make a spiral on the top of a cake. The just-frosted cake should be on a turntable. Touch the tip of the offset spatula to the center of the cake, apply-

ing gentle pressure, and begin spinning the turntable. As you spin, gradually move the spatula out toward the edge of the cake. When you reach the edge, gently lift the spatula off the cake. I usually go back around the sides of the cake, building a little wall of the excess frosting around my spiral (see opposite).

Spiky: An easy technique that's also super-fun. This works with any meringue-based frosting, as well as other soft frostings. Once you've frosted the cake, pick a place to start—I usually begin at the top, but it doesn't matter. Touch the tip of the spatula to the frosting, then pull upward quickly, making a little spike. Then repeat all over the cake. You can make the spikes close together for a very textured look, or space them apart.

PIPING

Piping the frosting makes a cake or cupcake look like a million bucks. Some people shy away from piping because they think it's hard to make it look even or perfect. But who says it has to be even? Or perfect? Sometimes I divide the frosting among a few disposable bags fitted with different tips and pipe random shapes all over the cake. It's fun, beautiful, and easy.

MY ADVICE: When you're filling a pastry bag, keep in mind that full isn't better—you want enough unfilled bag at the top that you can twist it closed, making it less likely that the frosting will splooge out of the top of the bag while you work. Fill the

bag two-thirds full at the most, then twist the top tightly together. Hold that twisted part of the bag in the crook of your hand, where your thumb meets your palm (using your dominant hand), and wrap your fingers around the top of the bag.

There are a few ways to hold a pastry bag when you're piping, but I usually use one of two methods. The first is to hold the bag straight up and down, perpendicular to the surface I'll be piping on; this is great for making individual piped shapes. The second is to hold the bag at a 45-degree angle; this is best for continuous shapes.

To pipe, begin to apply pressure from the top of the bag; you can use your nondominant hand as a sup-port while you work. Apply firm, even pressure and let the frosting flow out of the bag. When you've almost achieved the look you're aiming for, release the pressure on the bag to stop the flow and, in one quick motion, pull the bag away from the cake—I usually do this in a tight circle, which helps finish the piped shape cleanly.

You can achieve lots of different looks by piping.

Dots: Fit a pastry bag with a plain round tip—larger tips will make bigger dots, tiny tips will make itty-bitty ones. Hold the bag straight up and down, perpendicular to the surface you want to pipe on, apply pressure to the bag, and pipe until the circle is the size you want. Be sure not to move the bag—if you want large

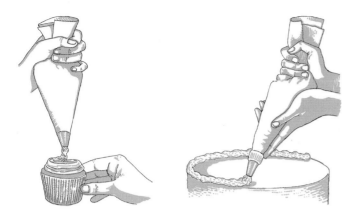

dots, just let the frosting flow out of the bag and over itself until the circle is big enough.

Rosettes: Fit a pastry bag with a star tip; a closed star tip will make a softer look, an open star tip will make a sharper, more defined shape. Hold the bag straight up and down, perpendicular to the surface you want to pipe on, apply pressure to the bag, and, as the frosting begins to flow, make a circle around the spot where the frosting first landed to make a rosette shape. Ideally you want the rosette to be an even round. You can also pipe a simple rose or star shape by holding the pastry bag straight up and down and applying pressure to the bag without moving the tip.

Stripes: There are several ways to achieve a striped effect with a pastry tip. One is to use a basket-weave tip—you can use the flat side or the fluted side. I find it's easier to start at the base of the cake and pipe strips up the sides of it—you can continue the strips across the top of the cake if you like, or just decorate the sides. Try to hold the tip as close to the cake as you can without disturbing the frosting underneath it. Apply pressure

PASTRY BAGS

Pastry bags are one of the most handy tools for baker. Besides frosting, I use them for everything from portioning desserts (like custard; see page 328) to creating different shapes or effects with batters. Because I use them so often, I opt for the disposable kind—then I don't have to worry about another thing to clean up! My favorite size is a 16- or 18-inch bag—any smaller, and it doesn't hold much; any bigger, and it can be difficult to handle.

to the bag and move slowly up the side of the cake, trying to keep the line straight. You can also make a striped effect by piping other shapes—dots, rosettes, or shells—in lines up and down the sides of the cake.

Ruffles: Fit a pastry bag with a rose tip. Place the wider side of the tip against the surface you're piping on, apply pressure to the bag, and, as the frosting begins to flow, move your hand back and forth to make a ruffled look. The wider you move your hand, the larger the ruffles will be. You can use this effect in a spiral on the top of a cake; I start in the center and work outward. You can also make long ruffles all around the sides of a cake, or pipe short ruffles up and down the sides.

Borders and Edges: Piping a border around the base of a cake is a great way to cover up any messiness at the base (or the cardboard cake circle, if you're using one). You can also pipe a border around the top edge of a cake. You can use almost any tip to pipe a border—I especially like a star tip for these—and you can make the border in one of two ways. You can pipe individual shapes next to one another all the way around the cake; hold the pastry bag straight up and down, perpendicular to the surface. Or you can make a continuous border by holding the bag at a 45-degree angle just above the piping surface; apply pressure to the bag and let the frosting flow out, drawing the tip downward as it flows. Rather than releasing the pressure, lessen the pressure when you want to end the shape and then, without lifting the bag, begin applying pressure again, so the next shape begins where the last one ended.

PASTRY TIPS

It's great to just buy a big set of pastry tips (I use Ateco). But unless you're doing lots of fancy piping techniques, you can get by with just a few. The chart below lists the ones I use often.

TIP SHAPE/SIZE	TIP NUMBER(S)	USE
ROUND (PLAIN)		
Small	1, 2, 3, 4, 5	Writing, fine-detail decor
Medium	6, 7, 8, 9, 10, 11, 12	Basic decor (dots, lines, swirls, borders)
Large	803, 804, 805	Fillings, toppings, frosting individual cakes
OPEN STAR		
Small	13, 14, 15, 16	Fine-detail decor
Medium	17, 18, 19, 20, 21, 22	Basic decor (stars, rosettes, borders)
Large	838, 839	Fillings, toppings, frosting individual cakes
CLOSED STAR		
Medium	29, 30, 31, 32, 33, 34, 35	Basic decor (stars, drop flowers, borders)
Large	848, 849	Fillings, toppings, frosting individual cakes
BASKET WEAVE		
Medium	895	Decor (basket weave, ruffles, borders)
ROSE		
Medium	406	Decor (roses, ruffles, swirls, borders)
ICING		
Large	789, 790	Large-scale decor, even coverage with filling or exterior icing
BISMARCK		
Large	229	Filling pastries or doughnuts

EDIBLE GARNISHES

Fresh flowers (nonpoisonous, of course) or elaborate sugar paste decorations make a cake look fancier, but I'm happier with something I don't have to remove when I slice the cake. Edible garnishes can be simple—a sprinkling of toasted coconut, a ring of candied nuts, or a pile of fresh fruit. Or you can go crazy and make little cookies or chocolate ruffles. Here are a few great ways to add edible garnishes:

Pile on Top: A big pile of edible garnishes such as chocolate shavings, fresh fruit, or citrus zest looks pretty on any kind of cake. I usually start the pile about 1 inch from the edge, and I advise always having more garnish than you think you'll need—a big pile is an impressive pile!

Side Coverage: If you're not great at frosting cakes, this technique looks sharp, tastes good, and can cover up any errors. Basically, just cover the sides of the cake with a garnish—it can be something with a fine texture, like sprinkles; something chunky, like chopped nuts; or carefully placed rows of chocolate shards or tiny cookies.

Borders: Sprinkling a garnish around the top or bottom edge of the cake (or both) works especially well with additions that are fine in texture, like sprinkles, chocolate shavings, or finely crushed candy or cookies. But you can also make a border of fresh fruit or larger candies or cookies for a pretty and polished look.

Asymmetrical: This is one of those "anything goes" categories. I love to make an off-center pile of cookies (meringues! macarons!) or fresh fruit on top of a cake. Let your imagination run wild.

Everywhere: Cover the whole thing with chopped nuts, coconut, sprinkles, cookie crumbs, or anything that sounds good to you. No one will see any frosting flaws, and the cake will taste amazing.

DIY SPRINKLES

You can make your own jimmies by piping thin lines of Royal Icing (page 163) onto parchment-lined baking sheets. Use a small round tip to pipe the lines, then let them dry at room temperature, uncovered, for 24 hours. Use a knife to cut them into pieces. You can dye the royal icing any color before you pipe, and you can use any sort of extract to add your own flavor.

Makes one 9-inch cake

DIFFICULTY: Easy

MAKE AHEAD AND STORAGE: Pound cake is delicious within 2 days of baking (store tightly in plastic wrap), but if tightly wrapped, it has a long shelf life—1 to 1½ weeks. Freeze slices, wrapped tightly in plastic wrap, then thaw at room temperature before serving.

Vanilla is my favorite flavor. Call it boring if you must (or compare me to a ninety-year-old woman, as many of my friends do), but I think a recipe that lets pure vanilla flavor shine is anything but dull. This cake is baked in a round pan, but it can be baked in a variety of pans (see page 80)—just remember to adjust the baking time.

Vanilla Pound Cake

1. Preheat the oven to 350°F / 175°C, with a rack in the middle. Grease and flour a 9-inch round cake pan.

2. In the bowl of a stand mixer fitted with the paddle attachment (or in a large bowl, using a hand mixer), cream the butter and vanilla sugar (or regular sugar) on medium-low speed until light and fluffy, 4 to 5 minutes.

3. Add the eggs one at a time, mixing until each one is fully incorporated. Scrape the bowl well. Add the vanilla extract, if using, and mix to combine.

4. In a medium bowl, whisk together the flour, baking powder, and salt. Add about one third of the mixture to the butter mixture and blend on low speed just until combined. Add about half of the milk and mix just until combined. Add another third of the flour mixture and mix until combined, then add the remaining milk. Mix in the remaining flour mixture just until incorporated.

5. Pour the batter into the prepared pan and spread it evenly. Sprinkle generously with turbinado sugar evenly over the surface.

6. Bake the cake until a toothpick inserted in the center comes out clean or with just a few moist crumbs attached, 45 to 50 minutes. Cool the cake in the pan for 15 minutes, then turn onto a wire rack to cool completely.

227 g / 8 oz unsalted butter, at room temperature

297 g / 1½ cups vanilla sugar (see Pro Tip), or 298 g / 1½ cups granulated sugar plus 5 g / 1 teaspoon vanilla extract

170 g / 3 large eggs

361 g / 3 cups all-purpose flour

6 g / 1½ teaspoons baking powder

2 g / ½ teaspoon fine sea salt

181 g / ¾ cup whole milk, at room temperature

Turbinado or coarse sugar, for sprinkling

❋ WHY IT WORKS

The original formula for pound cake dates back to the 1700s, and the recipe traditionally used one pound each butter, sugar, eggs, and flour. Today, most recipes have a higher ratio of sugar, to keep the cake moist, and more flour, to create a nice outer crust and interior crumb structure. The result is a cake that's rich, dense, and about as beautifully basic as it gets.

★ PRO TIP

To make vanilla sugar, dump 2 pounds / 907 g / 4⅔ cups granulated sugar into an airtight container. Add up to 5 leftover vanilla pods, mixing them into the sugar. As you use the sugar, replace it with an equal amount of uninfused granulated sugar.

Clockwise from left: Vanilla Pound Cake, Glazed Lemon Buttermilk Loaf (page 102), and Almond Pound Cake with Raspberry Swirl (page 98)

This recipe embraces the rich flavor and texture of almond flour, making a Bundt cake with a distinctively dense crumb. I like the dramatic and delicious raspberry swirl, but you can leave it out for a simpler cake. The photo is on page 97.

Makes one 10-inch Bundt cake

DIFFICULTY: Easy

MAKE AHEAD AND STORAGE: Although it is best within 2 days of baking, pound cake has a long shelf life if tightly wrapped—1 to 1½ weeks. Another option: Cut the cake into slices, wrap tightly in plastic wrap, and freeze. Thaw at room temperature before serving.

Almond Pound Cake with Raspberry Swirl

1. Preheat the oven to 350°F / 175°C, with a rack in the middle. Grease and flour a 10-inch Bundt pan.

2. Heat a large skillet over medium-low heat. Once the pan is hot, sprinkle in the almond flour in an even layer and toast, stirring occasionally, just until lightly golden and aromatic, 2 to 3 minutes. Transfer the almond flour to a medium bowl and let cool to room temperature.

3. Add the all-purpose flour, baking powder, and salt to the almond flour and whisk to combine.

4. In the bowl of a stand mixer fitted with the paddle attachment (or in a large bowl, using a hand mixer), cream the butter and sugar on medium-low speed until light and fluffy, 4 to 5 minutes.

5. Add the eggs one at a time, mixing until each one is fully incorporated before adding the next. Scrape the bowl well. Add the vanilla and almond extracts and mix to combine.

6. Add about one third of the almond flour mixture and blend on low speed just until combined. Add about half the milk and blend just until combined. Add another third of the flour mixture and mix until combined, then add the remaining milk. Add the remaining flour mixture and mix just until incorporated.

142 g / 1½ cups almond flour

181 g / 1½ cups all-purpose flour

6 g / 1½ teaspoons baking powder

2 g / ½ teaspoon fine sea salt

227 g / 8 oz unsalted butter, at room temperature

298 g / 1½ cups granulated sugar

170 g / 3 large eggs, at room temperature

5 g / 1 teaspoon vanilla extract

1 g / ¼ teaspoon almond extract

181 g / ¾ cup whole milk, at room temperature

102 g / ⅓ cup raspberry jam (seedless is best)

7. Pour half the cake batter into the prepared pan and tap the pan firmly on the counter a few times to remove any air pockets. Drizzle on half the jam (see Pro Tip). Try to keep the jam away from the edges of the pan—if it's exposed to too much heat, it can turn very dark in the oven. Repeat with the remaining cake batter and jam.

8. Bake the cake until a toothpick inserted into the center comes out clean or with just a few moist crumbs attached, 45 to 50 minutes. Cool the cake in the pan for 15 minutes, then invert onto a wire rack to cool completely.

✳ WHY IT WORKS

The fine texture of almond flour (almonds ground to a powder) allows it to replace all or part of all-purpose flour, which, because it contains gluten, provides structure. Here I use half all-purpose flour and half almond flour to produce what I think is a perfect Bundt—dense, moist, and flavorful.

★ PRO TIP

It's easiest to make the jam swirl with a disposable pastry bag. I snip a ¼-inch opening at the tip and drizzle half the jam randomly over the first layer of batter. Then I add the rest of the batter; I drop it in big dollops all over the pan to avoid disturbing the first layer of jam too much. Then I drizzle the remaining jam over the top. If you don't have a pastry bag (or a zip-top bag), you can just drizzle the jam with a spoon, but you may end up with some bigger pockets of jam instead of a swirl.

Baking with honey can be beyond delicious, but it also presents certain challenges. You've got to compensate for honey's fluidity compared to sugar and also find the right level of flavor. These cupcakes hit the mark on both counts. Bake them without papers to make miniature cakes or with liners for a more traditional look. The photo is on page 119.

Makes 12 cupcakes

DIFFICULTY: Easy

MAKE AHEAD AND STORAGE: The glazed cupcakes are best eaten within 3 days. You can freeze the unglazed cakes, well wrapped, for up to 1 month; thaw before glazing.

Honey Pound Cupcakes
with Honey-Caramel Glaze

1. Preheat the oven to 350°F / 175°C, with a rack in the middle. Grease and flour a 12-cup muffin pan (or line it with paper liners).

2. Make the cupcakes: In the bowl of a stand mixer fitted with the paddle attachment (or in a large bowl, using a hand mixer), cream the butter and brown sugar on medium-low speed until light and fluffy, 4 to 5 minutes. Add the honey and mix to combine.

3. Add the eggs one at a time, mixing until each one is fully incorporated before adding the next. Scrape the bowl well. Add the vanilla and mix to combine.

4. In a medium bowl, whisk together the flour, baking powder, and salt. Add about one third of the mixture to the butter mixture and mix on low speed just until combined. Add about half the yogurt and mix just until combined. Add another third of the flour mixture and mix to combine, then add the remaining yogurt. Mix in the remaining flour mixture just until incorporated.

5. Divide the batter among the prepared cups (I use a #16 / ¼-cup scoop).

6. Bake until a toothpick inserted into the center of a cupcake comes out

CUPCAKES

227 g / 8 oz unsalted butter, at room temperature

213 g / 1 cup packed light brown sugar

240 g / ¾ cup honey (see Pro Tip)

170 g / 3 large eggs, at room temperature

5 g / 1 teaspoon vanilla extract

402 g / 3⅓ cups all-purpose flour

6 g / 1½ teaspoons baking powder

2 g / ½ teaspoon fine sea salt

170 g / ¾ cup plain yogurt, at room temperature

HONEY CARAMEL

106 g / ⅓ cup honey

60 g / ¼ cup heavy cream

clean or with just a few moist crumbs attached, 27 to 29 minutes. Cool the cakes in the pan for 10 minutes, then turn out onto a wire rack and let cool completely before glazing.

7. Make the honey caramel: Bring the honey and cream to a simmer in a small saucepan over medium heat. Stir the mixture until it begins to simmer, but stop stirring as soon as it comes to a simmer. Attach a candy thermometer to the side of the pan and boil until the mixture reaches 235°F / 113°C. Remove the pan from the heat and cool the caramel to 150°F / 66°C before using.

8. Spoon 13 to 19 g / 2 to 3 teaspoons of the cooled caramel onto the top of each cupcake and use the back of the spoon to spread it to the edges. You can serve immediately, or let the caramel set so that it becomes firmer, like a glaze, at least 15 minutes.

❋ **WHY IT WORKS**
Honey can't be substituted in equal parts for sugar in a recipe, mainly because it's a liquid. Here, a little additional flour helps stabilize the batter, compensating for the slightly increased liquid content. Brown sugar complements the honey flavor, and the sugar helps to aerate the batter.

★ **PRO TIP**
Wildflower honey, ideally local, is one of my favorites for baking—it has a lovely flavor that is neither too strong nor too mild.

Lemon and buttermilk are a match made in dessert heaven. The light, bright, tangy flavors work well in many different types of desserts, including pound cake. If you can get them, Meyer lemons are great in this recipe—they are sweeter, more fragrant, and deeper in color, so the loaf will be even more delicious and prettier. The photo is on page 97.

The photo is on page 97.

Makes one 9-by-5-inch loaf cake

DIFFICULTY: Easy

MAKE AHEAD AND STORAGE: The unglazed cake can be stored, tightly wrapped in plastic wrap, at room temperature for up to 10 days. Once glazed, the cake can be stored, tightly covered, for up to 3 days.

Glazed Lemon Buttermilk Loaf

1. Preheat the oven to 350°F / 175°C, with a rack in the middle. Grease and flour a 9-by-5-inch loaf pan.

2. **Make the cake:** In the bowl of a stand mixer fitted with the paddle attachment (or in a large bowl, using a hand mixer), cream the butter, granulated sugar, and lemon zest on medium-low speed until light and fluffy, 4 to 5 minutes.

3. Add the eggs one at a time, mixing until each one is fully incorporated before adding the next. Scrape the bowl well. Add the lemon extract and mix to combine.

4. In a medium bowl, whisk together the flour, baking powder, and salt. Add about one third of the mixture to the butter mixture and beat on low speed just until combined. Add about half the buttermilk and mix just until combined. Add another one third of the flour mixture, followed by the remaining buttermilk. Mix in the remaining flour mixture just until incorporated.

5. Pour the batter into the prepared pan and spread it evenly. Bake the cake until a toothpick inserted into the center comes out clean or with just a few moist crumbs attached, 55 to 60 minutes. Cool the cake in the pan for 15 minutes, then invert onto a wire rack to cool completely.

CAKE

227 g / 8 oz unsalted butter, at room temperature

298 g / 1½ cups granulated sugar

6 g / 1 tablespoon grated lemon zest

170 g / 3 large eggs, at room temperature

1 g / ¼ teaspoon lemon extract

361 g / 3 cups all-purpose flour

6 g / 1¼ teaspoons baking powder

2 g / ½ teaspoon fine sea salt

181 g / ¾ cup buttermilk (see Pro Tip), at room temperature

⟶

6. Make the glaze: Whisk together the powdered sugar, lemon zest, and lemon juice in a bowl. Add enough cream to make a thick but pourable glaze.

7. Spoon the glaze over the loaf, letting the excess drip down the sides. Allow the glaze to set for at least 15 minutes before slicing and serving the cake.

❄ **WHY IT WORKS**

Creaming the lemon zest along with the butter and sugar extracts the most flavor from its essential oils. Buttermilk makes for a slightly lighter loaf than whole milk; it can be used interchangeably with milk in most recipes.

★ **PRO TIP**

No buttermilk? No problem. Make your own by adding 11 g / 2¼ teaspoons white vinegar or lemon juice to 181 g / ¾ cup whole milk and let sit for 10 minutes before using. (The easy formula to use for any recipe is 15 g / 1 tablespoon vinegar or lemon juice for every 242 g / 1 cup milk.)

GLAZE

113 g / 1 cup powdered sugar

4 g / 2 teaspoons grated lemon zest

30 g / 2 tablespoons freshly squeezed lemon juice

30 to 45 g / 2 to 3 tablespoons heavy cream

I love the combo of nuts and chocolate with bananas, and I add both to every banana cake I make. This cake isn't a far cry from banana bread, but the sweet add-ins put it squarely in dessert territory. The photo is on page 110.

Banana Cake
with Cocoa Nibs and Nutella Swirl

Makes one 9-by-5-inch loaf cake

DIFFICULTY: Easy

MAKE AHEAD AND STORAGE: This cake is even better after a day or so. The moist crumb means it won't dry out easily; you can keep it tightly wrapped in plastic wrap at room temperature for up to 1 week.

1. Preheat the oven to 325°F / 162°C, with a rack in the middle. Grease and flour a 9-by-5-inch loaf pan.

2. In a large bowl, whisk the butter and sugar to combine. Add the eggs one at a time, whisking well to combine. Beat in the vanilla and yogurt. Stir in the bananas and mix to combine, using a spatula to smoosh up any big chunks.

3. In a medium bowl, whisk together the flour, baking soda, cinnamon, and salt. Stir in the cocoa nibs. Fold into the banana mixture, mixing just until fully combined.

4. Pour half the batter into the prepared pan and top with half the Nutella. Use a small wooden skewer or the blade of a paring knife to swirl the Nutella into the batter. Pour in the remaining batter and finish with the last of the Nutella, swirling again.

5. Bake until the top of the loaf is golden brown, the sides pull slightly away from the edges of the pan, and a toothpick inserted into the center comes out with just a few moist crumbs attached (see Pro Tips), 75 to 90 minutes; check after 40 minutes, and if the cake is browning too quickly, tent loosely with aluminum foil. Cool the loaf in the pan for 15 minutes, then turn out onto a wire rack to cool completely.

85 g / 3 oz / 6 tablespoons unsalted butter, melted and cooled slightly

198 g / 1 cup granulated sugar

3.5 oz / 2 large eggs

5 g / 1 teaspoon vanilla extract

76 g / ⅓ cup whole-milk plain Greek yogurt

480 g / 4 very ripe medium bananas, mashed with a fork

241 g / 2 cups all-purpose flour

9 g / 1½ teaspoons baking soda

2 g / ½ teaspoon ground cinnamon

2 g / ½ teaspoon fine sea salt

71 g / ½ cup cocoa nibs (see Resources, page 369)

67 g / ½ cup Nutella, stirred well

❋ WHY IT WORKS

This cake is really a quick bread; I add more bananas than are commonly used, which keeps the cake extremely moist.

★ PRO TIPS

Remember that the toothpick test is tricky when the cake is swirled with something gooey—in this case, Nutella, which will stay melty throughout baking. Make sure you pick an unswirly spot to poke.

If you want to get fancy, cut a banana in half lengthwise and lay the halves on top of the batter, cut side up, then bake as directed.

I love cupcakes, but these mini cakes are a totally different kind of cute (and delicious). I use *brioche à tête* molds (classic French fluted molds that look a bit like metal cupcake liners), mini Bundt pans, or popover pans to make them. I often use different pan shapes and colors of glazes and arrange the little cakes on a platter or cake stand. These mini cakes deserve a pretty plate and a tiny fork.

Makes 10 mini cakes

DIFFICULTY: Easy

MAKE AHEAD AND STORAGE: The cakes can be stored airtight at room temperature for up to 3 days.

Glazed Mini Cakes

1. Preheat the oven to 350°F / 175°C, with a rack in the middle. Grease and flour ten mini cake pans with 4-ounce cups.

2. Make the cakes: In a large bowl, whisk the coconut oil and brown sugar to combine. Add the egg and mix well. Whisk in the vanilla.

3. In a medium bowl, whisk together the flour, baking powder, baking soda, cinnamon, and salt. Add half the mixture to the oil-and-sugar mixture and stir to combine. Add half the buttermilk and mix to combine. Repeat, alternating the remaining flour mixture and buttermilk, just until the ingredients are incorporated and the batter is smooth.

4. Scoop the batter into the prepared molds, filling each well about three-quarters full. Pick up the molds and slam them down on the counter a few times—hard—to eliminate any air bubbles trapped in the batter (this is especially important if the mold has lots of small details, ridges, or patterns).

5. Bake the cakes until a toothpick inserted into the center comes out clean, 16 to 20 minutes. Cool the cakes in the molds for 10 minutes, then run a small offset spatula around the edges of each mold and turn the cakes out onto a wire rack to cool completely.

6. Make the glaze: In a medium saucepan, bring the juice to a simmer over medium heat and simmer until it is syrupy and reduced to 80 g / ⅓ cup.

⟶

CAKES

60 g / ¼ cup coconut oil, melted and cooled slightly

213 g / 1 cup packed light brown sugar

57 g / 1 large egg

5 g / 1 teaspoon vanilla extract

241 g / 2 cups all-purpose flour

4 g / 1 teaspoon baking powder

3 g / ½ teaspoon baking soda

Scant 1 g / ¼ teaspoon ground cinnamon

3 g / ¾ teaspoon fine sea salt

181 g / ¾ cup buttermilk

FRUIT GLAZE

454 g / 2 cups pure fruit juice, such as pomegranate, cherry, or citrus (see Pro Tip)

142 g / 1¼ cups powdered sugar, or more as needed

14 g / 1 tablespoon heavy cream, or more as needed

7. Transfer the juice to a medium bowl and whisk in the powdered sugar. Add the cream and whisk to combine. Adjust the consistency of the glaze with more powdered sugar or cream if needed (see page 29).

8. Glaze the cakes: Use a serrated knife to level any of the bottoms of the cakes that aren't flat. Scoop a little glaze over the top of each cake (I use a #60 / 1-tablespoon scoop, but you can just eyeball it), letting it run down the sides. Let stand until the glaze is completely set before serving, at least 15 minutes.

❋ WHY IT WORKS

Being small, the cakes have a short baking time, which may vary depending on the size of the molds you're using. Overbaking is your enemy here; it will result in a thick outer crust.

★ PRO TIP

You can use whole fruit to make the glaze—an especially good way to go if you want the glaze to have a berry or stone fruit flavor: Cook 510 g / 3 cups (chopped, if applicable) fruit and 50 g / ¼ cup granulated sugar in a saucepan over medium heat until the fruit breaks down. Crush the fruit with a potato masher, then strain to remove any seeds, skin, or excess pulp. Return the juice to the saucepan and proceed as directed in step 7. The juice combines better with powdered sugar when warm. Also, fruits with naturally high levels of pectin (apples, pears, and blueberries, for example) will produce juice that firms up when reduced and cooled, so it's best to make the glaze while the juice is still warm.

This "dump it all in a pan and bake it forever" recipe makes a huge, flavorful cake that will probably look a little different every time you make it, depending on how you layer on the toppings. It's tender, moist, and dense all at the same time, and the streusel melts over the surface, enrobing the pears. It will make your whole house smell like fall, and it's just as great for breakfast as it is for dessert.

If you don't have a 10-inch springform or cake pan, you can bake this cake in two loaf pans; see Pro Tip.

Makes one 10-inch cake

DIFFICULTY: Easy

MAKE AHEAD AND STORAGE: The cake is delicious the day it's baked, but it can be stored, tightly wrapped in plastic wrap, at room temperature for up to 5 days.

Ginger Pear Cake

1. Preheat the oven to 350°F / 175°C, with a rack in the middle. Grease and flour a 10-inch springform pan or a round cake pan that is at least 2 inches tall.

2. **Make the streusel:** In a medium bowl, stir together the flour, oats, and brown sugar. Add the cubed butter and use your fingertips to cut it in until the mixture is homogeneously combined and clumps together in large crumbles. Add the walnuts and toss to incorporate.

3. **Make the cake:** In the bowl of a stand mixer fitted with the paddle attachment (or in a large bowl, using a hand mixer), cream the butter, both sugars, and ginger on medium-low speed until light and fluffy, 4 to 5 minutes.

4. Add the eggs one at a time, mixing until each is well incorporated before adding the next. Scrape the bowl well. Add the vanilla and mix to combine.

5. In a medium bowl, whisk together the flours, baking powder, ground ginger, cinnamon, and salt. Stir in the oats. Add the mixture to the butter mixture and blend on low speed just until incorporated, about 1 minute. Add the grated pears and crystallized ginger and mix just until incorporated.

6. Scoop the batter into the prepared pan and spread it evenly. Top the cake with the sliced pear in a single even layer, then sprinkle on the streusel.

STREUSEL

60 g / ½ cup all-purpose flour

25 g / ¼ cup old-fashioned oats

106 g / ½ cup packed dark brown sugar

85 g / 3 oz / 6 tablespoons cold unsalted butter, cut into ½-inch cubes

57 g / ½ cup chopped walnuts

CAKE

340 g / 12 oz unsalted butter, at room temperature

298 g / 1½ cups granulated sugar

106 g / ¾ cup packed dark brown sugar

17 g / 1 heaping tablespoon grated fresh ginger

228 g / 4 large eggs

→

Clockwise from top: Tomato Upside-Down Cake (page 112), Banana Cake with Cocoa Nibs and Nutella Swirl (page 104), and Ginger Pear Cake

7. Bake the cake until a toothpick inserted into the center comes out clean or with just a few moist crumbs attached, 80 to 90 minutes. Cool the cake in the pan for 30 minutes, then unmold it onto a wire rack to cool completely. Or eat it warm.

❄ **WHY IT WORKS**

Using the fruit's natural moisture instead of a liquid like milk makes this cake extra flavorful. Rye flour contains significantly less gluten than the traditional wheat flour, which makes for a more tender result. Recipes that use rye also typically need a higher ratio of liquid to properly hydrate the flour (due to the naturally occurring sugars present in rye, called pentosans). The pentosans can break apart easily with too much mixing, so it's important to not overmix this batter.

★ **PRO TIP**

If you don't have a 10-inch cake pan, you can bake this cake in two greased 9-by-5-inch loaf pans (or cut the recipe in half for one loaf pan). Line the pans with parchment paper (leave a 1-inch overhang on the two long sides to make it easy to lift the loaves out), then lightly grease the paper. Bake for 60 to 70 minutes (check halfway through and tent with aluminum foil if the cake is browning too quickly).

7.5 g / 1½ teaspoons vanilla extract

241 g / 2 cups all-purpose flour

103 g / 1 cup medium rye flour

6 g / 1½ teaspoons baking powder

3 g / 1 teaspoon ground ginger

3 g / 1 teaspoon ground cinnamon

2 g / ½ teaspoon fine sea salt

99 g / 1 cup old-fashioned oats

284 g / 1¼ packed cups coarsely grated cored, peeled pears (about 2 medium pears), plus 142 g / 1 medium pear, peeled, cored, and thinly sliced

92 g / ½ cup chopped crystallized ginger

My grandma once told me that her mom used to make a tomato jam that they ate on pancakes. I tried it once, using my dad's whole wheat pancakes. It was so good that I decided to experiment with it in my favorite upside-down cake recipe, which features graham flour for a nutty, crumby texture similar to those pancakes. Tomatoes are fruit, after all, so why not upside-down-cakeify them? The photo is on page 110.

The photo is on page 110.

Makes one 9-inch cake

DIFFICULTY: Easy

MAKE AHEAD AND STORAGE: This cake is best within 2 days of baking. Store tightly wrapped at room temperature.

Tomato Upside-Down Cake

1. **Make the jam:** In a medium saucepan, stir together the tomatoes, granulated sugar, cinnamon, cloves, and ginger and bring to a simmer over medium heat. Turn the heat down to low and cook, stirring occasionally, until the mixture thickens to a jam consistency, 35 to 45 minutes. Set aside to cool to room temperature (the jam will thicken a bit more as it cools).

2. Preheat the oven to 350°F / 175°C, with a rack in the middle. Use 43 g / 3 tablespoons of the butter to grease a 9-inch springform pan or a 9-inch round cake pan with sides at least 3 inches high. Line the bottom of the pan with a circle of parchment paper cut to fit and grease the paper. Line a baking sheet with parchment.

3. Spread the jam in an even layer over the bottom of the pan and place the pan on the lined baking sheet.

4. **Make the cake:** In the bowl of a stand mixer fitted with the paddle attachment (or in a large bowl, using a hand mixer), cream the butter and both sugars on medium-low speed until light and fluffy, 4 to 5 minutes.

5. Add the eggs one at a time, mixing until each one is fully incorporated before adding the next. Scrape the bowl well. Add the vanilla and mix to combine.

6. In a medium bowl, whisk together the all-purpose flour, graham flour, baking powder, baking soda, cinnamon, and salt.

TOMATO JAM

496 g / 2½ cups chopped ripe tomatoes

248 g / 1¼ cups granulated sugar

3 g / 1½ teaspoons ground cinnamon

1.5 g / ¾ teaspoon ground cloves

1.5 g / ¾ teaspoon ground ginger

CAKE

255 g / 9 oz unsalted butter, at room temperature

159 g / ¾ cup packed light brown sugar

99 g / ½ cup granulated sugar

113 g / 2 large eggs, at room temperature

5 g / 1 teaspoon vanilla extract

120 g / 1 cup all-purpose flour

113 g / 1 cup graham flour

7. Add one third of the flour mixture to the butter mixture and blend on low speed to combine, then add half of the crème fraîche, mixing to combine. Repeat, alternating the flour mixture and crème fraîche, until all the ingredients are incorporated and the batter is smooth.

8. Pour the batter into the prepared pan, spreading it evenly without disturbing the underlying bed of tomato jam. Bake the cake until a toothpick inserted into the center (but not deeply, or you'll poke into the juicy jam) comes out clean, 50 to 60 minutes. Cool the cake in the pan for 15 to 20 minutes.

9. If you used a springform pan, remove the ring, invert the pan onto a wire rack, and, while the cake is still warm, use the spatula to separate the base from the parchment and lift it away from the cake. Or, if you used a cake pan, run a small offset spatula around the outside of the cake and invert the cake onto the rack. Gently pull away the parchment; if any fruit is stuck to it, just pry it off and put it back where it belongs—it's easy to mash it back on there. Let cool completely.

✳ **WHY IT WORKS**
It's especially important to unmold upside-down cakes at the right time—10 to 15 minutes after removing them from the oven. That's when the cake will have firmed up a bit but the jam (or fruit) will still be warm and fluid, making it more likely to release from the base of the pan cleanly.

★ **PRO TIP**
You can make this recipe with 1¾ cups of any kind of jam, store-bought or homemade.

6 g / 1½ teaspoons baking powder

3 g / ½ teaspoon baking soda

2 g / 1 teaspoon ground cinnamon

3 g / ¾ teaspoon fine sea salt

302 g / 1⅓ cups crème fraîche, at room temperature

The best strawberry shortcakes are made with a biscuit base, but I took the idea and ran with it, creating a towering layer cake worthy of your fanciest summer soiree—although it is as easy to make as the traditional version. Bonus: The cheater's whipped cream filling is stable at room temperature, thanks to the addition of cream cheese, so no worries about it weeping or deflating if the cake doesn't all get eaten right away (although it probably will).

Makes one very tall 9-inch shortcake

DIFFICULTY: Easy

MAKE AHEAD AND STORAGE: The components for this recipe can all be made ahead and stored for up to 1 day— biscuits wrapped tightly in plastic wrap, at room temperature, and the strawberries and cream refrigerated in separate airtight containers. Once assembled, the cake should be kept refrigerated and served within 1 day.

Strawberry Not-So-Short Cake

1. Preheat the oven to 350°F / 175°C, with a rack in the middle. Grease three 9-inch round cake pans (see Pro Tip).

2. Make the biscuit layers: In the bowl of a food processor, pulse together the flour, brown sugar, baking powder, baking soda, and salt. Add the butter and pulse until the bits of butter are about the size of peas. Transfer the mixture to a large bowl.

3. In a container with a spout (such as a liquid measure) or in a medium bowl, whisk together the buttermilk, eggs, egg yolk, and vanilla. Make a well in the center of the flour mixture and pour in the buttermilk mixture. Use your hands to mix enough to begin moistening the flour mixture, then knead gently just until the mixture forms a homogeneous dough. Take care not to overwork the dough.

4. Divide the dough evenly among the prepared pans (about 525 g per pan). Press into an even layer—if the dough is sticky and hard to handle, lightly moisten your hands with water. Sprinkle each layer with turbinado sugar.

5. Bake until the biscuits are golden brown on the surface and a toothpick inserted into the center comes

BISCUIT LAYERS

602 g / 5 cups all-purpose flour

159 g / ¾ cup packed light brown sugar

24 g / 2 tablespoons baking powder

6 g / 1 teaspoon baking soda

3 g / ¾ teaspoon fine sea salt

453 g / 1 lb cold unsalted butter, cut into ½-inch cubes

302 g / 1¼ cups buttermilk

113 g / 2 large eggs

27 g / 1 large egg yolk

10 g / 2 teaspoons vanilla extract

Turbinado or coarse sugar, for sprinkling (optional)

⟶

My bestest bud, Terri, requested "black raspberry *anything*" for her bridal shower. I ultimately devised a black raspberry buttercream that's perfect for cupcakes—especially ones concealing more berries. Although black raspberry season is short, some orchards ship frozen berries year-round (see Resources, page 369)—and boy, are they worth it! Blackberries or red raspberries can be used in a pinch.

MAKE AHEAD AND STORAGE: The cooled unfrosted cupcakes can be stored tightly wrapped, for up to 2 days at room temperature. The buttercream can be made up to 1 week ahead and stored in an airtight container in the refrigerator (see page 151 for how to reconstitute before using). The frosted cupcakes should be eaten within 2 days.

Black Raspberry Cupcakes

1. Preheat the oven to 350°F/ 175°C, with a rack in the middle. Grease the cavities of a muffin pan or line with paper liners.

2. **Make the cupcakes:** In the bowl of a stand mixer fitted with the paddle attachment (or in a large bowl, using a hand mixer), cream the butter, granulated sugar, and lemon zest on medium-low speed until light and fluffy, 4 to 5 minutes.

3. Add the eggs one at a time, mixing until each is fully incorporated before adding the next. Scrape the bowl well.

4. In a medium bowl, whisk together the flour, baking powder, and salt. In a container with a spout (such as a 2-cup liquid measure) or a small bowl, whisk together the buttermilk and lemon juice to combine.

5. Add half the flour mixture to the butter mixture and mix on low speed just until combined. Add half the buttermilk mixture and mix just until combined. Repeat with the remaining flour mixture, followed by the remaining buttermilk mixture, mixing just until the ingredients are uniformly incorporated and the batter is smooth.

6. In a small bowl, toss the berries with the cornstarch to coat. If the berries don't appear fully coated, add more cornstarch 4 g / 1 teaspoon at a time.

CUPCAKES

113 g / 4 oz / 8 tablespoons unsalted butter, at room temperature

149 g / ¾ cup granulated sugar

6 g / 1 tablespoon grated lemon zest

170 g / 3 large eggs, at room temperature

151 g / 1¼ cups all-purpose flour

4 g / 1 teaspoon baking powder

2 g / ½ teaspoon fine sea salt

81 g / ⅓ cup buttermilk, at room temperature

30 g / 2 tablespoons freshly squeezed lemon juice

170 g / 1 cup fresh (or, if frozen, thawed and drained) black raspberries

7 g / 1 tablespoon cornstarch, plus more as needed

———→

From left: Peppermint–Devil's Food Hi-Hat Cupcakes (page 124), Black Raspberry Cupcakes, and Honey Pound Cupcakes with Honey-Caramel Glaze (page 100)

7. Scoop the batter into the prepared cups, filling each one about three-quarters full (I use a #16 / ¼-cup scoop, but you can just wing it). Drop a few raspberries into each cup and press them gently into the center (not down to the bottom) of the batter.

8. Bake the cupcakes until their centers spring back slightly when touched, 18 to 20 minutes. Let cool completely in the pan.

9. **Make the buttercream:** Combine the berries and granulated sugar in a medium saucepan and bring to a simmer over medium heat. Cook until the berries break down and are very juicy, 5 to 7 minutes. Mash the fruit with a potato masher or the back of a spoon.

10. Strain the berry juice into a small saucepan and bring to a simmer over medium heat. Simmer until the juice is reduced to 81 g / ⅓ cup. Let cool to room temperature (you can throw it in the fridge to speed this up).

11. Place the butter in the bowl of a stand mixer fitted with the paddle attachment (or use a large bowl and a hand mixer). Beat the butter for

1 minute, then gradually add the powdered sugar and cream the mixture on medium-low speed until light and fluffy, 4 to 5 minutes.

12. Add the reduced berry juice, vanilla, and the cream, if using, and beat until well combined, scraping the bowl well to make sure the juice has been evenly incorporated.

13. **Frost the cupcakes:** To pipe on the buttercream, transfer about half of it to a pastry bag fitted with a large star tip (such as #838 or #848; see page 93) and pipe a mound of frosting onto each cupcake, refilling the bag with the remaining frosting when you get low. Or spoon a dollop of frosting atop each cupcake and spread it with a small offset spatula.

❋ **WHY IT WORKS**
Tossing the berries with cornstarch helps prevent them from sinking to the bottom of the batter. Keeping them suspended in the center is significantly prettier, ensures even flavor and texture in each bite, and prevents the burnt bottoms that can result from an overrun of fruit juice.

BLACK RASPBERRY BUTTERCREAM

240 g / 2 cups fresh (or frozen) black raspberries

50 g / ¼ cup granulated sugar

113 g / 4 oz / 8 tablespoons unsalted butter, at room temperature

227 g / 2 cups powdered sugar

5 g / 1 teaspoon vanilla extract

30 g / 2 tablespoons heavy cream (optional)

★ **PRO TIP**
Using a fruit juice reduction to flavor buttercream is a great technique that works as well with an Italian buttercream (page 158) as it does with a simple buttercream like this one. Use a reduction made from fresh or frozen fruit, like berries or sliced stone fruit such as peaches, plums, apricots, or cherries. For a buttercream flavored with citrus, pomegranate, or tropical fruit, you're better off reducing pure fruit juice: Substitute 475 g / 2 cups juice for the fruit and skip the straining step unless the juice is very pulpy.

Rather than butter or oil, this batter gets most of its fat and richness from heavy cream. The cake is pillowy and soft, with a tight crumb structure. Apricots appear in three forms—dried apricots in the batter, apricot jam in the whipped cream topping, and roasted apricots on top—though you can skip the roasted apricots when they aren't in season.

Makes one 9-inch cake

DIFFICULTY: Easy

MAKE AHEAD AND STORAGE: This cake is best within 2 days of baking. Store airtight in the refrigerator. It's best to add the toppings just before serving.

Apricot Cream Cake

1. Preheat the oven to 350°F / 175°C, with racks in the upper and lower thirds. Grease and flour a 9-inch springform pan or a 9-inch round cake pan with sides at least 3 inches tall.

2. **Make the cake:** Whisk together the flour, baking powder, and salt.

3. In the bowl of a stand mixer fitted with the whisk attachment (or in a large bowl, using a hand mixer), whisk the eggs and granulated sugar on low speed to combine, then turn the speed up to high and whip the mixture until pale and thick, 5 to 6 minutes. Reduce the speed to medium and whip for 1 minute more to help stabilize the foam.

4. Sprinkle about one quarter of the flour mixture over the egg mixture and blend on low speed just until in-corporated. Add the remaining flour in 3 additions, mixing until just incorporated; take care not to overmix the batter. Slowly drizzle the cream into the batter, mixing on low speed just until incorporated. Add the vanilla and mix just to combine, then mix in the dried apricots.

5. Pour the batter into the prepared pan. Bake the cake on the upper rack until a toothpick inserted into the center comes out clean; 60 to 75 minutes—this is a big cake! Cool the cake completely in the pan.

6. **Meanwhile, roast the apricots, if using:** Line a baking sheet with parchment paper (or use a cast-iron skillet). Arrange the apricot halves on the lined baking sheet or in the skillet, cut side down. Sprinkle the granulated sugar over the fruit.

CAKE

421 g / 3½ cups all-purpose flour

12 g / 1 tablespoon baking powder

4 g / 1 teaspoon salt

248 g / 5 large eggs, at room temperature

397 g / 2 cups granulated sugar

484 g / 2 cups heavy cream

10 g / 2 teaspoons vanilla extract

142 g / 1 cup dried apricots, chopped

ROASTED APRICOTS (OPTIONAL; SEE PRO TIP)

324 g / 5 fresh apricots, halved and pitted

50 g / ¼ cup granulated sugar

APRICOT CREAM

242 g / 1 cup heavy cream

14 g / 2 tablespoons powdered sugar

113 g / ⅓ cup apricot jam

→

7. Roast the apricots on the lower rack until they are tender but still hold their shape, 15 to 20 minutes. Let cool completely.

8. Make the apricot cream: In the bowl of a stand mixer fitted with the whisk attachment (or in a medium bowl, using a hand mixer), whip the cream and powdered sugar to soft peaks. Add the jam and continue whipping until the cream reaches medium peaks.

9. Assemble the cake: Run a small offset spatula around the edges of the pan, then release the outer ring from the springform pan and unmold the cake (or, if using a traditional cake pan, turn out onto a wire rack). If you want a very flat top, you can use a long serrated knife to level off the cake (see page 82). Mound the whipped cream on top of the cake, and arrange the roasted apricots, if using, on top.

❋ **WHY IT WORKS**

This cake tastes like a butter cake but it is made using a method more similar to that for a sponge cake. Adding the cream at the end makes it moister and richer than a typical sponge. It's an excellent example of how using different ingredients with a familiar method will create different results!

★ **PRO TIP**

This cake is great in the summer, when you can get fresh apricots, but I make it year round. Just nix the roasted apricots and up the amount of dried apricots in the batter by 71 g / ⅓ cup to give it a little extra boost!

Hi-hat cupcakes can turn a sophisticated adult into a happy kid in five seconds flat. What makes this cupcake a hi-hat? A huge mound of marshmallowy frosting. It's flavored with peppermint and then covered with a thin layer of chocolate glaze. I love to make these cupcakes for the holidays.

Makes 18 cupcakes

DIFFICULTY: Medium

MAKE AHEAD AND STORAGE: The un-frosted cupcakes can be made up to 2 days ahead and stored, tightly covered, at room temperature. The glaze can be made ahead and kept airtight at room temperature for up to 1 week (remelt before using if it hardens). The frosted and glazed cupcakes will keep, tightly covered in the refrigerator, for up to 2 days.

Peppermint–Devil's Food Hi-Hat Cupcakes

1. Make the glaze: Combine the chopped chocolate and coconut oil in a medium heatproof bowl and place over a medium saucepan of barely simmering water (with the bowl not touching the water). Heat, stirring occasionally, until the mixture is fully melted and combined. Set aside to cool to room temperature.

2. Make the frosting: Combine the egg whites, sugar, water, and cream of tartar in a large heatproof bowl. Place the bowl over a medium saucepan of barely simmering water (with the bowl not touching the water) and heat, whisking constantly, until the sugar is dissolved and the mixture

is slightly warm to the touch (if you want to check with an instant-read thermometer, it should register about 140°F / 60°C), 2 to 3 minutes.

3. Transfer the mixture to a stand mixer fitted with the whisk attachment (or use a large bowl and a hand mixer) and whip on medium-high speed until the frosting is light and fluffy and holds medium peaks, 6 to 7 minutes. Add the peppermint and vanilla extracts and food coloring, if using, and mix to combine. Transfer the frosting to a disposable pastry bag fitted with a plain tip about ½ inch wide, or just cut a ½-inch opening in the tip of the bag (or the corner of a heavy-duty zip-top bag.

CHOCOLATE GLAZE

227 g / 8 oz milk chocolate, chopped

113 g / ½ cup coconut oil

PEPPERMINT SEVEN-MINUTE FROSTING

149 g / 5 large egg whites

397 g / 2 cups granulated sugar

60 g / ¼ cup water

Scant 1 g / ¼ teaspoon cream of tartar

2.5 g / ½ teaspoon peppermint extract

2.5 g / ½ teaspoon vanilla extract

3 or 4 drops red food coloring (optional)

18 Devil's Food Cupcakes (see Variation, page 134)

4. Frost the cupcakes: Place the cupcakes on a work surface and pipe a tall spiral of frosting onto each one, starting at the edge and working around the cupcake: After you've piped frosting all around the edge, let the frosting start to build upward once you reach the place where you started and continue building the spiral upward, layer by layer, until it's about 3 inches tall. When you've nearly finished piping, release the pressure on the bag and pull it away, giving the spiral a nicely curled tip. Chill the frosted cupcakes for 20 to 30 minutes.

5. Glaze the frosting: Line a baking sheet with parchment paper and set a wire rack on top. Transfer the cooled chocolate glaze to a tall container, such as a large liquid measuring cup (this makes for easier dipping; be sure the opening of the container is wide enough for the cupcakes). Hold each cupcake upside down and dunk it deep enough into the chocolate glaze to fully cover the frosting (let any excess glaze drip off; because the cupcakes are cold, though, the glaze should mostly start to set immediately), then set the glazed cupcake on the wire rack.

6. Transfer the cupcakes to the refrigerator and chill until the glaze is set, at least 5 minutes.

❋ **WHY IT WORKS**

The Devil's Food Cake recipe (page 133) produces cupcakes that bake flat, or with only a small dome. This is a sign that the batter has the proper amount of structure.

★ **PRO TIP**

The chocolate glaze for these cupcakes is a homemade version of the store-bought chocolate sauce that hardens when poured over ice cream. The coconut oil makes the chocolate more fluid and encourages it to set faster when it's applied to a chilled surface. You can use this glaze to make a drippy cake (see page 86), and it is excellent on top of Sweet Cream Ice Cream (page 362).

Petits fours are perfectly adorable, and there's perhaps no better way to flavor them than with delicate floral essences. The base recipe here is for rose petits fours, but you'll find orange blossom and lavender variations on page 129. If you want to really wow a crowd, make all three. I like to decorate them with edible flowers, but you really can't ever go wrong with sprinkles.

Makes 36 petits fours

DIFFICULTY: Medium

MAKE AHEAD AND STORAGE: The cake can be made ahead and stored, tightly wrapped in plastic, at room temperature for up to 1 day or frozen for up to 1 month. The glaze can be made up to 1 day ahead; reheat as directed. The filled and frosted cake can be frozen unglazed (whole or in pieces) airtight for up to 1 month. The glazed petits fours will keep at room temperature for up to 7 days airtight.

Rose Petits Fours

1. Preheat the oven to 350°F / 175°C, with a rack in the middle. Grease and flour a 9-inch square baking pan.

2. Make the cake: In the bowl of a stand mixer fitted with the paddle attachment (or in a large bowl, using a hand mixer), cream the butter and granulated sugar on medium-low speed until light and fluffy, 4 to 5 minutes.

3. Add the eggs one at a time, mixing on medium speed until each is fully incorporated. Scrape the bowl well. Add the vanilla and mix to combine.

4. In a medium bowl, whisk together the flour, baking powder, and salt. In a container with a spout (such as a 1-cup liquid measure), combine the milk and rose water. Add the flour mixture to the butter mixture and blend on low speed to combine, 1 to 2 minutes. Pour in the milk mixture in a slow, steady stream and mix to combine, 1 minute more.

5. Pour the batter into the prepared pan. Bake the cake until a toothpick inserted into the center comes out clean, 30 to 35 minutes (the cake will not spring back when you touch it in the middle). Cool the cake in the pan for 15 minutes, then turn out onto a wire rack to cool completely.

6. Make the frosting: In a small bowl, with a hand mixer, cream the butter and powdered sugar on medium-low

CAKE

227 g / 8 oz unsalted butter, at room temperature

298 g / 1½ cups granulated sugar

85 g / 3 large eggs, at room temperature

5 g / 1 teaspoon vanilla extract

271 g / 2¼ cups all-purpose flour

2 g / ½ teaspoon baking powder

1 g / ¼ teaspoon fine sea salt

121 g / ½ cup whole milk, at room temperature

60 g / ¼ cup rose water

→

speed until light and fluffy; scrape down the bowl as needed. Add the vanilla and cream and mix to combine.

7. Fill and frost the cake: Use a long serrated knife to cut the cake horizontally in half (see page 82). Place the bottom layer cut side up on a turntable or cake stand (or a platter). Spread the jelly evenly over the top. Top with the second layer. Pile the frosting onto the center of the cake and spread it in an even layer; use it to help fill in or conceal any ripples or marks, so that the surface of the cake is as flat and smooth as possible. Refrigerate the cake until it is thoroughly chilled, at least 30 minutes. (If you're short on time, you can freeze the cake for 15 to 20 minutes—the colder the cake is, the easier it will be to cut it cleanly.)

8. Make the icing: In a medium heat-proof bowl, whisk together the powdered sugar, corn syrup, water, vanilla, and food coloring, if using. Set the bowl over a medium saucepan of simmering water (with the bowl not touching the water) and heat, stirring occasionally, until the mixture is smooth and homogeneous. The icing should be fluid but not so warm it will melt the frosting (you can use an instant-read thermometer to make sure it's below 100°F / 38°C).

9. Glaze the petits fours: Use a long serrated knife to trim about ¼ inch off each side of the chilled cake, creating flat sides. To form 36 squares, cut the cake vertically into 6 equal strips and then horizontally into 6 equal strips.

10. Line a baking sheet with parchment paper and set a wire rack on top. Transfer the cut cakes to the rack. Use a ladle or a spoon to pour some icing over each cake. (The icing should easily run down and fully cover the sides of the cakes; if it gets too thick, you can warm it up slightly by setting the bowl in a shallow bowl of hot water.) To use the icing that falls onto the baking sheet, just lift off the rack of cakes, lift up the parchment, and squeeze the icing back into the bowl.

11. Garnish the cakes with rose petals or sprinkles and let sit until the icing is set, at least 30 minutes.

❊ **WHY IT WORKS**

The cake for these petits fours is on the dense side, which makes it easy to slice into tidy little squares. Only the cake component contains the floral flavoring, because it can become overwhelming. The jelly and icing help balance everything out with their fruitiness and sweetness.

FROSTING AND FILLING

58 g / 2 oz / 4 tablespoons unsalted butter, at room temperature

113 g / 1 cup powdered sugar, sifted

2.5 g / ½ teaspoon vanilla extract

15 g / 1 tablespoon heavy cream

170 g / ½ cup strawberry jelly

ICING

907 g / 8 cups / 2 boxes powdered sugar

312 g / ½ cup light corn syrup

161 g / ⅔ cup water

2.5 g / ½ teaspoon vanilla extract

3 or 4 drops red food coloring (optional)

Rose petals (dried, candied, or fresh, with bitter white base removed) or sprinkles, for finishing

★ **PRO TIP**

As with any recipe with multiple components, the whole process is much less daunting if you make some of them in advance. I usually make the frosting and icing ahead of time, so that after the cake is baked and cooled, I can just focus on the assembly. You can also make the cake ahead. See Make Ahead and Storage, page 127, for instructions on advance prep.

Variations

Orange Blossom Petits Fours: Replace the rose water with orange flower water. Replace the strawberry jelly with orange marmalade. If you want to tint the icing, use only 2 drops red food coloring and add 2 drops yellow food coloring. Garnish with fresh orange blossoms or sprinkles.

Lavender Petits Fours: Increase the milk to 161 g / ⅔ cup. Before making the cake, bring 81 g / ⅓ cup of the milk and 1 tablespoon organic dried lavender to a simmer in a small saucepan over medium heat. Remove the pan from the heat, cover, and let steep for 15 minutes, then strain the infused milk into a liquid measuring cup and add the remaining milk. (Be sure the mixture has cooled to room temperature before adding it to the cake batter.) Replace the strawberry jelly with quince or apple jelly. To tint the icing, use only 2 drops red food coloring and add 2 drops blue food coloring. Garnish with organic lavender flowers or sprinkles.

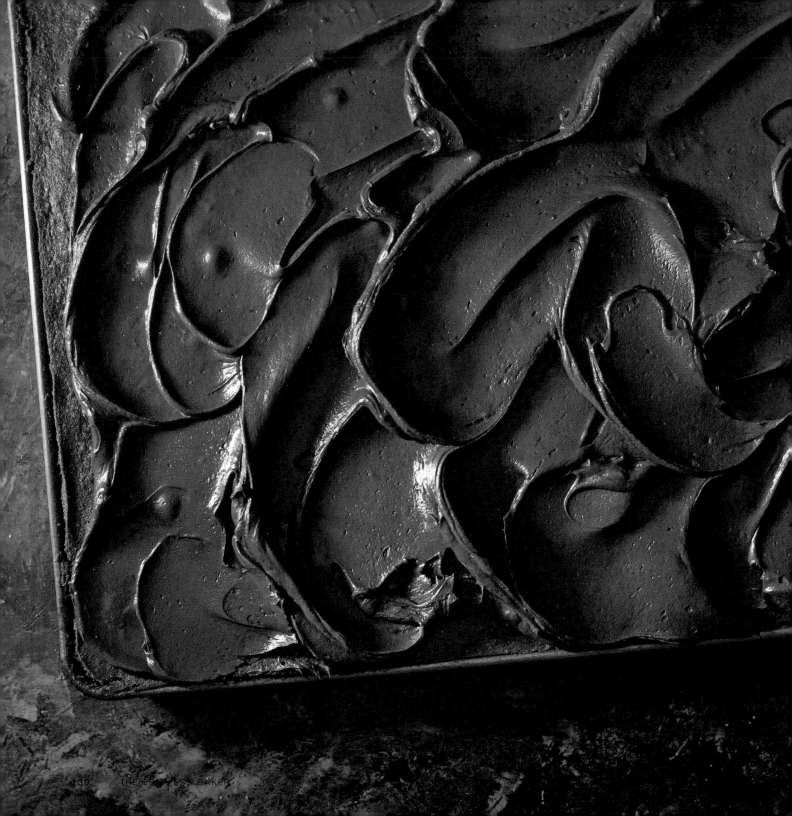

This cake is a dark horse: It's probably the one you remember from your childhood, bake sales, and church picnics. It's made using the high-ratio method. Yes, it uses shortening, which has become unpopular, but that plays an important role here (see Why It Works). High-ratio cakes are often made by large-scale bakeries, because they are sweet, moist, and tender. This is a good one to have in your arsenal.

Makes one 18-by-13-inch sheet cake

DIFFICULTY: Easy

MAKE AHEAD AND STORAGE: This cake keeps tightly covered at room temperature for up to 5 days.

Chocolate "High-Ratio" Sheet Cake

1. Preheat the oven to 350°F / 175°C, with a rack in the middle. Grease an 18-by-13-by-1-inch baking sheet.

2. Make the cake: Place the cocoa powder in a medium heatproof bowl. Pour in the boiling water and whisk to combine. Set aside to cool to room temperature.

3. In the bowl of a stand mixer fitted with the paddle attachment (or in a large bowl, using a hand mixer), cream the shortening, butter, and sugar on medium-low speed until light and fluffy, 4 to 5 minutes.

4. Add the eggs and egg yolks one at a time to the shortening mixture, mixing until each one is fully incorpo-

rated. Scrape the bowl well. Add the vanilla and mix to combine.

5. Sift together the cake flour, baking powder, baking soda, and salt in a medium bowl. Add one third of the mixture to the shortening mixture and mix on low speed to incorporate. Add half the cooled cocoa mixture and mix to incorporate. Repeat, alternating the flour mixture and cocoa mixture, until both are fully incorporated and the batter is smooth.

6. Pour the batter into the prepared pan and use an offset spatula to spread it evenly. Bake the cake until a toothpick inserted into the center comes out clean, 20 to 25 minutes. Let the cake cool completely in the pan.

CAKE

64 g / ¾ cup unsweetened cocoa powder

363 g / 1½ cups boiling water

227 g / 1 cup vegetable shortening, at room temperature

113 g / 4 oz / 8 tablespoons unsalted butter, at room temperature

447 g / 2¼ cups granulated sugar

227 g / 4 large eggs, at room temperature

54 g / 4 large egg yolks, at room temperature

15 g / 1 tablespoon vanilla extract

402 g / 3⅓ cups cake flour

8 g / 2 teaspoons baking powder

3 g / 1 teaspoon baking soda

3 g / ¾ teaspoon salt

⟶

7. Make the ganache: Place the chocolate in a medium heatproof bowl. Bring the cream to a boil in a small saucepan over medium heat and immediately pour it over the chocolate. Let the mixture sit, undisturbed, for 15 seconds, then stir, beginning in the center of the bowl with small circular motions and widening the circles, until the ingredients are uniformly combined and the ganache is smooth. Let the ganache cool to room temperature (you can park it in the refrigerator to speed this up, but don't let it firm up completely).

8. Transfer the cooled ganache to the bowl of a stand mixer fitted with the whisk attachment (or use a large bowl and a hand mixer). Whip the ganache on medium-high speed until lightened in color, 2 to 3 minutes. Scrape the bowl well and whip again to make sure the ganache is fully aerated.

9. Scoop the ganche onto the cooled cake in the pan and spread it evenly to the edges.

❈ WHY IT WORKS
High-ratio cakes traditionally use shortening, which is 100 percent fat, rather than butter, which is about 18 percent water—pure fat helps the ingredients in these ratios combine properly into a smooth batter. The texture of the cakes is light, tender, and moist, and it stays that way a bit longer than cakes made using other methods, all because of the higher ratios!

★ PRO TIP
This cake can also be baked in two 9-inch round cake pans—increase the baking time to 35 to 37 minutes.

WHIPPED GANACHE

340 g / 12 oz dark chocolate (I use 60% cacao), chopped

242 g / 1 cup heavy cream

Once upon a time, I took a six-month job as a baker on an island. The day I turned nineteen, I was given the task of making a devil's food cake frosted with thin layers of super-sweet American vanilla buttercream and covered in lots of coconut—which just so happens to be my favorite birthday cake. As I worked, I marveled at the coincidence, thinking, "This person and I have the same taste in cake." Turns out my parents wanted to surprise me with a cake for my birthday, but since I had arrived just a few days before, no one knew who I was, and the order was assigned to me!

Makes one 9-inch 2-layer cake

DIFFICULTY: Easy

MAKE AHEAD AND STORAGE: The cake layers can be made up to 2 days ahead and stored, tightly wrapped, at room temperature. The buttercream can be made ahead and stored airtight in the refrigerator for up to 1 week (see page 151 for how to reconstitute before using). The frosted cake can be refrigerated airtight for up to 2 days.

Devil's Food Cake
(My Favorite Birthday Cake)

1. Preheat the oven to 350°F / 175°C, with a rack in the middle. Grease and flour two 9-inch round cake pans.

2. **Make the cakes:** Place the cocoa powder in a medium heatproof bowl. Whisk in the boiling water until fully combined. Stir in the milk and set aside.

3. In the bowl of a stand mixer fitted with the paddle attachment (or in a large bowl, using a hand mixer), cream the butter and granulated sugar on medium-low speed until light and fluffy, 4 to 5 minutes. Add the eggs one at a time, mixing until each is fully incorporated before adding the next.

Scrape the bowl well. Add the vanilla and mix to combine.

4. In a medium bowl, whisk together the flour, baking powder, baking soda, and salt. Add one third of the mixture to the butter mixture and mix on low speed to combine. Add half the cocoa-and-milk mixture and mix to incorporate. Repeat, alternating between the dry and wet ingredients, until both are fully incorporated and the batter is smooth.

5. Divide the batter between the prepared pans (about 652 g per pan). Bake the cakes until a toothpick inserted into the center comes out

CAKE

128 g / 1½ cups unsweetened cocoa powder

242 g / 1 cup boiling water

285 g / 1¼ cups whole milk

255 g / 9 oz unsalted butter, at room temperature

595 g / 3 cups granulated sugar

284 g / 5 large eggs

15 g / 1 tablespoon vanilla extract

361 g / 3 cups all-purpose flour

8 g / 2 teaspoons baking powder

6 g / 1 teaspoon baking soda

3 g / ¾ teaspoon fine sea salt

⟶

clean, 40 to 45 minutes. Cool the cakes in the pans for 10 to 15 minutes, then turn out onto a wire rack to cool completely.

6. Make the buttercream: In the bowl of a stand mixer fitted with the paddle attachment (or in a large bowl, using a hand mixer), cream the butter and powdered sugar on medium-low speed until light and fluffy, 4 to 5 minutes. Add the vanilla and cream and mix until thoroughly combined, about 1 minute.

7. Assemble the cake: Use a serrated knife to level the top of each cake (see page 82). Place one layer on a turntable or cake stand (or a platter). Scoop a heaping ¾ cup of the frosting onto the layer and use an offset spatula to spread the frosting evenly over it. Top with the other cake layer, flat side up. Apply a crumb coat of frosting (see page 87) to the top and sides of the cake and refrigerate to set, 15 to 30 minutes.

8. Frost the sides and top of the cake (for more detailed frosting instructions, see page 87). Use your hands to pat the coconut all over the top and sides of the cake. Refrigerate the cake for at least 15 minutes before slicing and serving (it will slice more cleanly).

❄ **WHY IT WORKS**

Like many of the best chocolate cake recipes, this recipe starts by drowning cocoa powder in boiling water—a step that brings out its intense chocolaty flavors. You want to make sure that this mixture isn't too hot when you add it to the batter, or it could melt the butter and possibly break the batter.

★ **PRO TIP**

To avoid having to wait for the liquid to cool, I stir the cold milk into the cocoa mixture, lowering the temperature, so it is good to go right away.

AMERICAN BUTTERCREAM

227 g / 8 oz unsalted butter, at room temperature

454 g / 4 cups powdered sugar

10 g / 2 teaspoons vanilla extract

61 g / ¼ cup heavy cream (optional)

255 g / 3 cups sweetened or unsweetened flaked or shredded coconut (whatever you like)

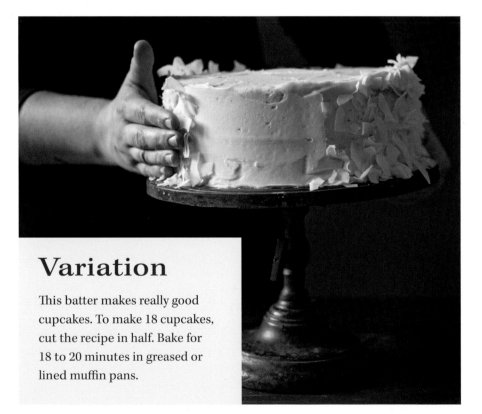

Variation

This batter makes really good cupcakes. To make 18 cupcakes, cut the recipe in half. Bake for 18 to 20 minutes in greased or lined muffin pans.

For those times when you want to have your coffee and eat it too! The point of departure for this recipe was my deep, dark Devil's Food Cake (page 133), which I reworked to infuse it with plenty of rich coffee flavor.

Makes one 9-inch 3-layer cake

DIFFICULTY: Hard

MAKE AHEAD AND STORAGE: The cake layers can be made up to 2 days ahead and stored, tightly wrapped, at room temperature. The ganache can be made up to 1 week ahead and refrigerated (see page 151 for how to reconstitute before using). The frosted cake keeps at room temperature for up to 2 days.

Mocha Cake
with Coffee–White Chocolate Ganache

1. Make the ganache: Place the white chocolate in a large heatproof bowl. In a medium saucepan, bring the cream to a simmer over medium heat, then stir in the espresso powder and bring to a full boil.

2. Pour the hot cream over the white chocolate. Let the mixture sit, undisturbed, for 15 seconds, then stir, beginning in the center of the bowl with small circular motions and widening the circles, until the ingredients are uniformly combined and the ganache is smooth. Let the ganache cool to room temperature (you can briefly park it in the refrigerator—just don't let it firm up completely).

3. Meanwhile, make the cakes: Preheat the oven to 350°F / 175°C, with a rack in the middle. Grease and flour two 9-inch round cake pans.

4. Place the cocoa powder in a medium bowl. In a spouted measuring cup, whisk the milk into the coffee. Slowly add the mixture to the cocoa powder, whisking constantly to fully combine.

5. In the bowl of a stand mixer fitted with the paddle attachment (or in a large bowl, using a hand mixer), cream the butter and sugar on medium-low speed until light and fluffy, 4 to 5 minutes. Add the espresso powder and mix for 1 minute.

COFFEE–WHITE CHOCOLATE GANACHE

765 g / 1 lb 11 oz white chocolate, chopped

181 g / ¾ cup heavy cream

43 g / 1½ tablespoons instant espresso powder

MOCHA CAKE

128 g / 1½ cups unsweetened cocoa powder

302 g / 1¼ cups whole milk

181 g / ¾ cup freshly brewed coffee (preferably espresso)

255 g / 9 oz unsalted butter, at room temperature

595 g / 3 cups granulated sugar

43 g / ¼ cup instant espresso powder

→

6. Add the eggs one at a time, mixing until each is fully incorporated before adding the next. Scrape the bowl well. Add the vanilla and mix to combine.

7. In a medium bowl, whisk together the flour, baking powder, baking soda, and salt. Add one third of the mixture to the butter mixture and mix on low speed to combine. Add half the cocoa mixture and mix to incorporate. Repeat, adding alternate additions of the dry ingredients and wet ingredients, until they are fully incorporated and the batter is smooth.

8. Pour the batter into the prepared pans (about 652 g per pan). Bake the cakes until a toothpick inserted into the center comes out clean, 50 to 60 minutes. Cool the cakes in the pans for 10 to 15 minutes, then turn them out onto a wire rack and cool completely.

9. Whip the ganache: Transfer the cooled ganache to the bowl of a stand mixer fitted with the whisk attachment (or use a medium bowl and a hand mixer) and whip on medium-high speed until it has lightened in color, 2 to 3 minutes. Scrape the bowl well and whip the ganache again just to make sure it's homogeneous.

10. Assemble the cake: Use a long serrated knife to level the top of each cake (see page 82). Cut each in half horizontally to make 2 layers, for 4 layers total. Place one layer on a turntable or cake stand (or platter). Scoop on about ½ cup of the frosting and use an offset spatula to spread it evenly over the top. Top with another of the cake layers, applying frosting to the top and then topping with the next layer. Repeat with another layer of frosting and the final layer of cake.

11. Apply a crumb coat of frosting (see page 87) to the top and sides of the cake. Refrigerate to set, 15 to 30 minutes.

12. Apply a final coat of frosting to the sides and top of the cake (for more detailed instructions, see page 87).

❊ **WHY IT WORKS**

The Devil's Food Cake (page 133) uses hot water, which is easily replaced here with coffee. But the coffee flavor wasn't strong enough, so I added espresso powder to both the cake and the frosting.

★ **PRO TIP**

Looking for even more coffee flavor? Crush some chocolate-covered espresso beans, then sprinkle them on top of the ganache filling and/or use them to decorate the cake.

284 g / 5 large eggs, at room temperature

15 g / 1 tablespoon vanilla extract

361 g / 3 cups all-purpose flour

8 g / 2 teaspoons baking powder

6 g / 1 teaspoon baking soda

3 g / ¾ teaspoon fine sea salt

Variation

Mocha Cake with Ganache Drizzle: Prepare and frost the cake as directed, then chill for at least 1 hour. While the cake chills, make the ganache for the drizzle: Place 227 g / 8 oz / 1⅓ cups dark chocolate, chopped (I use 60% cacao) in a medium heatproof bowl. In a small saucepan, bring 181 g / ¾ cup heavy cream to a boil over medium heat. Pour the hot cream over the chocolate and let sit for 15 seconds, undisturbed, then stir to combine (see Step 2 for more detailed instructions). Let the ganache cool to room temperature. Pour the ganache over the cake as directed on page 86.

My dad sent me a photo of a wall of tall, clustered flowers known as Dame's Rocket. "Maybe you could make a cake called Dame's Rocket," he said. "It's such a good name." Dame's Rocket flowers are edible—a little mustardy and spicy—so I made a spice cake inspired by them, in the style my dad prefers, with bare sides.

This recipe makes a tall, narrow cake, but if you don't have 6-inch round pans, you can bake it in regular 9-inch cake pans; see Pro Tip.

Makes one very tall 6-inch 6-layer cake

DIFFICULTY: Medium

MAKE AHEAD AND STORAGE: The uncut cake can be made ahead and kept at room temperature for up to 1 day. Once it's sliced, keep the leftover cake wrapped tightly at room temperature for up to 2 days.

Dame's Rocket Cake

1. Preheat the oven to 350°F / 175°C, with a rack in the middle. Grease and flour three 6-inch round cake pans (see Pro Tip).

2. **Make the cakes:** In the bowl of a stand mixer fitted with the paddle attachment (or in a large bowl, using a hand mixer), cream the butter and granulated sugar on medium-low speed until light and fluffy, 4 to 5 minutes.

3. Add the eggs one at a time, mixing on medium speed until each is fully incorporated before adding the next. Scrape the bowl well. Add the vanilla and mix to combine.

4. In a medium bowl, whisk together the flour, spices, salt, baking powder, and baking soda. Add one third of the mixture to the butter mixture and beat on low speed just until combined. Add half the milk and mix just until combined. Repeat, alternating between the flour mixture and the milk, just until the batter is uniformly combined.

5. Divide the batter between the prepared pans (about 458 g per pan), spreading it evenly. Bake the cakes until a toothpick inserted into the center comes out clean or with just a few moist crumbs attached, 25 to 32 minutes. Cool the cakes in the pans for 15 minutes, then turn out onto a wire rack to cool completely.

6. **Make the frosting:** In the bowl of a stand mixer fitted with the paddle attachment (or in a large bowl, using a hand mixer), whip the cream cheese, butter, and powdered sugar until light and fluffy, 3 to 4 minutes. Add the

CAKE

226 g / 8 oz unsalted butter, at room temperature

397 g / 2 cups granulated sugar

227 g / 4 large eggs, at room temperature

7.5 g / 1½ teaspoons vanilla extract

361 g / 3 cups all-purpose flour

4 g / 2 teaspoons ground cinnamon

1 g / ½ teaspoon ground cloves

1 g / ½ teaspoon ground allspice

1 g / ½ teaspoon ground ginger

1 g / ½ teaspoon freshly grated nutmeg

2 g / ½ teaspoon fine sea salt

6 g / 1½ teaspoons baking powder

3 g / ½ teaspoon baking soda

242 g / 1 cup whole milk, at room temperature

$\longrightarrow$

molasses and vanilla and mix until fully incorporated.

7. Assemble the cake: Use a long serrated knife to level each cake (see page 82), then cut each one horizontally in half to create a total of 6 layers. Place one layer on a turntable or cake stand (or a platter). Scoop ½ cup of the frosting onto the layer and use an offset spatula to spread it evenly. (For a different look, try piping the frosting instead—see page 89.) Top with another cake layer and another ½ cup of the frosting, spreading it evenly. Repeat until you get to the last layer; leave the last layer bare.

8. Use an offset spatula to smooth the frosting that has squeezed out between the layers. If you like, you can add a very thin layer of frosting to the sides and/or the top of the cake. Or leave them as is—naked (see page 85)! Refrigerate the cake for at least 20 minutes to help firm it up before slicing and serving.

❋ **WHY IT WORKS**
This cake recipe is perfect for building a tall layer cake. It isn't as delicate as a sponge cake—the layers are a little easier to handle, both in slicing and stacking, and it's less likely they'll tear.

★ **PRO TIP**
Tall skinny cakes can be spectacular, but if you don't have 6-inch pans, simply use two 9-inch round cake pans instead (about 723 g of batter per pan) and bake for 45 to 50 minutes.

MOLASSES CREAM CHEESE FROSTING

454 g / 1 lb cream cheese, at room temperature

113 g / 4 oz / 8 tablespoons unsalted butter, at room temperature

284 g / 2½ cups powdered sugar

43 g / 2 tablespoons molasses

5 g / 1 teaspoon vanilla extract

Based on classic Southern-style caramel cake, this recipe starts with a version of my favorite cream cake. The cake is very soft and moist—which makes it the perfect pairing for the fudgy, slightly crystallized icing.

Makes one 9-inch 3-layer cake

DIFFICULTY: Medium

MAKE AHEAD AND STORAGE: This cake can be stored tightly wrapped at room temperature for up to 4 days.

Caramel Cake

1. Preheat the oven to 350°F / 175°C, with a rack in the middle. Grease and flour three 9-inch round cake pans (see Pro Tips).

2. Make the cakes: In a large bowl, whisk together the flour, baking powder, and salt.

3. In the bowl of a stand mixer fitted with the whisk attachment (or in a large bowl, using a hand mixer), whisk the eggs and brown sugar on low speed to combine, then turn the speed to high and whip the mixture until it's thick, 5 to 6 minutes. Reduce the speed to medium and whip for 1 minute more to help stabilize the foam.

4. Sprinkle about one quarter of the flour mixture over the egg mixture and mix on low speed just until incorporated. Add the remaining flour in 3 additions, mixing just until incorporated.

5. Gradually drizzle the cream into the batter, mixing just until incorporated. Add the vanilla and mix just to combine.

6. Divide the batter among the prepared pans (about 694 g per pan). Bake the cakes until a toothpick inserted in the center comes out clean or with just a few moist crumbs attached, 22 to 26 minutes. Cool the cakes in the pans for 15 minutes, then turn out onto wire racks to cool completely.

7. When you're ready to assemble the cake (see Pro Tips), make the frosting: First level off each cake (see page 82) and place one layer on a turntable or cake stand (or a platter).

CAKE

542 g / 4½ cups all-purpose flour

12 g / 1 tablespoon baking powder

4 g / 1 teaspoon fine sea salt

347 g / 7 large eggs, at room temperature

532 g / 2½ cups packed dark brown sugar

665 g / 2¾ cups heavy cream, at room temperature

15 g / 1 tablespoon vanilla extract

CARAMEL FUDGE FROSTING

227 g / 8 oz unsalted butter

425 g / 2 cups packed dark brown sugar

121 g / ½ cup heavy cream

3 g / ¾ teaspoon fine sea salt

½ vanilla bean, split lengthwise

680 g / 6 cups powdered sugar

→

8. In a medium saucepan, melt the butter over medium heat. Stir in the brown sugar, cream, and salt. Scrape the seeds from the vanilla bean and add the seeds and pod to the pan. Bring the mixture to a boil and cook, stirring frequently to prevent scorching or sticking, until it has thickened slightly, 3 to 4 minutes.

9. Transfer the mixture to the bowl of a stand mixer fitted with the whisk attachment (or use a large bowl and a hand mixer) and mix on low speed for 30 seconds. Gradually add the powdered sugar, mixing to combine—the frosting should be smooth, creamy, and thick.

10. Scoop about ½ cup of the frosting onto the cake layer on the turntable and use an offset spatula to spread it evenly. Top with another layer and spread on another ½ cup of the frosting. Top with the third layer and frost the sides and top of the cake with the remaining frosting (see page 87 for more detailed frosting instructions). Let the frosting set for at least 15 minutes to allow it to crystallize before slicing and serving.

❉ **WHY IT WORKS**

The dark brown sugar gives the cake and frosting deep caramel notes without the work of cooking sugar to make caramel. Whipping the frosting helps crystallize the sugar, giving it the classic fudgelike texture.

★ **PRO TIPS**

If you don't have three cake pans, remove one third of the batter (694 g) and hold it in a bowl at room termperature, covered with plastic wrap, until you're ready to bake.

As the sugar crystallizes, the frosting will set up relatively firmly—and this happens quickly as it begins to cool. Don't try for a sharp, clean-edged finish here; just sweep the frosting onto the cake in big swirly swoops—and then grab the forks.

After much experimentation, I finally developed my own roulade that reliably delivers exactly what it should bring to the table: a short baking time, a nearly 1:1 ratio of pillowy cake to creamy filling, and a classic look that never disappoints. This roulade is made using a thin sponge cake—known in French as *biscuit* (pronounced *biss*-QUEE, not to be confused with our American word *biscuit*)— that's easily rolled up around the filling.

Makes one 17-inch roulade
(about 10 servings)

DIFFICULTY: Medium

MAKE AHEAD AND STORAGE: The roulade is best within 2 days of baking. Store airtight in the refrigerator. The purple color of the blueberry filling may bleed a little into the cake.

Blueberry Cream Roulade

1. Preheat the oven to 400°F / 205°C, with a rack in the middle. Grease a 12-by-17-inch jelly-roll pan. Line it with parchment paper, leaving a 1-inch overhang on the two shorter ends, and grease the parchment.

2. Make the sponge cake: In a small bowl, whisk the cake flour, all-purpose flour, and salt together.

3. In the bowl of a stand mixer fitted with the whisk attachment (or in a large bowl, using a hand mixer), whip the eggs and egg yolks on medium speed until slightly pale, 1 to 2 minutes. Gradually add 74 g / 6 tablespoons of the granulated sugar, then turn the speed up to medium-high and whip until the mixture is pale and thick and has quadrupled in volume, 4 to 5 minutes.

4. Sprinkle about half the flour mixture over the egg yolk mixture and mix on low speed just until incorporated. Add the remaining flour, mixing just until it is incorporated.

5. In a clean dry mixer bowl (or other large bowl), combine the egg whites with the cream of tartar. Using the cleaned and dried whisk attachment or beaters, whip the whites on low speed until slightly foamy, 1 to 2 minutes. Turn the speed up to medium-high and whip the whites to soft peaks, 4 to 5 minutes. With the mixer running, gradually add the remaining 74 g / 6 tablespoons sugar in a slow, steady stream, then continue whipping until the mixture reaches medium peaks, 1 to 2 minutes more.

⟶

SPONGE CAKE

30 g / ¼ cup cake flour

15 g / 2 tablespoons all-purpose flour

1 g / ¼ teaspoon fine sea salt

113 g / 2 large eggs, at room temperature

81 g / 3 large egg yolks, at room temperature

149 g / ¾ cup granulated sugar

89 g / 3 large egg whites, at room temperature

Scant 1 g / ¼ teaspoon cream of tartar

3 g / ½ teaspoon vanilla extract

Powdered sugar, for dusting

BLUEBERRY CREAM

363 g / 1½ cups heavy cream

14 g / 2 tablespoons powdered sugar

170 g / ½ cup blueberry jam

5 g / 1 teaspoon vanilla extract

6. Add about one quarter of the egg white mixture to the batter, folding it in with a silicone spatula and mixing thoroughly (this first addition helps temper the batter, making it easier to incorporate the rest of the whites without deflating them). Add the remaining whites in 2 or 3 more additions, gently folding in just until incorporated.

7. Pour the batter into the prepared pan and use an offset spatula to spread it evenly. (Work quickly—too many swipes can deflate your batter, but do your best to make it an even layer.)

8. Bake the cake until the edges are just starting to turn golden and the center springs back when lightly touched, 7 to 9 minutes.

9. While the cake bakes, scoop some powdered sugar into a sieve and set on a plate. Line a work surface with a large sheet of parchment paper.

10. As soon the cake comes out of the oven, dust the surface evenly with powdered sugar. Use an offset spatula to loosen the cake from the edges of the pan. Use the parchment overhang to lift the cake out of the pan and invert it onto the clean piece of parchment. Carefully peel away the parchment from the cake and discard. With one of the longer sides of the cake facing you, use the underlying sheet of parchment to help roll it up into a tight cylinder. Let the cake cool completely, still rolled up.

11. Make the blueberry cream: In the bowl of a stand mixer fitted with the whisk attachment (or in a large bowl, using a hand mixer), whip the cream and powdered sugar to soft peaks. Add the jam and vanilla and continue whipping until the mixture reaches medium peaks. Refrigerate until ready to use.

12. Assemble the roulade: Unroll the cake and position it, on the parchment paper, with one of the long sides facing you. Dollop the cream all over the cake and spread it in an even layer all the way to the edges. Starting with the side closest to you, gently roll the cake up into a log. It won't be as tight this time because of the filling, but try to make it as rounded as possible; use the paper to help you—it adds a protective layer so you can apply a little pressure if needed without risk of damaging the cake.

13. Chill the roulade for at least 15 minutes and up to overnight before cutting into 2-inch-thick slices and serving.

❋ **WHY IT WORKS**

Keeping the batter light and airy is key to a soft roulade—if you overwork the batter at any stage, you'll end up with a tough cake that will likely tear when you roll it up. Rolling up the just-baked cake while it's warm makes it easier to roll it up again later when filled.

★ **PRO TIPS**

The key to a good sponge cake is proper baking. The cake should appear "set" on the surface, and it should spring back relatively quickly when touched in the center. Unlike many cakes, roulades should be immediately removed once baked—they're so thin that the residual heat of the pan can result in an overbaked cake.

To help keep the base of the filled cake from flattening out, find a curved surface to chill the roulade. I take a cardboard tube from a roll of wrapping paper, cut it open, and nestle the roulade inside, seam side down.

This cake can be used in a million different ways. Light and soft, it's perfect for layering, and it stands up well to being soaked with flavorful syrup. Here I pair the cake with dark chocolate Italian buttercream, which I highly recommend salting—with a little sprinkle of flaky sea salt over each slice!

Makes one 9-inch 4-layer cake

DIFFICULTY: Medium

MAKE AHEAD AND STORAGE: This cake is best served within 4 days of baking: Store tightly wrapped at room temperature.

Basic Yellow Sponge Cake
with Dark Chocolate Italian Buttercream

1. Preheat the oven to 350°F / 175°C, with a rack in the middle. Grease and flour two 8-inch round cake pans.

2. Make the cakes: Sift the cake flour, baking powder, and salt together into a medium bowl. In a container with a spout (such as a 2-cup liquid measure), whisk together the oil, milk, and vanilla.

3. In the bowl of a stand mixer fitted with the whisk attachment (or in a large heatproof bowl, using a hand mixer), beat the eggs and sugar to combine. Set the bowl over a medium saucepan of barely simmering water (with the bowl not touching the water) and heat, whisking constantly, until the mixture registers 105°F / 41°C on an instant-read thermometer.

4. Remove the bowl from the saucepan and whip the mixture on high speed until pale and thick, 5 to 6 minutes. Reduce the speed to medium and beat for 2 to 3 minutes more (this will help stabilize the foam).

5. Sprinkle about one quarter of the flour mixture over the egg mixture and mix on low speed just until incorporated. Add the remaining flour mixture in 2 to 3 additions, mixing just until incorporated into the batter. Gradually drizzle the milk mixture into the batter, mixing just until incorporated.

CAKE

322 g / 2⅔ cups cake flour

8 g / 2 teaspoons baking powder

2 g / ½ teaspoon fine sea salt

198 g / 1 cup vegetable oil

181 g / ¾ cup whole milk, at room temperature

15 g / 1 tablespoon vanilla extract

934 g / 8 large eggs, at room temperature

463 g / 2⅓ cups granulated sugar

6. Divide the batter between the prepared pans (about 730 g per pan). Bake the cakes until the centers spring back when touched, 45 to 55 minutes. Cool in the pans for 15 minutes, then invert onto a wire rack to cool completely.

7. **Make the buttercream:** Place the egg whites in the bowl of a stand mixer fitted with the whisk attachment (or use a large bowl and a hand mixer).

8. In a medium saucepan, combine the sugar and water and bring to a boil over medium heat, stirring constantly to help dissolve the sugar. Once the mixture comes to a boil, stop stirring (if any sugar clings to the sides, use a pastry brush dipped in cool water to brush it back down into the syrup). Attach a candy thermometer to the side of the saucepan (or have an instant-read thermometer at the ready).

9. When the syrup reaches 235°F / 113°C, begin whipping the egg whites on medium-high speed. (The goal is to get the whites to soft peaks by the time the sugar reaches 240°F / 115°C.)

10. When the whites are at soft peaks and the syrup has reached 240°F / 115°C, with the mixer running, pour the syrup into the whites in a slow, steady stream. Then continue whipping on medium-high until the meringue is firm, glossy, and cool and the bowl is no longer warm to the touch, 5 to 6 minutes.

11. With the mixer running on medium speed, gradually add the butter, 1 to 2 tablespoons at a time, to the meringue, waiting until each addition is incorporated before adding more. Add the melted chocolate and mix to combine. Set aside.

12. **Assemble the cake:** Use a serrated knife to level the top of each cake and then cut each one into two layers (see page 82).

13. Place one layer on a turntable or cake stand (or a platter). Scoop ½ cup of the buttercream onto the layer and use an offset spatula to spread it evenly. Repeat with 2 more layers and more buttercream. Top the cake with the fourth layer. Apply a crumb coat of buttercream (see page 87) to the top and sides of the cake and refrigerate to set, 15 to 30 minutes.

⟶

DARK CHOCOLATE ITALIAN BUTTERCREAM

119 g / 4 large egg whites

347 g / 1¾ cups granulated sugar

81 g / ⅓ cup water

454 g / 1 lb unsalted butter, at room temperature

10 g / 2 teaspoons vanilla extract

454 g / 1 lb dark chocolate, coarsely chopped, melted, and cooled slightly

Flaky sea salt, such as Maldon, for sprinkling (optional)

14. Frost the sides and top of the cake (see page 87 for detailed instructions). Refrigerate the cake for at least 15 minutes before slicing (it will slice more cleanly this way).

15. Slice the cake and sprinkle each slice with a little flaky sea salt, if desired.

❉ **WHY IT WORKS**

For this basic sponge cake, the key is to achieve full volume when beating the eggs and then deflate them as little as possible when adding the remaining ingredients. As the cake bakes, the air incorporated expands so the cake rises. In this cake, the addition of baking powder helps make the cake extra light and rise even higher and more evenly. For the Italian meringue, adding a hot sugar syrup to beaten egg whites and continuing to beat them allows you to achieve up to eight times their original volume.

★ **PRO TIP**

It's especially important not to overmix a sponge cake batter—you'll lose the volume created by aerating the eggs and end up with a dense, flat disk. But it's also important to make sure the flour is fully incorporated, because you don't want "flour bombs"—pockets of flour that don't get mixed in. If you're unsure, mix the flour in by hand, adding it a little at a time and folding it in gently with a silicone spatula until incorporated.

HOW TO RECONSTITUTE BUTTERCREAM

Let the buttercream soften at room temperature for 15 to 20 minutes. Transfer it to the bowl of a stand mixer fitted with the whip attachment (or to a large bowl, using a hand mixer). Heat the buttercream by warming the bowl. My preferred method for this is to use a kitchen torch to apply flames to the side of the bowl while you whip the buttercream on medium speed. If you don't have a torch, you can warm the bowl over a medium pot of simmering water for 5- to 10-second bursts.

I may look like an adult, but on the inside, I fluctuate between the ages of four and thirteen: I love balloons and gummy candy, and I drop just about anything to hold a baby animal. Oh—and I love caramel corn. And what makes caramel corn better? Putting it on a cake—a cake that tastes like caramel . . . and corn. But there's some bourbon in there too, because I'm a grown-up now (I think).

Corn flour is readily available in many markets.

Makes one 8-inch 2-layer cake

DIFFICULTY: Hard

MAKE AHEAD AND STORAGE: This cake is best within 2 days of baking—any longer, and the layer of caramel corn in the middle tends to get soggy. Store tightly wrapped at room temperature.

Caramel Corn Layer Cake

1. Preheat the oven to 350°F / 175°C, with a rack in the middle. Grease and flour two 8-inch round cake pans.

2. Make the cakes: Sift the corn flour, cornstarch, cake flour, baking powder, baking soda, and salt together into a medium bowl.

3. In the bowl of a stand mixer fitted with the whisk attachment (or in a large bowl, using a hand mixer), whip the eggs and granulated sugar on high speed until the pale and thick, 5 to 6 minutes. Turn the speed down to medium and whip for 2 to 3 minutes more to help stabilize the foam.

4. Sprinkle about one quarter of the flour mixture over the egg mixture and fold in just to combine. Add the remaining flour mixture in 3 addi-tions, folding just until incorporated into the batter.

5. Add the vanilla to the melted but-ter, then slowly pour the mixture into the batter, folding just until incorpo-rated.

6. Divide the batter between the prepared pans (about 517 g per pan). Bake the cakes until the centers spring back when lightly touched, 25 to 30 minutes. Cool in the pans for 15 minutes, then turn out onto a wire rack to cool completely.

7. Make the buttercream: In a medium saucepan, combine 298 g / 1½ cups of the granulated sugar and the water and bring to a boil over medium heat, stirring constantly to help dissolve the sugar. Once the

CORN SPONGE CAKE

151 g / 1⅓ cups corn flour

7 g / 1 tablespoon cornstarch

241 g / 2 cups cake flour

8 g / 2 teaspoons baking powder

3 g / ½ teaspoon baking soda

2 g / ½ teaspoon fine sea salt

454 g / 8 large eggs, at room temperature

265 g / 1⅓ cups granulated sugar

7.5 g / 1½ teaspoons vanilla extract

85 g / 3 oz / 6 tablespoons unsalted butter, melted and cooled slightly

⟶

mixture comes to a boil, stop stirring (if any sugar clings to the sides, use a pastry brush dipped in cool water to brush it back down into the syrup). Boil the syrup until it darkens to a medium amber color, then remove it from the heat (see Pro Tip). Stir in the evaporated milk. If the caramel clumps up, return the pan to low heat and stir constantly until it smooths back out, then remove from the heat.

8. In a medium heatproof bowl, whisk together the flour and the remaining 49 g / ¼ cup granulated sugar. Gradually pour about one third of the hot caramel mixture into the bowl, whisking constantly to combine. Then pour the resulting mixture back into the pan and whisk vigorously to combine. Cook the mixture over low heat, stirring constantly with a silicone spatula, until the pudding thickens and comes to "first boil" (a single large bubble comes to the surface in the center), 3 to 4 minutes. Stir in the vanilla.

9. Pour the pudding into a shallow heatproof dish and cover with plastic wrap pressed directly against the surface of the pudding. Refrigerate the pudding to cool it to room temperature (no longer warm to the touch), 30 to 45 minutes.

10. Combine the butter and powdered sugar in the bowl of a stand mixer fitted with the paddle attachment (or use a large bowl and a hand mixer) and cream on medium-low speed until light and fluffy, 4 to 5 minutes. Add the pudding about ¼ cup at a time, mixing until fully incorporated after each addition before adding the next. Set the buttercream aside at room temperature.

11. **Make the caramel corn:** Preheat the oven to 350°F / 175°C, with a rack in the middle. Line a baking sheet with parchment paper and grease the paper. Spread the popcorn on the baking sheet.

12. In a medium saucepan, heat the butter, brown sugar, granulated sugar, and corn syrup over medium heat, stirring, until the mixture begins to simmer. Then cook the mixture, without stirring, until it is a medium amber color (see Pro Tip). Stir in the bourbon, vanilla, and salt, then drizzle the caramel evenly over the popcorn. Mix it around a little with a silicone spatula.

13. Bake the caramel corn, stirring once halfway through, until the kernels are evenly coated, 12 to 15 minutes. Cool it to room temperature, then break it up into bite-size pieces.

CARAMEL PUDDING BUTTERCREAM

347 g / 1¾ cups granulated sugar

81 g / ⅓ cup water

340 g / 1⅓ cups evaporated milk

10 g / 2 teaspoons vanilla extract

60 g / ½ cup all-purpose flour

340 g / 12 oz unsalted butter, at room temperature

113 g / 1 cup powdered sugar

CARAMEL CORN

45 g / 6 cups freshly popped popcorn (from about 45 g / ¼ cup kernels)

43 g / 1.5 oz / 3 tablespoons unsalted butter

53 g / ¼ cup packed light brown sugar

50 g / ¼ cup granulated sugar

39 g / 2 tablespoons light corn syrup

45 g / 3 tablespoons bourbon

5 g / 1 teaspoon vanilla extract

2 g / ½ teaspoon fine sea salt, or more to taste

14. Assemble the cake: Place one layer on a turntable or cake stand (or a platter). Scoop about 1½ cups of the frosting onto the top of the cake and spread it evenly, then scatter on one quarter of the popcorn, pressing lightly to firmly embed it in the frosting. Top with the remaining cake layer, then frost the top and sides of the cake with the remaining frosting (see page 87 for tips and techniques on frosting). Pile the remaining caramel corn on top of the cake.

✳ WHY IT WORKS

Corn flour, which has a finer texture than cornmeal, replaces some of the cake flour in this basic sponge recipe. Corn flour is significantly denser than cake flour, but here, that works in the recipe's favor, yielding a flat cake that doesn't need to be leveled before filling and frosting. If your corn flour seems coarse, sift it twice before measuring it, discarding any granules that won't pass through the sieve.

★ PRO TIP

When you are making caramel, remember that the sugar syrup is very hot and retains heat even after you remove it from the stovetop. For this reason, it is a good idea to stop cooking caramel just before it reaches the desired color. Adding room-temperature ingredients (like the evaporated milk in the buttercream recipe here) helps lower the temperature and stop caramelization as well.

Created as a love letter to the number one lemon lover in my life, this cake has yet to disappoint a single citrus fan. Soft lemon chiffon cake is soaked with lemon syrup and layered with tart lemon curd, and then the whole thing is frosted with lemon curd buttercream. Use fragrant Meyer lemons if you can get them—that sends this cake completely over the top.

Lemon-Love Chiffon Layer Cake

Makes one 9-inch 4-layer cake

DIFFICULTY: Hard

MAKE AHEAD AND STORAGE: The cakes can be wrapped tightly in plastic wrap and refrigerated for up to 1 day, or double-wrapped and frozen for up to 3 months; thaw at room temperature before using. The syrup can be made up to 1 week ahead and refrigerated airtight. The frosting can be made up to 1 week ahead and refrigerated airtight (see page 151 for how to reconstitute before using). Slices can be refrigerated tightly wrapped in plastic for up to 2 days.

1. Preheat the oven to 325°F / 162°C, with a rack in the middle. Grease and flour two 9-inch round cake pans.

2. Make the cakes: Sift together the cake flour, baking powder, and salt into a medium bowl. In a container with a spout (such as a 2-cup liquid measure), whisk together the oil, milk, vanilla, and lemon extract.

3. In the bowl of a stand mixer fitted with the whisk attachment (or in a large bowl, using a hand mixer), whip the egg yolks on medium speed until

slightly pale, 1 to 2 minutes. Gradually add 198 g / 1 cup of the granulated sugar and whip the mixture on medium-high speed until it becomes pale and thick and has quadrupled in volume, 4 to 5 minutes. Reduce the speed to low and add the lemon zest, then whip for 1 minute more to help stabilize the foam.

4. Gradually add the milk mixture to the egg yolk mixture in a slow steady stream, mixing on low speed to combine.

LEMON CHIFFON CAKE

361 g / 3 cups cake flour

12 g / 1 tablespoon baking powder

2 g / ½ teaspoon fine sea salt

121 g / ½ cup vegetable oil (or other neutral oil; see page 69)

161 g / ⅔ cup whole milk, at room temperature

7.5 g / 1½ teaspoons vanilla extract

2.5 g / ½ teaspoon lemon extract

215 g / 8 large egg yolks, at room temperature

298 g / 1½ cups granulated sugar

→

5. Sprinkle about one quarter of the flour mixture over the egg yolk mixture and mix on low speed just until incorporated. Add the remaining flour in 3 more additions, mixing just until incorporated.

6. In a clean, dry mixer bowl or other large bowl, combine the egg whites with the cream of tartar and, using the mixer (fitted with the cleaned and dried whisk attachment/beaters), beat on low speed until lightly foamy, 1 to 2 minutes. Turn the speed up to medium-high and whip the egg whites to soft peaks, 4 to 5 minutes. Gradually add the remaining 100 g / ½ cup granulated sugar and continue whipping the mixture until it reaches medium peaks, 1 to 2 minutes more.

7. Fold about one quarter of the whipped egg whites into the batter, mixing thoroughly (this first addition helps temper the batter, making it easier to incorporate the rest of the whites without deflating them). Add the remaining whites in 2 or 3 more additions, gently folding them in just until incorporated.

8. Divide the batter between the prepared pans (about 652 g per pan). Bake until the cakes spring back sli-

ghtly when touched in the center, 50 to 55 minutes. Cool the cakes in the pans for 10 to 15 minutes, then turn out onto a wire rack to cool completely.

9. **Meanwhile, make the lemon syrup:** Combine the lemon juice and granulated sugar in a small saucepan and bring to a boil over medium-high heat, stirring to help dissolve the sugar. Set aside to cool to room temperature.

10. **Make the buttercream:** Start with an Italian meringue. Place the egg whites in the bowl of a stand mixer fitted with the whisk attachment (or use a large bowl with a hand mixer). In a medium saucepan, combine the sugar and the water and bring to a boil over medium heat, stirring constantly to help the sugar dissolve. Once the mixture comes to a boil, stop stirring (if any sugar clings to the sides, use a pastry brush dipped in cool water to brush it back down into the syrup). Attach a candy thermometer to the side of the saucepan (or have an instant-read thermometer at the ready).

11. When the syrup reaches 235°F / 113°C, begin whipping the egg whites on medium-high speed. (The goal is to get the whites to soft peaks by the time the sugar reaches 240°F / 115°C.)

12 g / 2 tablespoons grated lemon zest

238 g / 8 large egg whites, at room temperature

Scant 1 g / ¼ teaspoon cream of tartar

LEMON SYRUP

80 g / ⅓ cup freshly squeezed lemon juice

66 g / ⅓ cup granulated sugar

LEMON CURD BUTTERCREAM

149 g / 5 large egg whites

347 g / 1¾ cups granulated sugar

181 g / ¾ cup water

397 g / 14 oz unsalted butter, at room temperature

239 g / 1 cup Lemon Curd (page 338)

FILLING

340 g / 1½ cups Lemon Curd (page 338)

12. When the whites reach soft peaks and the syrup has reached 240°F / 115°C, with the mixer running, pour the syrup into the whites in a slow, steady stream, then continue whipping until the meringue has reached its full volume (it will be very white and glossy) and the bowl is no longer warm to the touch, 5 to 6 minutes.

13. With the mixer running on medium speed, gradually add the butter, 1 to 2 tablespoons at a time, waiting until each addition is incorporated before adding more. Add the lemon curd and mix to combine.

14. Transfer about one quarter of the buttercream to a disposable pastry bag or a heavy-duty zip-top bag and snip off a ½-inch opening at the tip/ one corner.

15. Assemble the cake: Use a long serrated knife to level the tops of the cakes and then slice each one horizontally in half to create a total of 4 layers (see page 82).

16. Place one layer on a turntable or cake stand (or a platter) and brush the top evenly with lemon syrup, fully soaking the layer. Pipe a ring of buttercream all around the outer edge of the cake. Scoop ½ cup of the lemon curd into the center of the ring and use a small offset spatula to spread it evenly. Repeat with the remaining cake layers, more buttercream, and the remaining lemon curd. Leave the top layer naked.

17. Apply a crumb coat of frosting (see page 87) to the top and sides of the cake and refrigerate to set, 15 to 30 minutes.

18. Frost the sides and top of the cake with an offset spatula (for more detailed frosting instructions, see page 87). Refrigerate the cake for at least 15 minutes before slicing (it will slice more cleanly this way).

❋ **WHY IT WORKS**

Whipping the yolks and whites separately provides double aeration for maximum lightness, with the whipped yolks serving as a strong base to which the other ingredients can be added to form the batter. The egg whites are folded in at the end to take the cake to towering, light-as-air heights.

Piping a ring of frosting around the outer edge of each cake layer acts as a sort of "retaining wall" to help keep the soft lemon curd from oozing out the sides as you layer the cake.

★ **PRO TIP**

Many recipes for delicate cakes like this call for the dry ingredients to be folded in by hand, and that is generally my preferred method. But for many people, this can be tricky to do without overmixing the batter. Using the mixer (carefully and minimally) allows you to achieve a homogeneous batter faster, which means a better chance for a loftier cake. Once you've made a chiffon cake successfully, try folding the ingredients together by hand for an even lighter cake!

A mousse cake, or *entremet*, is made by sandwiching layers of cake with jam and mousse, with the mousse also serving as the "icing." This utterly gorgeous cake looks (and tastes!) like it came from a fancy bakery—the "ooohs" and "aaaahs" alone make it worth the effort.

The best way to tackle the cake is to break up the preparation, although it can be done in a single day (see Pro Tips). Reserve space in your fridge or freezer to chill for at least 3 hours.

You will need an 8-inch cake ring—or a reasonable facsimile—to make this recipe; see Pro Tips.

Makes one 8-inch 4-layer cake

DIFFICULTY: Hard

MAKE AHEAD AND STORAGE: The assessmbled cake can be refrigerated (unmolded) for up to 2 days or frozen, well wrapped, for up to 1 week. Once the cake is glazed, it can be stored in the refrigerator for up to 2 days.

Vanilla Strawberry Mousse Cake

1. Preheat the oven to 350°F / 175°C, with a rack in the middle. Grease and flour two 6-inch round cake pans.

2. Make the cakes: In a medium bowl, whisk together the flour, baking powder, and salt.

3. In the bowl of a stand mixer fitted with the whisk attachment (or in a large bowl, using a hand mixer), whisk the eggs, egg yolk, and sugar on low speed to combine. Turn the speed up to high and whip the mixture until pale and thick, 4 to 5 minutes. Reduce the speed to medium and whip the mixture for 1 minute more to help stabilize the foam.

4. Sprinkle about one quarter of the flour mixture over the egg mixture and mix on low speed just until incorporated. Add the remaining flour in 3 additions, mixing just until incorporated.

5. Gradually drizzle the cream into the batter, mixing just until incorporated. Add the vanilla and mix to combine.

6. Divide the batter between the prepared pans (about 411 g per pan). Bake until a toothpick inserted into the center comes out clean or with just a few moist crumbs attached, 40 to 45 minutes. Cool the cakes in

CAKE

211 g / 1¾ cups all-purpose flour

6 g / 1½ teaspoons baking powder

2 g / ½ teaspoon fine sea salt

113 g / 2 large eggs, at room temperature

27 g / 1 large egg yolk, at room temperature

198 g / 1 cup granulated sugar

242 g / 1 cup heavy cream, at room temperature

5 g / 1 teaspoon vanilla extract

the pans for 15 minutes, then turn out onto a wire rack to cool completely.

7. Use a long serrated knife to level the tops of the cakes, then slice each cake in half horizontally, creating a total of 4 layers (see page 82). Scoop ¼ cup of the strawberry jam onto each layer and spread it evenly.

8. **Assemble the cake:** Line a baking sheet with wax paper or parchment paper. Place an 8-inch cake ring (3½ to 4 inches tall) on the baking sheet. Ladle or scoop the mousse to make an even layer—about 2 inches deep—in the ring and smooth the surface. (This will eventually be the top of the cake.) Lift up one cake layer, jam side up, and set it on top of the mousse, gently pressing on the cake just enough to nestle it into the mousse. Ladle or spoon another layer of mousse on top about 1 inch deep (note how many ladlesful you use so that you can use the same amount for the other layers).

9. Invert a second cake layer, jam side down, onto the mousse, lightly press it down, and add another layer of mousse. Repeat the process with another cake layer, jam side down, and cover it with another layer of mousse.

10. Set the fourth layer jam side down on the mousse. You will be close to the top of the ring, and when you gently press the cake down, the mousse will flood out of the edges of the ring. Ladle on the remaining mousse using an offset spatula to smooth it evenly. (This isn't a full layer of mousse, just a little bit to "seal" that bottom layer in place.)

11. Transfer the cake, still in the ring and on the baking sheet, to the freezer. Chill until the mousse is firm, at least 3 hours.

12. Make the glaze: Bring the jam to a boil in a small saucepan over medium heat and cook until it's slightly reduced, 3 to 4 minutes. Strain the glaze and set aside to cool to room temperature.

13. Several hours before you want to serve the cake, remove it from the freezer. Use a kitchen torch to warm the outside of the ring to release the mousse, then lift the ring off the cake. (If you do not have a torch, dampen a couple of kitchen towels with very hot water and wrap them around the ring to warm it.) Invert the cake onto a cake stand or serving platter. (You can use the parchment paper to help lift the cake up and turn it over; as long as the cake is properly chilled, this should be easy!) Peel off the paper.

14. Spoon or pipe the cooled glaze onto the top of the cake, letting the excess drip down the sides (see page 86). Let the cake thaw at room temperature and serve, or refrigerate until ready to serve.

❋ **WHY IT WORKS**

Mousse cakes are beautiful because they have straight, perfect edges—the mousse conforms perfectly to whatever shape you pour it into. The gelatin gives the mousse structure, so it's firm enough to slice and eat easily.

★ **PRO TIPS**

Cake rings are available in baking supply stores, and they aren't terribly expensive (around $20). If you don't have one, you can use the ring of an 8-inch springform pan or an 8-inch silicone cake pan (the cake will easily slide out of a silicone pan). The ring or pan needs to be 4 inches tall. If yours is not, wrap a folded piece of wax paper or parchment paper around the ring to create additional height. Wrap the paper tightly, so it's flush against the ring, secure it with tape, and trim it as needed.

To stagger the preparation, on day 1, bake the cakes and make the crème anglaise base for the mousse. On day 2, make the mousse and assemble the cake, then chill as directed. On day 3, unmold the cake, garnish, and serve.

FILLING

340 g / 1 cup strawberry jam

Double recipe Vanilla Bean Mousse (page 335), made just before you're ready to assemble the cake

GLAZE

170 g / ½ cup strawberry jam

Royal icing is a super-sweet white icing that hardens when exposed to air. It's ideal for fine details on cookies or cakes. You can also use it to make your own sprinkles (see page 95).

Royal Icing

1. In the bowl of a stand mixer fitted with the whisk attachment (or in a large bowl, using a hand mixer), whip the egg whites on medium speed until lightly frothy, about 1 minute. Gradually add the powdered sugar, mixing on low speed, and then mix until the icing is glossy and smooth, 1 to 2 minutes. Add the vanilla and mix to combine. If the icing is too thick to pipe, thin it out with water; if it is too thin, add more powdered sugar, mixing until smooth (see photo, page 29).

2. Keep the icing covered with plastic wrap placed directly against the surface until ready to use—it hardens in seconds when exposed to air.

❈ **PRO TIP**
You can also make the icing with meringue powder (available at cake supply stores or online). Substitute 30 g / 3 tablespoons meringue powder and 91 g / 6 tablespoons water for the egg whites.

Makes about 475 g / 3 cups

DIFFICULTY: Easy

MAKE AHEAD AND STORAGE: The royal icing can be made ahead and stored at room temperature, covered directly with plastic wrap, in an airtight container for up to 5 days.

89 g / 3 large pasteurized egg whites

482 g / 4¼ cups powdered sugar

5 g / 1 teaspoon vanilla extract

CHAPTER 3

Pies & Tarts

It's no secret that pie is my favorite dessert: tender, flaky, buttery dough encasing smooth custard, toasty nuts, or seasonal fruit. Pies aren't too sweet—often they are even a little sour. They have multiple textures in every bite. And even when they are wonky and imperfect, they still look amazing.

Pie is great anytime: to take on a picnic, to eat after a swanky dinner, to enjoy in the middle of the afternoon for no reason at all, or even for breakfast (frankly, my favorite time for pie). Plus, anything that begs for a dollop of whipped cream or a scoop of ice cream is always a winner in my book.

Pies' cousins, tarts, are similar in all the right ways, with a few notable differences. Tarts usually have a single crust that's "shorter," less flaky, crumblier, and often cookielike. Many are more delicate looking, with a thin crust that fits neatly in the pan. And, unlike pies, tarts are meant to be removed from the pan, so all their pretty finishes can really shine.

Mastering the crust is what scares many people away from trying their hand at these desserts, so I'm here to show you the way! Understanding when, how, and why to do certain steps will get you on the right track, producing delicious pies or tarts every time.

KEYS TO ROLLING OUT DOUGH

* Lightly flour the work surface—excess flour can make dough tough or dry—and work quickly so the dough doesn't warm up too much. If you have trouble with the dough sticking, try rolling it out between two pieces of parchment (some folks like plastic wrap, but I find it often bunches up and leaves dents and marks in the dough—though it can be a good solution for stickier doughs).

* Rather than focusing on the diameter of the rolled-out dough, I prefer to use the proper thickness as my guideline (the correct size falls right in line). Roll the dough out to between ⅛ inch and ¼ inch thick, depending on your preferences and/or the recipe. You can use the pan as a guide as you roll—just place it upside down on top of the dough and you'll see when you're getting close.

WHY, WHEN, AND HOW TO CHILL PIE DOUGH

Chilling dough is an important step for several reasons. Skipping it at any required stage will be the difference between "YOU made that?!?" and "What IS that?"

* Chilling gives the dough time to relax. No matter how carefully you mix the dough, you're still

developing gluten, those tricky protein strands that form during mixing. Excess gluten formation can not only make your dough tough, but also make it more likely to shrink. Chilling the dough allows the gluten strands to "retract," so to speak. It relaxes the gluten so the dough will stay the size and shape you want.

* Chilling is good for the fat (usually butter). When the cold fat hits the heat of the oven, the moisture in it evaporates, creating steam. The steam pushes the dough upward, creating those crisp, flaky layers you know and love. If the fat isn't cold enough when it hits the oven, it will melt before enough steam can be produced, and it can often even seep out of the crust. The result? Not only less flakiness, but also a solid chance for sogginess.

* Dough benefits from chilling at all of the following points: after mixing, after rolling, after crimping, and after filling the shell. You can make the dough ahead of time to give yourself a head start. Note, however, that pie dough can turn gray, due to oxidization if you leave it in the refrigerator for more than 2 to 3 days, and that tinge can linger even after baking. So, for longer storage, keep the dough in the freezer (tightly wrapped in plastic wrap and then foil or sealed in a zip-top plastic bag to prevent

MIXING INFO: BUTTER SIZE MATTERS!

Pie dough is made using the cut-in method, where fat is "cut into" flour, and then liquid is added to bind the dough. This method is also used to make other flaky doughs, like those for biscuits and scones. There are a few rules that are especially important to keep in mind. First, what kind of pie are you making? The type will determine how you need to mix your crust. If you want a flaky crust, as for most fruit pies, you want the butter in large pieces, the size of walnut halves. I can't emphasize that enough. When I teach someone how to make pie dough, they inevitably say to me, "The butter should be *that big*?" Yup. Keeping the butter in larger pieces will increase your chances of perfectly flaky success. For a less flaky or "mealy" crust with a shorter crumb, often used for custard pies, the butter should be in smaller pieces, slightly larger than peas.

Tart doughs can be mixed in several ways. Some are mixed like pie dough, with the butter cut in, though they generally have a mealier consistency to stand up to moister fillings. Others are mixed like cookie dough, using the blending or creaming method. Regardless, be careful not to overwork the dough, which can result in a crust that's overly tough.

EGG WASH

Egg wash helps make all kinds of desserts more evenly golden brown. It also adds just a bit of sheen to the surface anywhere it's brushed. In short, it makes doughs of all sorts look even better! I make my egg wash by whisking 1 large egg with 15 g / 1 tablespoon water and a pinch of salt to combine. Egg wash can be stored in an airtight container in the refrigerator for up to 5 days.

freezer burn). Thaw frozen dough in the refrigerator overnight or at room temperature until it's pliable.

✽ Refrigerate pie dough until well chilled, 20 to 30 minutes, depending on the temperature of your dough and your fridge. If you're short on time, you can chill the dough in the freezer for 10 to 15 minutes or so. If the dough gets too cold, just let it soften for a moment at room temperature, or hit it with your rolling pin until it becomes malleable (this is also excellent for anger management purposes).

NOTE: Unlike pie dough, tart dough only needs to be lightly chilled before rolling—it's generally hard to roll it out if it's *too* cold. So steer clear of the freezer, wrap the dough well, and chill in the refrigerator just until it's firm, usually 10 to 15 minutes. (It should also be noted that some tart doughs don't require chilling.) For longer storage, use the freezer and thaw overnight in the fridge before using.

PARBAKING AND BLIND-BAKING CRUSTS

I prebake a lot of my pie and tart crusts—even the bottom crusts for fruit pies with double crusts. There are two ways to do this. The first is called **parbaking:** You partially bake the crust before filling it, helping to ensure that the bottom crust is fully baked (nice and crisp!) by the time the filling is cooked. **Blind-baking** refers to fully baking a crust before filling it—it's a technique used for cold-filled pies like lemon meringue or coconut cream. To parbake or blind-bake a crust, start with a fully chilled crust.

Prick the crust: Whether you are parbaking or blind-baking, you gotta prick that dough. There's no need to go crazy or be perfect with placement, just poke it all over with the tines of a fork.

Use pie weights: For most crusts, pricking isn't enough; you also need to weigh the crust down to prevent it from puffing up as it bakes. Cut a square of parchment paper that is slightly larger than your pie pan. Place it, centered, over the dough and fill the pan one-third full with pie weights—reusable ceramic ones, or just plain ol' dried beans. I don't like those stainless steel pie chains, since they only cover the bottom of the crust, not the sides.

Bake: For a parbaked crust, bake the crust at 425°F / 218°C for 15 to 20 minutes, just until the edges look set and barely begin to color. Remove the paper and weights and continue baking for 2 to 4 minutes to get rid of any excess moisture that built up between the parchment and crust.

For a blind-baked crust, bake the weighted crust at 425°F / 218°C for 15 to 20 minutes, until fully golden and crisp. As with parbaking, you'll want to remove the pie weights and parchment once the crust begins to turn golden to get rid of any excess moisture on the crust, then bake until the crust is fully baked, 12 to 17 minutes more.

PRESS-IN CRUSTS

Press-in tart crusts are amazing for all the right reasons: They're fast, they're easy, and there's usually no waiting around for chilling. There are basically two types of press-in crusts: crumb crusts and what I call "cookie crusts." **Crumb crusts** are made by processing cookies or crackers into coarse crumbs, adding a little sugar and/or flavoring, and binding it together with fat (usually melted butter). Pour the crumbs into the pan (greasing isn't necessary) and press into an even layer—I like to use the bottom of a small dry measure to help press the crust evenly. If you want a crumb crust on the sides of the pan as well, press the cup against the edges as you near the sides, and the crumbs will begin to work their way up. Use your fingers to get even coverage on the sides. If you're going to build your own recipe, the chart on page 170 can help you figure out how much crumb crust you need for a given pan size.

CHOOSING THE RIGHT PIE PAN

Go for glass: I always recommend glass pie pans for beginners or for anyone who struggles with getting that crisp bottom crust. Glass conducts heat well and, even better, you can see through it so you can see when it's golden brown. Once you've got the hang of it, you can opt for ceramic or metal pans if you prefer.

Look for a pan with a wide edge: A wider rim on a pie pan gives crimped edges a place to rest, which makes them less likely to break off or become misshapen during baking. This is especially nice for cutouts and braids (see page 183), which are relatively fragile.

PIE / TART PANS		
6-inch	---	91 g / ⅔ cup
8-inch	---	170 g / 1¼ cups
9-inch	---	204 g / 1½ cups
10-inch	---	272 g / 2 cups
11-inch	---	318 g / 2⅓ cups
12-inch	---	363 g / 2⅔ cups
SPRINGFORM / CAKE PANS	BOTTOM ONLY	BOTTOM AND SIDES
6-inch	45 g / ⅓ cup	102 g / ¾ cup
8-inch	102 g / ¾ cup	204 g / 1½ cups
9-inch	170 g / 1¼ cups	272 g / 2 cups
10-inch	238 g / 1¾ cups	408 g / 3 cups
11-inch	318 g / 2⅓ cups	499 g / 3⅔ cups
12-inch	408 g / 3 cups	578 g / 4¼ cups

NOTE: Exact weights will vary depending on the type of crumbs you're using (graham crackers versus sugar cookies versus gingersnaps, and so on).

Press-in **cookie crusts** are made like cookie doughs, using either the blending or creaming method. Most are ready to use as soon as they are mixed, but it's still advisable to pop the dough into the refrigerator or freezer for 15 to 30 minutes before baking. To press in a cookie crust, start at the sides, adding the dough to the sides by pressing it in one clump at a time. This may seem counterintuitive, but it helps ensure that you don't get too much dough in the corners—you want the dough to be the same thickness everywhere: bottom, sides, and where they meet. Once you have an even layer around the sides, place the remaining dough in the center of the pan and press it outward toward the edges.

TYPES OF PIES

Fruit Pies are my favorite. The fillings don't usually have many ingredients: fruit, sweetener, and a thickening agent, plus whatever flavorings you're feeling (or not). Regardless of the recipe, it's always advisable to taste the fruit before you make your filling. If it's extra juicy, you may need additional thickener. If the fruit is rock hard, you may want to add a little extra sweetener.

It's best to let your fruit pies cool completely before slicing—if you cut them while they're still warm, they may be too juicy. Then again, that's not a terrible problem—if you can't wait, ice cream can help.

MY ADVICE: Too much juiciness is one of the biggest problems with fruit fillings. There are a few things you can do to manage it. One is to reduce the juices. For fresh fruit, combine the fruit with the sugar and let macerate for 15 to 20 minutes. Drain and reserve the juices. Transfer the juices to a small saucepan and bring to a simmer over medium heat, then turn down the heat to low and simmer until reduced; you're looking for about 60 g / ¼ cup of reduced juice. From here, you can make a slurry with the thickener (add a small amount of liquid to the bowl with the thickener and whisk to combine—no lumps), then add the remaining liquid and proceed with the recipe. This technique works with frozen fruit too—thaw completely, add the sugar and macerate, then drain the juices and reduce them.

You can also opt to precook your pie filling, which allows you to see how thick it is before you pour it into the crust. The downside of this method is that you have to let the filling cool completely before you add it to the crust. The plus side is that it can be done ahead, which can streamline your pie baking down the line.

Custard Pies have fluid egg-based fillings. The proteins in the eggs coagulate during baking, setting the filling. Some custards are very simple—the ingredients are combined and then poured into the crust. Others require some cooking to warm the liquid and/or dissolve the sweetener. This warm liquid is then gradually added to the egg mixture, and the filling is added to a warm, parbaked piecrust.

Custard fillings are relatively sensitive, and so custard pies need to be baked at a lower temperature than other pies (325° to 375°F / 162° to 175°C). Be sure not to overbake a custard filling. Overbaked fillings have an unpleasant texture and an overly eggy flavor, and they often crack at the surface or separate from the edges of the crust. Bake the pie just until the filling is set around the edges but the center still jiggles slightly when you shake it gently—as the pie cools, the custard will finish setting and have an evenly creamy texture.

MY ADVICE: Custard pies are especially prone to soggy bottom crusts. An egg wash makes a great seal for the bottom crust (see page 168), but chocolate works smashingly too, for both parbaked and blind-baked crusts. If the flavor goes well with your pie, spread melted dark, milk, or white chocolate (about 113 g / 4 oz / 1 cup chopped chocolate for a standard 9-inch pie) evenly over the bottom of the

---

crust, all the way to the edges. Let the chocolate cool completely before you proceed with the recipe. Or, if you're making a savory pie, a layer of grated hard cheese, like Parmesan, will create a similar (and delicious!) barrier.

Nut Pies are almost in a category of their own, but they're usually made with a custard base, so they have some of the same issues; see Custard Pies on page 171.

MY ADVICE: A quick tip that's unique to nut pies: Place the nuts in the crust first, then pour the filling over them. If the nuts are lightweight, they are likely to float to the surface (and stay there once the pie has baked and set). If you want a specific appearance or pattern in the nuts—say, for a pecan pie—pile some of the nuts in the bottom of the crust and then arrange the top layer exactly as you want it (such as concentric circles). Then fill with enough custard to reach slightly below (⅛ to ¼ inch) this top layer; the custard will rise slightly during baking.

Cold-Filled Pies include chiffon and cream pies. **Chiffon pies** are made from a cooked starch-thickened custard base that is combined with whipped cream, whipped egg whites, or both (much like mousse). **Cream pies** are also custard based, often lightened with whipped cream. Yes, these two categories are quite similar, and in fact, what you call them depends largely on your location and the pie traditions in your area. These fillings are added to a fully blind-baked and cooled piecrust and then chilled before serving.

MY ADVICE: Chiffon and cream fillings can leach some of their moisture into the crust, so these pies especially benefit from a seal to help keep the crust crisp. When the pie is nearly finished baking, remove it from the oven and brush the bottom and sides with egg wash. Return the pie to the oven for 1 to 2 minutes more, until the egg wash is lightly golden and set. This layer will act as a protective barrier against high-moisture fillings (the aforementioned layer of chocolate works too—you can even do both)! I actually like to do this for par-baked crusts too, for any pies with a high-moisture filling.

MAKE IT PRETTY: CRIMPING A PIECRUST

I actually believe that any pie is a beautiful pie—even when it's crooked or has a few dark spots or (especially) when the filling bubbles up or leaks out somewhere along the way. But I'm happy to share all my tips and tricks for making gorgeous pies and tarts.

When I was in pastry school, one of my close friends was stellar at making chocolates, but not so good at making pies. She would sometimes carry her crusts over to me, and I would help her beautify her edges—in exchange for some help with my chocolates. I find that I dole out more advice on how to make pretty piecrusts than almost anything else. Don't fear the crust—just work confidently and quickly. And when you can't be quick, the freezer is your best friend.

Here are the most common decorative edges for piecrusts:

Fork Crimp: Basic and classic. Choose a fork with long tines—and, not that you need to be too finicky, crimps made with thin tines look better than big fat ones. Dip the fork into a small amount of flour before each press, or as necessary: You can usually get away with not dipping every time—just use your judgment, and flour the tines when things start to look sticky or the presses aren't as clean. If you want to be extra precise, start each press by placing the last (or first, depending on which way you are working around the pie) tine in the final imprint of the press you made before. Repeat all around the crust.

Chevron Fork Crimp: Press your floured fork into the crust at a 45-degree angle to make a sort of half-triangle shape; the tine on the left will make a longer indentation and the tine on the right will make a shorter one. Then turn the fork and make a second indentation at a 45-degree angle in the opposite direction. The marks should line up at their points to make a chevron shape. Repeat all around the crust.

Crisscrossing Fork Crimp: Press your floured fork into the crust at a 45-degree angle to make a half-triangle shape. The tine on the left will make a longer indentation and the tine on the right will make a shorter one. Then turn the fork and make a second indentation at a 45-degree angle in the opposite direction, overlapping the first indentation to make a crisscross shape. Repeat all around the crust.

Decorative Fork Crimp: Fork crimps also look great paired with other decorative edges. If you make a scalloped edge (see opposite), you can use a fork to crimp the interior of each scallop. Or you can do alternating fork crimps and scallops, creating multiple textures in one crust.

Spoon Crimp: Dip the bowl of the spoon lightly into flour and press it gently into the crust, moving inward and using your fingers to guide the outer edge. Repeat all around the crust. The larger the bowl of the spoon, the bigger the waves will be.

Basic Finger Crimp: Form a V-shape with the thumb and forefinger of your dominant hand, place at the outer edge of the piecrust, and use the index finger of your nondominant hand to press down lightly and push outward toward the V; press in slightly with your V at the same time. This looks good with both small crimps, very close together, or larger crimps, farther apart. Repeat all the way around the pie.

Scalloped Edge: This is the reverse of the basic finger crimp. Form a wider shape with the thumb and forefinger of your dominant hand (at least 1 inch apart), place on the inner edge of the piecrust, and use the forefinger of your dominant hand to pull the dough outward to create a rounded, scalloped edge. To create a sharper finish, you can use a paring knife to push in the outer edge.

Rope Crimp: Pinch the dough at a 45-degree angle between your two forefingers (use the side of your fingers, not the fingertips) to squeeze the dough upward between them. Repeat all the way around the pie, rotating the pie as you work and taking care to match the angle with each pinch. This crimp can also be done

Chevron Fork Crimp

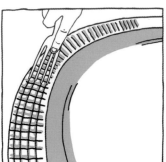
Crisscrossing Fork Crimp

Decorative Fork Crimp

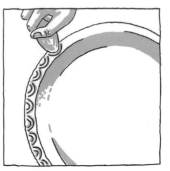
Spoon Crimp

Basic Finger Crimp

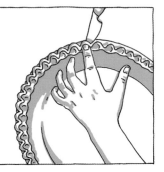
Scalloped Edge

Rope Crimp

Checkerboard

one handed, using the thumb and forefinger of your dominant hand.

Checkerboard: This is a classic edge for chess or other custard pies. Use a paring knife to make cuts through the edge of the dough all around the pie. Use a ruler to measure the distance between each cut if you want this to look really sharp—I like about 1 inch between cuts. Then fold every other flap inward over the filling to create a checkerboard pattern.

Foldover: This is an easy technique often used to finish galettes, but it looks great on a traditional pie too. When you line the pie plate, leave 1 to 1½ inches of excess dough all around the plate. For a more precise look, trim the rough edges away with scissors—otherwise, you can leave it as is. Add the filling to the pie plate, ideally filling so it's flush to the edge of

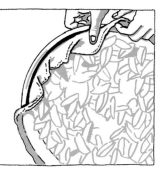
Foldover

the pan. Fold one piece of the dough over onto the filling. Fold the next piece over, allowing it to overlap on the first fold. Repeat all the way around the pie.

MAKING A LATTICE CRUST

There are two main types of lattice—woven and unwoven   but within those two types are multiple different styles. An unwoven lattice, the simplest, is made by laying half of the dough strips onto a pie, then laying the remaining strips over them in a different direction. A woven lattice is made by weaving the strips together in a pattern. A few tips for any kind of lattice:

* Use a ruler. Whether you're trying to be super-precise or not, a ruler—or even a spatula handle—can help you maintain straight, even lines when you cut the strips. If you're a fan of eyeballing (I hear you!), just take care when you cut the first strip, then use that strip as a guide for the remaining ones.

* Cut more, rather than fewer, strips. It can be hard to say exactly how many strips you'll need, as that can vary depending on the size of your pie pan, the amount of filling, and your personal preferences for look and style. Always plan on having a little more dough handy, just in case—I save scrap dough from past pies in my fridge/freezer for this purpose. But I do give approximations on the following pages for a guideline.

* It's ideal to have each strip the diameter of your pan, but remember that it's OK for some pieces to be shorter—use those at the edges.

* Rotate the pan or baking sheet as you work. In my lattice method, I pull the lattice strips halfway across the pie, starting on the right side (since I'm right-handed). Then I rotate the pie so the unwoven

left side is on the right and pull the strips hallway across and weave the lattice.

❋ Chill the pie after making the lattice. This is especially important in the heat of summer. Pop it into the fridge for 20 to 30 minutes or in the freezer for 10 to 15 minutes before you throw it in the oven. A cold lattice bakes up best.

HOW TO MAKE A WOVEN LATTICE

1. For a 9-inch pie pan, using a pastry wheel (fluted or straight) and a ruler, cut twelve 1-inch-wide strips from the rolled-out dough.

2. Lay half the strips vertically across the pie, spacing them evenly (with about ½ inch between them). Then rotate the pie 90 degrees so the strips run horizontally.

3. Pull every other strip back halfway across the pie. Now place another strip vertically slightly off the center of the pie. Fold the horizontal pieces you pulled back down over this strip.

4. Repeat the process, but this time pull back the strips you did not move the first time. Then place another strip vertically across the pie, about ½ inch from the first vertical strip. Fold the horizontal pieces you pulled back over this strip.

5. Repeat with a third vertical strip on this half of the pie. Now rotate the pie 180 degrees and repeat the process on the other side with the remaining 3 strips.

6. Trim away the excess dough from the lattice and/or fold it under the edge of the bottom crust. Crimp as desired and chill.

HOW TO MAKE AN UNWOVEN LATTICE

1. For a 9-inch pie, using a pastry wheel (fluted or straight) and a ruler, cut twelve 1-inch-wide strips from the rolled-out dough.

2. Lay half the strips vertically across the pie, spacing them evenly (with about ½ inch between them). Then rotate the pie 90 degrees so that the strips run horizontally.

3. Lay the remaining strips vertically across the pie, spacing them evenly (a slight angle, which makes diamonds of visible filling instead of squares, is nice too).

4. Trim away the excess dough from the lattice and/or fold it under the edge of the bottom crust. Crimp as desired and chill before baking.

Unwoven Lattice

OTHER LATTICE STYLES

Fat Lattice: This is my favorite lattice, and it is especially awesome for beginners. I affectionately call it a "fattice," and I adore it, because it always looks good and the crust always gets nice and crisp (thinner lattices can have some wet spots due to juices bubbling up, but the fattice has more surface area for browning). It's great for folks just starting out because there are fewer lattice strips than for most pies and they are less fragile, which makes handling them easier. I love a super-fat lattice (about 2-inch-wide strips), but you can do this same style with a lesser width. This style also works well for the tightly woven lattice (see right).

Skinny Lattice: This lattice is adorable, but it is a test of your patience, as it takes almost twice as long to weave as a traditional lattice. Otherwise, it's no harder! Remember to keep your lattice strips nice and cold—warm strips will be harder to manipulate and can cause you grief. The concept is identical to the traditional lattice, except you use much narrower strips, ⅛ to ¼ inch wide. (See photo page 182.)

Random Lattice: This is for anyone who is scared of a lattice. One of my favorite pie bakers does this style effortlessly, and it's always gorgeous. Cut the strips into all different widths (it doesn't even matter if they're crooked) and arrange them in a random order on the pie using the same method as traditional lattice. I like to use a variety of widths ranging from ⅛ inch to 1½ inches, and I find the lattice looks best when the strips are relatively tightly woven, without much space between them. The finished pie looks put-together and rustic at the same time. And since it's random, there's really no way to mess it up! (See photo page 182.)

Tightly Woven Lattice: This technique is increasingly popular, and for a very good reason: It looks very sleek. This technique works with lattice strips of any width, but it is easiest with the traditional (1-inch) or fattice (2-inch) lattice. It is a little bit tougher to accomplish with skinnier strips unless you have a very steady hand. Essentially you weave the lattice so that there is almost no space between the strips. Steam can still escape from between them, so there's no need to cut vents, but the finished look is very swanky. (See photo page 182.)

Diagonal Lattice: This is similar to a traditional lattice, but instead of placing the first strips vertically, you lay them across the pie on a diagonal. Then, just as with a traditional lattice, rotate the pie 90 degrees and lay the remaining strips (for a woven or unwoven lattice) on a diagonal. This style looks nice with a tightly woven lattice. (See photo page 182.)

Slattice: This is an easy unwoven lattice made by slightly overlapping strips of dough all the way across the pie. I call it a "slattice" because it resembles the slats of a closed window shade. Although you can do this with dough strips of any width, I prefer medium size, about 1 inch wide. (See photo page 183.)

Braided Lattice: This unwoven lattice is made by laying strips of braided pie dough across a pie in one direction only. For each braid, cut 3 long strips of dough with a knife or a pastry wheel; the strips can range

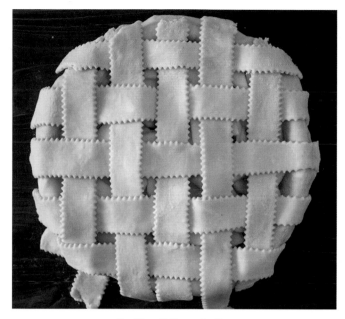

Traditional Woven Lattice

Fat Lattice (Fattice)

USING A BAKING STONE FOR PIES

If you're struggling to get crisp bottom crusts, try a baking stone. Preheat the oven with the baking stone on the bottom rack. Then place your pie pan on the stone. The stone helps regulate overall oven temperature as well as ensure that the bottom of your pie gets golden brown and crisp. If you're using a glass or ceramic pie pan, it is not a good idea to put the pie straight from the fridge, or especially from the freezer, onto the stone. Instead, bake the pie on a different rack for the first 15 minutes, then transfer the pie to the stone for the remainder of the baking. And if the crust is actually browning too much, you can just move the pie to another rack to finish baking.

Skinny Lattice

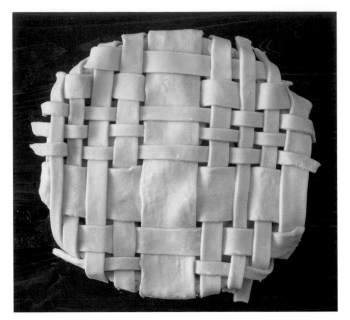

Random Lattice

Tightly Woven Lattice

Diagonal Lattice

Slattice

Braided Lattice

from ½ to 1 inch wide, depending on how thick you want the braid to be. Pinch the 3 strips together at the top and braid them together; pinch the ends together to seal. Hold the strand at both ends and stretch it out gently. If you opt for thinner braids, you'll need 7 or 8 braids to cover the pie; if you opt for wider strips, you'll need 4 or 5 braids. Lay the braids across the pie, spacing them evenly, then trim away the excess dough and finish the edge as desired. (Note: Mealy dough works best for this technique; flaky dough may look uneven after baking.)

OTHER DECORATIVE FINISHES

Braids: For a great decorative edge, make an extra batch of pie dough (mealy, page 188, is best) and roll it out ⅛ inch thick, making the piece of dough as long as possible. A standard 9-inch pie pan is slightly more than 28 inches in circumference, so either go for it and roll out the dough to 29 inches long and make a single braid, or take a more sensible route and roll it out in two 15-inch-ish sections and make 2 braids (you can always place cutouts over the seam where the ends of the braids overlap). For each braid, cut 3 long strips about ¼ inch wide, using a chef's knife or pastry wheel. Pinch the strips together at one end and braid together; when the strips are almost fully braided, pinch the ends together to seal. Hold the braid at both ends and stretch it gently. Brush the edge of the crust lightly with water and press the braid (or braids) onto it (if you made 2 braids, overlap the ends slightly to achieve a seamless effect). This technique also works with just

REHEATING FRUIT PIE

Sometimes you want to make your pie ahead of time, but some pies are just dreamier fresh and warm and they can also get a little soggy when they sit too long. Reheating the pie before serving can be a delicious choice and a crust-saving grace. My best advice is to reheat the pie on a baking stone. Preheat the oven to 425°F / 218°C, to ensure that the baking stone is hot, then lower the oven temperature to 375°F. Cover the pie with foil to prevent overbrowning and bake until it is heated through—10 to 15 minutes for a standard 9-inch pie. The baking stone will recrisp the bottom crust, and then you can slice that bad boy and top it with ice cream. If you are reheating a single slice, for breakfast, for example, wrap the whole thing with foil and reheat on a stone for 6 to 8 minutes.

2 long strips of dough twisted together. It's best to use mealy dough for this—flaky dough is more likely to puff up unevenly around the edge during baking.

Cutouts are such fun to decorate a pie with. You can use them to make a decorative edge, which looks especially great if you overlap the pieces slightly. (Don't use cutters much wider than the edge of the pie pan, though.) You can also use cutouts as the top crust of a pie, arranging them in concentric circles (or another pattern) before baking. Or you can cut shapes out of the top crust for a double-crust pie before placing it on the pie for sort of an open, easier version of lattice. You can also bake the cutouts separately and use them to decorate the finished pie. I find it's best to use scraps of rolled-out dough or mealy dough for cutouts. (Scraps work well for when you make just a few cutouts; for a border [see opposite], you'll need another disk of dough.) Flaky dough is more likely to puff up unevenly, and your cutouts will suffer as a result. Cutouts are generally sturdier if you roll the dough fairly thick—¼ to ⅓ inch. And try to pick cutters without too many tiny details, since pie dough will not hold a shape as well as, say, sugar cookie dough.

To make the cutouts, dip your cutter into flour and press it into the dough. Then, if you're applying the cutouts to the pie before baking, brush the undersides with water and apply the cutouts to the edge, or build concentric circles over the filling. If you're applying the cutouts after baking, brush the surface of each cutout with egg wash and bake them on a baking sheet in a 425°F / 218°C oven until golden and crisp. Arrange the cutouts on the pie once they have cooled.

TYPES OF TARTS

You can really fill tarts with almost anything you fill pies with, but since the structure of the dough and shell are different, the process of filling a tart can also be quite different. The most common kinds of tarts are:

Custard Tarts are filled with a liquid custard before baking. Tart crusts are often parbaked because the layer of filling is much thinner than in a pie and so takes less time to bake.

Nut Tarts have fillings that are usually bound with custard, so they're governed by the same rules that apply to custard tarts.

Cold-Filled Tarts are made with a crust that is fully blind-baked and cooled before it is filled with a pre-made filling, such as whipped cream, fruit curd, and so on. Allowing the dough plenty of time to chill in the pan before blind-baking is key; that helps prevent the dough from shrinking, resulting in the prettiest edge.

MAKING TARTS BEAUTIFUL

It's easy to make tart shells look beautiful, because the pans themselves usually have scalloped edges or attractive sharp corners. But the pan can't do all the work. The most important thing to remember when making a tart is to be certain that the crust is even, since imperfections are more obvious than with a slightly uneven piecrust. See the instructions for lining a tart pan on page 193, taking special note of the method for trimming away the excess.

Here are some other special looks for tarts:

Make a rope border. Line the tart pan as described on page 193, but leave ¼ inch of excess dough all the way around (cut away any excess beyond this with scissors). Press the excess dough down, making it even all the way around; essentially you want a slightly fatter top edge. Press a paring knife on a diagonal into the dough at one of the divots in the tart pan. Repeat on the next divot, at the same angle, and repeat all the way around the tart pan. Chill well before baking.

Drizzle on a smooth surface. If you have a tart filling with a smooth surface (such as custard, ganache, or caramel), a drizzle looks fantastic and—best of all—doesn't need to be perfect (or the same on each tartlet, if you are making individual ones). Try contrasting colors of chocolate or make a thick fruit glaze for a splash of color—see the Sweet Cream Tartlets on page 240.

Pipe on a topping. This method works well for both tarts and tartlets. Use a large tip for a grander, swoopier look (I like a star tip for this). Try piping meringue or whipped cream on top of a tart as you would frosting on a cupcake (see page 85). A small tip will make a tart look fancier, and it's quite easy when you get the hang of it (I like a plain round tip for this). For best results, make sure each piped shape sits snugly next to the one beside it. If you're not good at making the piped shapes even, just make them random. Piped shapes look especially good with a meringue or marshmallow topping, especially if you toast it!

Try a swirl. If your tart has two fillings, swirl them together for an awesome look. The key to a good swirl is to not do it too much, or the two colors will blend together and not be distinct. Start with the bottom filling, then plop large dollops of the second filling randomly over it. Use a skewer or the tip of a small knife to swirl and swoop through the fillings—use a figure-eight motion, but switch direction every so often—until you achieve the look you like.

Take care when arranging your fruit. Part of what makes a fruit tart so appealing is the attractive presentation of the fruit on top. You can arrange fruit by color (use a variety of red fruits, for example) or by size. A generous amount of one kind of fruit is always impressive, and arranging the fruit—whole berries or sliced other fruit—in patterns like spirals or lines is an easy way to make a simple dessert look professional.

It all starts with the dough, and this all-butter dough is hard to beat. But different combinations of fats, flours, and flavorings can also make some pretty tasty crusts; see the Variations.

Makes one 9-inch single or double crust

DIFFICULTY: Medium

MAKE AHEAD AND STORAGE: The tightly wrapped disk(s) of dough can be refrigerated for up to 3 days. Wrapped in plastic and then in aluminum foil, the dough can be frozen for up to 3 months. Thaw overnight in the refrigerator.

All-Buttah Pie Dough

1. To mix the dough by hand: In a large bowl, whisk together the flour and salt. Add the butter cubes, tossing them through the flour until each piece is well coated. Cut the butter into the flour by pressing the pieces between your palms or your fingers, flattening the cubes into big shards and continuing to toss them through the flour, recoating the shingled pieces.

For a flaky crust, continue cutting the butter into the flour just until the pieces of butter are about the size of walnut halves. *Or, for a mealy crust,* continue to work the mixture together until the pieces of butter are about the size of peas.

To mix the dough in a food processor: See Pro Tip.

2. Make a well in the center of the flour mixture. Add 3 tablespoons ice water for a single crust or 6 table-spoons for a double crust and mix to incorporate. Then add more ice water 1 tablespoon at a time and continue mixing just until the dough comes together. As it begins to come together, you can knead it a few times to make sure it's fully combined. It's important not to add too much water to the dough, which should never be sticky—it should hold together easily in a ball but still feel almost dry to the touch.

3. Form the dough into an even disk if making a single crust; or divide in half and shape into 2 equal disks if making a double crust. Wrap tightly in plastic wrap and chill for at least 30 minutes or up to overnight.

4. For a single-crust pie: Lightly flour the work surface. Roll out the dough to a circle ¼ inch thick: Start in the center of the disk of dough and push

SINGLE CRUST

151 g / 1¼ cups all-purpose flour

Pinch of fine sea salt

113 g / 4 oz / 8 tablespoons cold unsalted butter, cut into ½-inch cubes

45 g / 3 tablespoons ice water, plus more as needed

DOUBLE CRUST

302 g / 2½ cups all-purpose flour

Pinch of fine sea salt

226 g / 8 oz cold unsalted butter, cut into ½-inch cubes

90 g / 6 tablespoons ice water, plus more as needed

Egg wash: 57 g / 1 large egg, beaten with 15 g / 1 tablespoon water and a small pinch of fine sea salt

Flaky (left) versus mealy crust

away from you using even pressure. Return to the center and repeat, this time moving toward you. Continue, rotating the dough occasionally and reflouring as needed to prevent the dough from sticking. This produces a more even result than just rolling back and forth, which can often yield thin edges and a thick center.

To transfer the dough to the pie pan, roll the dough up onto the rolling pin, starting at the far edge of the round. With the pie pan in front of you, start at the edge closest to you and gently unfurl the dough into the pan. Press gently to make sure the crust settles all the way to the bottom, but be careful not to poke any holes in the dough. Trim away the excess dough, leaving a ½-inch overhang all around. Chill in the refrigerator for 20 to 30 minutes or freeze for 5 to 10 minutes.

Tuck the excess dough under at the edges, pressing lightly to help "seal" the dough to the outer rim of the pie pan. Return the dough to the refrigerator for 20 to 30 minutes or to the freezer for 5 to 10 minutes.

Crimp the edges of the piecrust as desired (see page 173). The crust is now ready to be parbaked, blind-baked, or filled and baked as directed in the individual recipes.

5. For a double-crust pie: Using one disk of dough, follow the instructions for a single-crust pie and chill the bottom crust in the pie pan. Roll out the second disk of dough on a lightly floured surface to ¼ inch thick and place on a parchment-lined baking sheet. Chill in the refrigerator for 10 to 15 minutes.

Fill the bottom crust as directed in the recipe. Roll the top crust up onto the rolling pin, starting at the far edge of the dough. With the pie pan in front of you, start at the edge closest to you and gently unfurl the dough onto the filling. Trim the excess dough from the edges, leaving a ½-inch overhang all around. Use your fingers to press the edges of the bottom and top crusts together so they are lightly sealed. Chill the pie in the refrigerator for 15 to 30 minutes or freeze for 5 minutes.

Tuck the excess dough under at the edges, pressing lightly to help "seal" the dough to the rim of the pie pan. Return the dough to the refrigerator for 15 to 30 minutes or to the freezer for 5 to 10 minutes.

Crimp the edges of the piecrust as desired (see page 173).

Bake as directed in the recipe.

✳ **WHY IT WORKS**

Manipulated properly, four simple ingredients—flour, fat, salt, and water—make a dough that's crisp and tender. The key takeaways: Keep everything cold; don't be afraid to leave the butter in large pieces; and don't overmix. And, come baking time, don't be afraid of the high temperature, which turns this dough into all it can be through the magic of moisture evaporation and steam!

★ **PRO TIP**

I prefer mixing my dough by hand, but it can be made in the food processor. Start by cutting the butter into ¾-inch cubes instead of ½ inch. Toss the butter in the flour to coat before adding both to the food processor, then pulse in 3-second bursts until the pieces of butter are the desired size, depending on whether you want a flaky (walnut size) or mealy (pea size) crust. I find 10 to 15 pulses usually do the trick. Even when using the food processor, it's best to add the water by hand to prevent overmixing.

TO PARBAKE A SINGLE PIECRUST

1. Preheat the oven to 425°F / 218°C, preferably with a baking stone on the bottom rack. Cut a square of parchment paper slightly larger than the pie pan.

2. Prick the chilled dough all over with a fork. Place the parchment over the crust and fill with pie weights or dried beans (see page 168).

3. Bake the crust on the stone or bottom rack just until the edges barely begin to turn golden, 15 to 20 minutes.

4. Take the pan out of the oven and remove the parchment and weights, then return the pan to the oven and bake the crust for another 2 to 4 minutes, just until lightly golden around the edges.

5. Immediately brush the bottom of the crust with a thin layer of egg wash. The residual heat should cook the egg, but if it looks wet, throw it back in the oven for 1 minute more. Cool the crust completely before filling it and returning it to the oven to finish baking, as directed in the individual recipes.

TO BLIND-BAKE A SINGLE PIECRUST

1. Follow the instructions for parbaking through step 3.

2. Take the pan out of the oven and remove the parchment and weights. Brush the bottom and crimped edges of the dough with a thin layer of egg wash.

3. Return the pie pan to the oven and bake for another 12 to 17 minutes, until the dough is evenly golden brown. Cool the crust completely before filling it.

Variations (for a single crust; all can be doubled)

Whole Wheat Pie Dough: Reduce the all-purpose flour to 75 g / ⅔ cup and add 89 g / ¾ cup whole wheat pastry flour. Start with 60 g / 4 tablespoons ice water, then add more as needed. Whole wheat flour absorbs water differently—blame the bran and the germ—so it's necessary to start with a little bit more water, and know that you might need to add more than for a dough using only all-purpose flour. Also, take care not to overmix once the water is added, as the whole wheat flour makes it especially easy to end up with a tough crust.

Even-Flakier Piecrust: Replace 57 g / 2 oz / 4 tablespoons of the butter with an equal amount of very cold shortening or lard.

Chocolate Pie Dough: Replace 30 g / ¼ cup of the all-purpose flour with 28 g / ⅓ cup unsweetened cocoa powder (preferably dark). Be aware that the increased fat content from the cocoa makes the dough more prone to becoming sticky if overmixed and/or handled excessively.

Cream Cheese Pie Dough: Replace 57 g / 2 oz / 4 tablespoons of the butter with an equal amount of cream cheese.

Peanut Butter Pie Dough: Cut a piece of parchment about 5 inches square. Spread 68 g / ¼ cup creamy peanut butter in a ½-inch-thick layer on the paper and freeze until fairly firm, about 1 hour. Cut into cubes and use in place of 57 g / 2 oz / 4 tablespoons of the butter.

I can never make a tart without thinking of Rose Levy Beranbaum. I've been a huge fan of hers since I was about sixteen. When I was working with her styling the food for her book *The Baking Bible,* she taught me how to fold a small amount of the excess dough over the edges of the tart pan so the dough wouldn't shrink. Rose was kind enough to let me borrow part of her technique for this book.

Makes one 9- to 11-inch crust (or enough dough for 12 tartlets)

DIFFICULTY: Medium

MAKE AHEAD AND STORAGE: The tightly wrapped dough can be refrigerated for up to 4 days. Wrapped in plastic wrap and then in aluminum foil, it can be frozen for up to 3 months. Thaw overnight in the refrigerator before using.

Tart Dough

1. In a food processor, pulse together the flour, sugar, and salt. Add the butter and pulse until the mixture resembles coarse meal, about 1 minute.

2. Transfer the mixture to a medium bowl. Make a well in the center and pour in the water. Knead the mixture gently with your hands until it forms a smooth dough that holds together when squeezed. It should not be wet or sticky.

3. Tightly wrap the dough in plastic wrap and chill it in the refrigerator for at least 30 minutes and up to overnight.

4. When ready to roll out the dough, let it rest at room temperature for 5 to 10 minutes. Start in the center of the disk of dough and push, using even pressure, away from you. Return to the center and repeat, this time moving toward you. Continue, rotating the dough occasionally and reflouring as needed.

5. Lightly flour a work surface. Roll the dough out to a ¼-inch-thick circle, using as little flour as possible. Aim for the circle to be about 2 inches wider than the tart pan all around.

6. Roll the dough up onto the rolling pin and gently transfer it to the tart pan, unfurling the dough off the pin and into the pan. Lift the dough up at the edges and nudge it downward to make sure it fits snugly into the corners; press firmly to make sure it settles all the way to the bottom

241 g / 2 cups all-purpose flour

37 g / 3 tablespoons granulated sugar

2 g / ½ teaspoon fine sea salt

151 g / 5 oz / 10 tablespoons cold unsalted butter, cut into ½-inch cubes

60 g / ¼ cup ice water, plus more as needed

but be careful not to make any holes in the dough. Chill the dough in the refrigerator for 20 to 30 minutes or freeze it for 5 to 10 minutes.

7. Use scissors to trim the dough to a 1-inch overhang. Fold the excess dough under itself (it will reach about halfway down the side of the pan). Then use your fingers to smooth out the dough in any places where it's thicker. It will rise above the edge of the tart pan as you do so—that's OK! Using a paring knife held flush against the rim of the pan, trim the excess dough, leaving a clean edge. Prick the dough all over with a fork. Freeze for at least 45 minutes (see Pro Tip).

8. Bake as directed in the recipe.

❊ **WHY IT WORKS**

Processing the butter more finely than for pie dough results in a mealier crust that's tender and lightly crisp—like a cookie— that can hold up to any tart filling.

★ **PRO TIP**

For best results, the dough should be handled with care and kept nice and cool. It's especially important to chill tart dough thoroughly before parbaking or blind baking. The colder the dough is, the less likely it is to shrink as it bakes. I like to freeze it thoroughly—preferably 2 hours or up to overnight for best results.

TO PARBAKE A TART CRUST

1. Preheat the oven to 400°F / 204°C, preferably with a baking stone on the bottom rack.

2. Cut a square of parchment paper slightly larger than the tart pan. Place it over the chilled crust and fill with pie weights or dried beans (see page 168).

3. Bake the crust on the stone or bottom rack just until the edges barely begin to turn golden, 12 to 17 minutes.

4. Take the pan out of the oven and remove the parchment and weights, then return the pan to the oven and bake the crust for another 2 to 3 minutes, just until lightly golden at the edges.

5. Cool the crust completely before filling it and returning to the oven to finish baking as directed in the individual recipes.

Vanilla Mascarpone Cream Pie (page 203)

Makes one 10-inch crust (or enough dough for 12 tartlets)

DIFFICULTY: Easy

MAKE AHEAD AND STORAGE: The tightly wrapped dough can be refrigerated for up to 4 days; bring to room temperature before using. Wrapped in plastic wrap and then in aluminum foil, the dough can be frozen for up to 3 months. Thaw overnight in the refrigerator before using.

This fuss-free tart dough is mixed a lot like cookie dough. Then you just press it into the pan with your hands, and you're ready to bake.

Press-In Tart Dough

1. In the bowl of a stand mixer fitted with the paddle attachment (or in a large bowl, using a hand mixer), cream the butter and sugar on medium-low speed until smooth, 2 to 3 minutes.

2. Add the egg yolk and mix on medium speed to combine. Scrape the bowl well. Add the flour and salt and mix on low speed until fully incorporated, 45 seconds to 1 minute. Add the water and mix just until the dough is smooth, 1 minute more.

3. Turn out the dough and use your fingers to press it into a 10-inch tart pan (see Pro Tip). Once the sides and bottom of the pan are fully covered, smooth the dough with your fingers to even out any thicker spots. Use a

paring knife held flush against the rim of the pan to trim the excess dough, leaving a clean edge. Prick the dough all over with a fork. Freeze for at least 30 minutes and up to overnight.

4. To parbake the crust, follow the basic instructions on page 194, but preheat the oven to 425°F / 218°C. Bake the crust with the weights just until the edges barely begin to turn golden, 15 to 20 minutes. Then remove the parchment and weights and bake for another 5 to 7 minutes, just until lightly golden at the edges. Immediately brush the bottom of the crust with a thin layer of egg wash. The residual heat should cook the egg wash, but if it looks wet, throw it back in the oven for 1 minute more. Cool the crust completely.

113 g / 4 oz / 8 tablespoons unsalted butter, at room temperature

50 g / ¼ cup granulated sugar

27 g / 1 large egg yolk

211 g / 1¾ cups all-purpose flour

2 g / ½ teaspoon fine sea salt

15 g / 1 tablespoon water

Egg wash: 57 g / 1 large egg, beaten with 15 g / 1 tablespoon water and a small pinch of fine sea salt

To blind-bake the crust, follow the instructions for parbaking on page 194, but as soon as you remove the parchment and weights, brush the bottom and crimped edges of the dough with a thin layer of egg wash. Then bake for another 12 to 17 minutes, until the dough is evenly golden brown. Cool the crust completely before filling.

✻ WHY IT WORKS

Creaming the butter and sugar for less time than you would for a cookie dough helps keep the crust from puffing up too much in the oven.

★ PRO TIP

When pressing the tart dough into the pan, I start at the edges and work my way inward (see page 170). This helps make the sides even (the hardest part, I think!), preventing too much buildup in the corners.

Variation

Chocolate Press-In Dough: Replace 30 g / ¼ cup of the all-purpose flour with 21 g / ¼ cup unsweetened cocoa powder.

TO BLIND-BAKE A TART CRUST

1. Follow the instructions for parbaking on page 194 through step 3.

2. Take the tart pan out of the oven and remove the parchment and weights. Return the pan to the oven and bake for another 10 to 15 minutes, until the dough is evenly golden brown.

3. Cool the crust completely before filling it.

From top: Jammy Hand Pies and Rice Pudding Tarts (page 355)

Make these hand pies when you want homemade pie in as short a time as possible; when you have scraps of pie dough piling up in your fridge or freezer; or when you want a fruit pie but have no fresh fruit.

Jammy Hand Pies

1. Line two baking sheets with parchment paper.

2. On a lightly floured surface, roll one chilled disk of dough out to a ¼-inch-thick square a little larger than 12 inches across. Trim the edges to even them, then cut the dough into 8 equal rectangles. (For round pies, use a round cutter.)

3. Transfer 4 of the rectangles to one of the prepared baking sheets. Place about 56 g / 2½ tablespoons jam in the center of each one and lightly brush the edges of the dough with water. Top with the remaining 4 dough rectangles, laying them down gently and pressing to remove excess air so the dough tightly encloses the jam. Press gently around the edges to seal, then crimp with a fork all around (see Pro Tip). Repeat, using the remaining

dough and jam, for 12 pies total, 6 per baking sheet.

4. Transfer the hand pies to the refrigerator and chill thoroughly, at least 30 minutes, or freeze for 15 minutes.

5. Preheat the oven to 425°F / 218°C, preferably with a baking stone on the bottom rack.

6. Brush the pies with the egg wash and sprinkle with turbinado sugar. Cut steam vents in the tops with a sharp paring knife—a few small lines or a tiny X in each one.

7. Bake the pies on the stone or bottom rack until golden brown—the jam may bubble through the vents a bit—19 to 22 minutes. Cool for at least 5 minutes before serving.

Makes 12 individual pies

DIFFICULTY: Easy

MAKE AHEAD AND STORAGE: These pies are best eaten the same day they're baked, preferably warm from the oven. Store leftover pies airtight at room temperature for up to 2 days. The unbaked pies can be frozen for up to 3 months; freeze them on the baking sheets, then transfer to an airtight container for storage.

Triple recipe All-Buttah Pie Dough (page 188; mixed for a flaky crust) divided into 3 portions, shaped into disks, and chilled

About 680 g / 2 cups jam (any flavor)

Egg wash: 57 g / 1 large egg, beaten with 15 g / 1 tablespoon water and a small pinch of fine sea salt

Turbinado or coarse sugar, for sprinkling

✳ **WHY IT WORKS**

The jam melts a little in the oven, flattening into an even layer inside the dough. The moisture level is less than that of fresh fruit, so there are no worries of leakage as long as the edges are well sealed.

★ **PRO TIP**

The key to successful hand pies is proper crimping, so make sure those edges are sealed so that jam doesn't splooge out the sides. Dip your fork in flour every few crimps to keep the crimps clean.

A galette is a great way to learn to make pie—no pie pan needed, and randomness is encouraged! I usually make this galette as a square or rectangle, but you can go free-form—whatever shape works for you. Just make sure you seal the edges well so you don't have leaks.

Makes one 10-by-5-inch galette

DIFFICULTY: Easy

MAKE AHEAD AND STORAGE: The galette is best eaten the same day it's baked, preferably fresh out of the oven. But it can be stored airtight at room temperature for up to 2 days.

Double-Crust Berry Galette

1. Line a baking sheet with parchment paper. On a lightly floured surface, roll one disk of dough out into a narrow ¼-inch-thick rectangle; it should measure a little larger than 10 by 5 inches. Trim the edges so they are straight. Transfer the dough to the prepared baking sheet and chill in the freezer for at least 15 minutes, or in the refrigerator for 20 to 30 minutes.

2. In a large bowl, toss the berries with the lemon juice. In a small bowl, whisk the sugar and flour to combine, then add the mixture to the berries and toss to coat.

3. Roll out the remaining disk of dough as you did the first. (See Pro Tip if you want to make a lattice crust.)

4. Remove the bottom crust from the refrigerator and pile the berries evenly on top, leaving a 1-inch margin all the way around. Brush the exposed edges of the dough with water. Carefully place the second crust on the berries. Press the edges of the crusts gently with your fingers to seal all the way around, then crimp as desired (see page 173; I just use a fork). Chill the galette in the fridge or freezer for at least 15 minutes.

5. Preheat the oven to 425°F / 218°C, preferably with a baking stone on the bottom rack.

6. Brush the top crust of the galette with the egg wash and sprinkle generously with turbinado sugar. Cut steam vents into the top with a sharp paring knife—a few small lines or an X.

All-Buttah Pie Dough for a double crust (page 188; mixed for a flaky crust), divided in half, shaped into 2 disks, and chilled

1.19 kg / 2⅔ pounds / about 7 heaping cups fresh berries (blueberries, strawberries, raspberries, or blackberries, or a mixture)

9 g / 2 teaspoons freshly squeezed lemon juice

99 g / ½ cup granulated sugar

30 g / ¼ cup all-purpose flour

Egg wash: 57 g / 1 large egg, beaten with 15 g / 1 tablespoon water and a small pinch of fine sea salt

Turbinado or coarse sugar, for sprinkling

⟶

7. Bake the galette on the stone or bottom rack until the crust is golden brown (the fruit may bubble up through the vents or seams a bit), 45 to 50 minutes. Cool for at least 15 minutes before serving.

✳ **WHY IT WORKS**

Galettes are great because they are easier to bake properly than a traditional pie— they are thinner and they brown more evenly. And it isn't as difficult to get the bottom to brown, because the whole surface is against the hot baking sheet. (Though underbaking can still lead to a soggy bottom.)

★ **PRO TIP**

Lattice ain't just for pies! To top the galette with a lattice crust, follow the instructions on page 177, but rather than tucking the ends of the dough strips under the edge of the bottom crust, fold the edges of the bottom crust up and over the ends of the lattice strips. Then crimp as desired (see page 173).

This is the easiest pie in the book, and it's infinitely adaptable. The cookie crumb crust means no fussing over flaky pastry, and the filling is cold-set, not baked. It's one of my favorite summer pies, because I don't have to turn the oven on for long, but since it can be finished with nearly any fruit, it's great year-round.

Vanilla Mascarpone Cream Pie

Makes one 9-inch single-crust pie

DIFFICULTY: Easy

MAKE AHEAD AND STORAGE: This pie is best served the same day it's made, since the crust can get soggy quickly, but if made 1 day ahead, it will still be good—do hold off adding the fruit until the last minute, though, as it may weep. Store in the refrigerator, tightly covered with plastic wrap.

1. Preheat the oven to 375°F / 190°C, preferably with a baking stone on the bottom rack.

2. Make the crust: In a medium bowl, stir the cookie crumbs and salt to combine. Add 43 g / 1.5 oz / 3 tablespoons of the melted butter and mix just until the mixture clumps together. If it looks dry, add the remaining 14 g / 0.5 oz / 1 tablespoon butter.

3. Press the crumb mixture in evenly over the bottom of a 9-inch pie pan and up the sides (I use a small dry measure to help press it into the corners and keep things even).

4. Bake the crust on the stone or bottom rack until golden brown, 8 to 12 minutes. Cool completely.

5. Make the filling: Pour the water into a shallow dish and sprinkle the gelatin evenly over it. Let soak for 5 minutes, then heat it in the microwave until liquid, 30 to 60 seconds.

6. In the bowl of a stand mixer fitted with the whisk attachment (or in a large bowl, using a hand mixer), whip the heavy cream on medium-low speed until frothy. Gradually add the sugar and continue whipping to soft peaks, 2 to 3 minutes. Add the mascarpone, vanilla, and melted

CRUST

213 g / 2 cups fine sugar cookie crumbs

1 g / ¼ teaspoon fine sea salt

57 g / 2 oz / 4 tablespoons unsalted butter, melted

FILLING

30 g / 2 tablespoons cold water

4 g / 1 teaspoon powdered gelatin

302 g / 1¼ cups heavy cream

99 g / ½ cup granulated sugar

454 g / 16 oz / 2 cups mascarpone cheese

4 g / ¾ teaspoon vanilla extract

→

gelatin and mix on medium speed until the mixture reaches medium peaks, 2 to 3 minutes more.

7. Pour the mascarpone mixture into the cooled crust and spread it evenly; work quickly, as it will set fast. Arrange the fruit on top of the filling.

8. In a small saucepan, warm the honey until fluid. Gently brush the fruit with the warm honey. Refrigerate the pie until ready to serve.

❋ **WHY IT WORKS**
Refrigerator pie recipes like this one are great to have in your back pocket—the simple crust and cold filling mean they come together in less than half the time of traditional fruit or custard pies. I use gelatin to firm up and stabilize the rich, creamy filling, making it easily sliceable.

★ **PRO TIP**
Sometimes I go monochromatic and decorate this pie with a few fruits of the same color. Other times, I mix it up for a bold and bright pie. Here are some of my fave fruit combos, by season:

Spring: sliced or whole strawberries and sliced rhubarb (sautéed or poached, cooled)

Summer: any whole berries and halved or quartered stone fruit

Fall: sliced or halved pears, grapes, or figs and whole raspberries

Winter: citrus suprêmes (peeled sections with membranes removed) and pomegranate seeds

About 2 cups seasonal fruit, cut into large wedges or trimmed and left whole, depending on the fruit (see Pro Tip)

43 g / 2 tablespoons honey (preferably wildflower)

From left: Vanilla Mascarpone Cream Pie (page 203) and Dulce de Leche Ice Cream Pie (page 206)

This is my go-to ice cream pie. You can use store-bought dulce de leche, but homemade is simple. If you prepare it in advance (it does need to cook on the stove for a few hours), then whenever you feel like pie, it's bim-bam-boom.

I like to add a little crunch with Marcona almonds, a delicious almond roasted in olive oil and salted—but you can substitute regular almonds (or salted peanuts) if you like. The photo is on page 205.

Makes one 9-inch single-crust pie

DIFFICULTY: Medium

MAKE AHEAD AND STORAGE: Tightly wrapped in plastic wrap, the pie, without the whipped cream topping, can be kept in the freezer for up to 2 weeks.

Dulce de Leche Ice Cream Pie

1. Make the dulce de leche: In a medium saucepan, combine the milk, sugar, salt, and cinnamon stick. Scrape the seeds from the vanilla bean and add the seeds and pod to the pan. Bring to a simmer over medium heat, stirring until the sugar dissolves. Stir in the baking soda—be careful, the mixture may bubble up slightly—and turn the heat down to low. Cook the mixture for 2½ to 3 hours, stirring occasionally, until thick and golden brown. About halfway through the cooking, when the mixture begins to darken in color, remove the vanilla bean pod and cinnamon stick, which can be difficult to get at once the caramelizing and thickening have begun.

2. Strain the dulce de leche into a heatproof container and cool completely.

3. Preheat the oven to 375°F / 190°C, preferably with a baking stone on the bottom rack.

4. Make the crust: In a medium bowl, stir the cookie crumbs and salt to combine. Add 43 g / 1.5 oz / 3 tablespoons of the butter and mix just until the mixture clumps together. If it looks dry, add some or all of the remaining 14 g / 0.5 oz / 1 tablespoon melted butter.

5. Press the crumb mixture evenly over the bottom and up the sides of a 9-inch pie pan (I use a small dry

DULCE DE LECHE
(MAKES 538 G / 2 CUPS)

967 g / 4 cups whole milk

298 g / 1½ cups granulated sugar

2 g / ½ teaspoon fine sea salt

One 1-inch piece cinnamon stick

½ vanilla bean, split lengthwise

3 g / ½ teaspoon baking soda

CRUST

213 g / 2 cups fine chocolate cookie crumbs (such as chocolate wafers)

1 g / ¼ teaspoon fine sea salt

57 g / 2 oz / 4 tablespoons unsalted butter, melted

⟶

measure to help press it into the corners of the pan and keep things even). Bake on the stone or bottom rack until the crust appears set, 10 to 12 minutes. Cool completely.

6. Spread 67 g / ¼ cup of the dulce de leche evenly over the bottom of the cooled crust.

7. Soften the ice cream to the point that it can be stirred relatively easily, then transfer to a large bowl and stir a few times with a silicone spatula to loosen it. Drizzle 202 g / ¾ cup of the dulce de leche over the ice cream and fold a few times to swirl the two together. Scoop the ice cream into the crust and smooth into an even layer. Transfer to the pie to the freezer and chill for at least 45 minutes.

8. In the bowl of a stand mixer (or in a large bowl, using a hand mixer), whip together the cream, sugar, and vanilla on medium speed until the mixture reaches medium peaks. Spread or pipe the whipped cream on top of the pie (see Pro Tip). Drizzle with the remaining 269 g / 1 cup dulce de leche. Sprinkle the almonds on top, if using.

9. Freeze the pie until firm, at least 1 hour and preferably overnight, before serving.

❊ WHY IT WORKS

Dulce de leche is traditionally made by heating sweetened condensed milk until the sugars caramelize, making a thick, caramel-like sauce. But the traditional method can be a bit scary, as you're basically pressure-cooking the can to get the milk to caramelize (something that can lead to the occasional explosion if done improperly). This recipe goes in a slightly safer direction by starting with whole milk and sugar. The cooking process takes a while—first to reduce the milk, simmering away some of the water content and resulting in a higher ratio of the natural sugars. These sugars, combined with added sugar, make the mixture caramelize evenly and result in a perfect (if not totally traditional) dulce de leche.

★ PRO TIP

Ice cream pies come together quickly, especially if you're using store-bought ingredients, but it's easy to add a little flair with the garnish. For this one, you can pipe the whipped cream on—shells, rosettes, dots, anything works! Drizzles (of one or more sauces) and a sprinkling of chocolate shavings, nuts, or sprinkles will also give it a wow effect.

479 g / 4 cups vanilla ice cream

242 g / 1 cup heavy cream

37 g / 3 tablespoons granulated sugar

2.5 g / ½ teaspoon vanilla extract

128 g / 1 cup Marcona almonds, roughly chopped, for garnish (optional)

Clockwise from top left: Hazelnut Pie with Chocolate Crust (page 212), Brownie Pie, and Chocolate Cream Pie with Whipped Peanut Butter Cream (page 210)

Brownies are good. Pie is good. So brownie pie is obviously . . . really good. Brownie batter studded with almonds and chocolate chunks goes into a piecrust, which bakes up crisp and golden while the filling becomes soft and fudgy. This is a good pie to make with and serve to kids—don't forget the ice cream!

Makes one 9-inch single-crust pie

DIFFICULTY: Easy

MAKE AHEAD AND STORAGE: The pie can be made ahead and stored at room temperature for up to 2 days; leftovers can be stored airtight for up to 2 days more.

Brownie Pie

1. Preheat the oven to 350°F / 175°C, preferably with a baking stone on the bottom rack.

2. **Make the filling:** In a medium heatproof bowl, combine the butter, oil, and bittersweet chocolate. Set the bowl over a medium saucepan of simmering water (with the bowl not touching the water) and heat, stirring occasionally, until the mixture is fully melted and combined. Let cool slightly.

3. Add both sugars to the chocolate mixture and mix well with a silicone spatula. Add the eggs one at a time, mixing until each one is fully incorporated. Whisk in the vanilla. Add the flour and salt and mix well to ensure there are no flour pockets, but do not overmix. Fold in the semisweet chocolate and almonds.

4. Pour the batter into the piecrust and bake until a toothpick inserted into the center of the brownie comes out with moist, clumpy crumbs, 45 to 50 minutes. Do not overbake! Let the pie cool for at least 20 minutes before slicing and serving—with ice cream or whipped cream, or both.

❈ **WHY IT WORKS**
Brownie batter baked in a piecrust has an extra advantage—slightly different depths of the batter mean that the edges are chewier, while the off-center and center parts are softer and extra-fudgy. It's the best of both worlds for any brownie lover.

★ **PRO TIP**
You can make this pie using any brownie—or blondie—batter! I've even made it with a chocolate chip cookie dough filling—just take special care not to overbake. Most brownies are high in chocolate and will continue to firm up as they cool; err on the side of underbaking the filling for best results.

FILLING

57 g / 2 oz / 4 tablespoons unsalted butter

60 g / ¼ cup neutral oil (such as vegetable, canola, or peanut oil)

227 g / 8 oz bittersweet chocolate (I use 70% cacao), chopped

106 g / ½ cup packed light brown sugar

99 g / ½ cup granulated sugar

168 g / 3 large eggs

10 g / 2 teaspoons vanilla extract

80 g / ⅔ cup all-purpose flour

2 g / ½ teaspoon fine sea salt

170 g / 6 oz semisweet chocolate, chopped

113 g / 1 cup chopped almonds

Ice cream and/or whipped cream, for serving

One 9-inch piecrust made with All-Buttah Pie Dough (page 188; mixed for a mealy crust), parbaked, brushed with egg wash, and cooled completely (see page 191)

For this pie, my favorite dark chocolate pudding, made with a hint of espresso to deepen the chocolate flavor, is nestled in a flaky peanut butter crust and topped with a mixture of whipped peanut butter and cream. Chocolate cream pie purists, you can certainly skip the PB whip and throw the pudding in whatever crust you like (consider a chocolate cookie crumb crust). The photo is on page 208.

Makes one 9-inch single-crust pie

DIFFICULTY: Medium

MAKE AHEAD AND STORAGE: The filled pie can be refrigerated, loosely covered with plastic wrap, for up to 3 days, but it's best to add the peanut butter whip the day that you serve the pie.

Chocolate Cream Pie
with Whipped Peanut Butter Cream

1. Make the filling: In a medium saucepan, heat the milk, cream, and chocolate over medium-low heat, stirring constantly, until the chocolate has fully melted. Turn the heat up to medium and bring the mixture to a gentle simmer.

2. Meanwhile, whisk the sugar, cornstarch, and espresso powder together in a medium heatproof bowl. Whisk in the egg yolks until well combined.

3. When the chocolate mixture has come to a simmer, pour about half of it into the egg yolk mixture in a slow, steady stream, whisking constantly. Then pour the egg yolk mixture into the saucepan and cook the pudding over low heat, stirring constantly with a silicone spatula, until it gets very thick and comes to a first boil (a single large bubble comes up to the surface in the center of the pudding), 3 to 4 minutes. Stir in the butter and vanilla until well combined.

4. Pour the warm pudding into the cooled piecrust and cover with plastic wrap pressed directly against the surface of the pudding. Let cool at room temperature until the filling is completely set, 35 to 45 minutes.

5. Make the peanut butter cream: In the bowl of a stand mixer fitted with the whisk attachment (or in a large bowl, using a hand mixer), whip the

CHOCOLATE CREAM FILLING

605 g / 2½ cups whole milk

121 g / ½ cup heavy cream

113 g / 4 oz unsweetened chocolate, chopped

198 g / 1 cup granulated sugar

37 g / ⅓ cup cornstarch

3 g / 1 teaspoon instant espresso powder

135 g / 5 large egg yolks

28 g / 1 oz / 2 tablespoons unsalted butter, at room temperature

10 g / 2 teaspoons vanilla extract

One 9-inch piecrust made with Peanut Butter Pie Dough (page 192; mixed for a mealy crust), blind-baked, brushed with egg wash, and cooled completely (see page 191)

⟶

peanut butter and sugar on medium-high speed until light and fluffy, 2 to 3 minutes. Add the cream and continue whipping until the mixture reaches medium peaks. Add the vanilla and mix to combine.

6. Finish the pie: Dollop the peanut butter cream on top of the cooled pie and swirl it around with an offset spatula (easier), or transfer it to a pastry bag and pipe it on (fancier—see Pro Tip). Refrigerate until ready to serve.

❄ **WHY IT WORKS**

Perfect pudding relies on proper cooking. Adding a small amount of the warm liquid to the eggs (while whisking vigorously and constantly) gradually warms up the egg mixture, bringing it closer to the temperature of the rest of the warm liquid, a process called tempering. If the eggs are added directly to the warm milk mixture, they are more likely to scramble, resulting in a grainy, chunky pudding.

★ **PRO TIP**

For a fancier finish, I like to use a flat side of a basket-weave tip to pipe on the whip in concentric circles, working toward the center of the pie. But plenty of other techniques would fly here—think big fat rosettes or even random-sized dots all over!

WHIPPED PEANUT BUTTER CREAM

135 g / ½ cup smooth peanut butter

25 g / 2 tablespoons granulated sugar

121 g / ½ cup heavy cream

3 g / ½ teaspoon vanilla extract

This is a seriously decadent nut pie—large chunks of hazelnuts in a sweet filling, all wrapped in a chocolate piecrust. I leave the hazelnuts in pretty big pieces, because I dig the texture, but you can chop them up a bit finer if you like. The photo is on page 208.

Makes one 9-inch single-crust pie

DIFFICULTY: Medium

MAKE AHEAD AND STORAGE: The pie is best eaten the same day it's made, but it can be stored airtight in the refrigerator for up to 2 days.

Hazelnut Pie *with Chocolate Crust*

1. Preheat the oven to 375°F / 190°C, preferably with a baking stone on the bottom rack.

2. Make the crust: Place the chocolate in a small heatproof bowl. In a small saucepan, bring the cream to a simmer over medium heat. Pour the hot cream over the chocolate and let sit, undisturbed, for 15 seconds. Using a silicone spatula, stir, beginning in the center of the bowl and widening the circles, until the ganache is smooth and glossy.

3. Pour the ganache into the piecrust and spread it evenly over the bottom. Set aside.

4. Make the filling: In a medium bowl, whisk the butter, brown sugar, maple syrup, salt, and vanilla to combine. Add the eggs one at a time, whisking until incorporated before adding the next.

5. Assemble and bake the pie: Arrange the nuts in an even layer over the bottom of the prepared crust. Pour in the custard.

6. Bake the pie on the stone or bottom rack just until the custard is set at the edges but still slightly jiggly in the center, 33 to 36 minutes; the nuts should look lightly golden and the crust should be evenly browned. Cool completely.

❈ **WHY IT WORKS**
Much like a traditional pecan pie, this pie relies on the gentle coagulation of egg proteins to make a silky filling—an ideal contrast to the crisp hazelnuts and flaky pie dough.

★ **PRO TIP**
Want to up the ante? Throw 170 g / 6 oz chopped bittersweet chocolate in with the nuts before you add the filling.

CRUST

113 g / 4.5 oz bittersweet chocolate (I use 60% cacao), finely chopped

61 g / ¼ cup heavy cream

One 9-inch piecrust made with Chocolate Pie Dough (page 192; mixed for a mealy crust), parbaked, brushed with egg glaze, and cooled completely (see page 191)

FILLING

71 g / 2.5 oz / 5 tablespoons unsalted butter, melted

213 g / 7.5 oz / 1 cup packed light brown sugar

191 g / ½ cup maple syrup

2 g / ½ teaspoon fine sea salt

5 g / 1 teaspoon vanilla extract

170 g / 3 large eggs

255 g / 2 cups skinned hazelnuts, roughly chopped

This classic custard pie is popular in some parts of the Midwest (helloooooo Indiana!) and Canada (where it's flavored with maple). The filling is silky smooth and sinfully rich. I like it in a cream cheese crust, but it is neutral enough to work with nearly any kind of pastry. Not that it should be relegated to holidays only, but the lovely hint of nutmeg makes this perfect for Christmastime.

Makes one 9-inch single-crust pie

DIFFICULTY: Medium

MAKE AHEAD AND STORAGE: This pie is best the same day it's made, but it can be stored, tightly wrapped in plastic wrap, in the refrigerator for up to 2 days.

Sugar Pie

1. Preheat the oven to 375°F / 190°C, preferably with a baking stone on the bottom rack.

2. **Make the filling:** In a medium bowl, whisk together the granulated sugar and flour. Add the brown sugar and mix to combine. Scrape the seeds from the vanilla bean and add the seeds to the bowl (you can use the pod for vanilla sugar; see Pro Tip, page 97). Whisk in the milk, cream, and nutmeg just enough to combine; too much whisking will lead to lots of air bubbles on the surface of the pie.

3. Pour the custard into the cooled piecrust. Use the tip of a paring knife or a toothpick to pop any large bubbles on the surface. Bake the pie until the custard appears set at the edges but is still slightly jiggly in the center, 28 to 32 minutes. Cool completely.

4. Dust the pie with powdered sugar before slicing and serving.

❊ **WHY IT WORKS**

Many custards are made with eggs—and plenty of them—but this one is cream-based and depends on the gelatinization of the starch (flour) to help it set in the oven. As a result, the custard has the silky texture of an egg-based custard pie but the sweet cream flavor really sings because it's not competing with eggs. (And the color is nice and pale.) You can substitute maple sugar for the brown sugar if you want to give the Canadian version a try.

★ **PRO TIP**

The surface of this custard is so smooth, it makes a perfect background for a pattern. I like to lay a stencil over the top of the pie and then dust it with powdered sugar. Peel the stencil away, and the beautiful pattern is left behind. You can use any kind of stencil, or even make a simple one from a piece of paper. But my favorite way is to do this using a doily; see the photo on page 215.

FILLING

99 g / ½ cup granulated sugar

60 g / ½ cup all-purpose flour

106 g / ½ cup packed light brown sugar

½ vanilla bean, split lengthwise

242 g / 1 cup whole milk

302 g / 1¼ cups heavy cream

2 g / ½ teaspoon freshly grated nutmeg

One 9-inch piecrust made with Cream Cheese Pie Dough (page 192; mixed for a mealy crust), parbaked, brushed with egg wash, and cooled completely (see page 191)

Powdered sugar, for dusting

Sugar Pie with doily finish
(see Pro Tip, page 213)

This custard is made a lot like the filling for pumpkin pie, but with mashed sweet potatoes. Then the whole thing is topped with toasted molasses marshmallow. For an easier pie, you can swap the marshmallow for meringue or just plenty of whipped cream.

Makes one 9-inch single-crust pie

DIFFICULTY: Hard

MAKE AHEAD AND STORAGE: The pie can be made up to 1 day ahead, but it's best to add the topping the same day you serve it. The finished pie can be stored, loosely covered, at room temperature for up to 3 days.

Sweet Potato Pie

1. Preheat the oven to 375°F / 190°C, preferably with a baking stone on the bottom rack.

2. Make the filling: In a large bowl, whisk together the eggs and both sugars until well combined, about 1 minute. Add the vanilla, melted butter, and cream and whisk to combine. Add the sweet potatoes and whisk until combined—the mixture should be relatively smooth. Stir in the spices.

3. Pour the filling into the piecrust, smoothing it into an even layer.

4. Bake the pie on the stone or bottom rack until the filling is set at the edges but still slightly jiggly in the center, 40 to 45 minutes. Cool completely.

5. Make the marshmallow topping: Pour 81 g / ⅓ cup of the water into a small heatproof bowl, and sprinkle the gelatin over it. Let soak for at least 5 minutes. Grease a silicone spatula and an offset spatula with nonstick spray; set aside.

6. Meanwhile, combine the remaining 81 g / ⅓ cup water, the granulated sugar, molasses, and corn syrup in a medium saucepan and bring the mixture to a boil over medium-high heat. You can stir the mixture before it comes to a boil to help dissolve the sugar, but stop stirring the moment it starts to boil. Attach a candy thermometer to the side of the pan (or have an instant-read thermometer ready). Boil the mixture until it registers 240°F / 115°C.

FILLING

149 g / 3 large eggs

160 g / ¾ cup packed light brown sugar

99 g / ½ cup granulated sugar

5 g / 1 teaspoon vanilla extract

57 g / 2 oz / 4 tablespoons unsalted butter, melted

161 g / ⅔ cup heavy cream

510 g / 2 cups mashed sweet potatoes (from about 2 large sweet potatoes, peeled and boiled)

6 g / 2 teaspoons ground cinnamon

4 g / 1 teaspoon ground ginger

1 g / ½ teaspoon ground allspice

Scant 1 g / ¼ teaspoon freshly grated nutmeg

One 9-inch single piecrust made with All-Buttah Pie Dough (page 188; mixed for a mealy crust), parbaked, brushed with egg wash, and cooled (see page 191)

→

7. Meanwhile, place the egg whites in the bowl of a stand mixer fitted with the whisk attachment (or use a large bowl and a hand mixer) and whip on low speed until lightly frothy. Melt the gelatin over a water bath (or in a heat-proof bowl set over a pan of boiling water) or in the microwave, about 30 seconds.

8. When the sugar mixture registers 240°F / 115°C, increase the mixer speed to medium-high and add the syrup to the bowl in a slow, steady stream. Pour in the melted gelatin with the mixer running and whip on high speed until the mixture is bright white, fluffy, and aerated and holds medium peaks, 4 to 5 minutes.

9. Use the greased spatula to transfer the molasses marshmallow to the top of the cooled pie. Working quickly, use the spatula to spread the marshmallow over the filling, making lots of peaks and valleys.

10. Let the marshmallow topping set for 5 minutes, then use a kitchen torch to toast the surface. Yes, you can skip this step, but it looks cool and tastes all campfire-y.

❋ **WHY IT WORKS**

Sweet potatoes make an excellent base for a custard pie, and while these pies are often compared to pumpkin pies, there's an important difference. Sweet potatoes have a higher level of starch than pumpkin does, so it's important not to overmash them, which can make them gluey. I like my sweet potato pie a bit rustic—I just use a fork to coarsely mash the potatoes while they're hot. If you want your filling a bit smoother, use a potato masher or a food mill.

★ **PRO TIP**

The marshmallow layer is easier to slice through if you spray your knife (and pie server) with nonstick spray before you cut.

MOLASSES MARSHMALLOW TOPPING

162 g / ⅔ cup cool water

12 g / 1 tablespoon powdered gelatin

198 g / 1 cup granulated sugar

113 g / ⅓ cup molasses

78 g / ¼ cup light corn syrup

59 g / 2 large egg whites

Scant 1 g / ¼ teaspoon cream of tartar

5 g / 1 teaspoon vanilla extract

Variation

Purple Sweet Potato Pie: Replace the regular sweet potatoes with an equal amount of mashed purple sweet potatoes. Increase the sugar to 198 g / 1 cup, decrease the brown sugar to 53 g / ¼ cup, and leave off the marshmallow so you can see the pretty purple color!

This recipe is solid: classic enough to satisfy die-hard pumpkin pie fans, but with enough interesting warm spice notes to intrigue the rest of us. A hefty dollop of whipped cream on every slice is a must.

Makes one 9-inch single-crust pie

DIFFICULTY: Medium

MAKE AHEAD AND STORAGE: This pie can be made up to 1 day ahead and kept at room temperature. It can be stored airtight in the refrigerator for up to 4 days more.

Five-Spice Pumpkin Pie

1. Preheat the oven to 375°F / 190°C, preferably with a baking stone on the bottom rack.

2. Make the filling: In a large bowl, whisk the eggs and both sugars until well combined, about 1 minute. Whisk in the vanilla, five-spice powder, and salt. Add the pumpkin and whisk until the mixture is relatively smooth. Gradually add the half-and-half, whisking until the filling is smooth.

3. Pour the filling into the cooled piecrust and spread it evenly with a spatula. Bake the pie until the filling is set at the edges but still slightly jiggly in the center, 40 to 45 minutes. Cool completely before serving.

❄ **WHY IT WORKS**

Pumpkin pie is a classic custard pie, so proper baking is key. The filling should look fully set at the edges, but the center should still jiggle slightly when you move the pie. Be careful not to overbake. Cracks on the surface are a sign of an overbaked custard. (Though if all else fails, just slap a smear of whipped cream on top of the cooled pie and be all, "Cracks? What cracks?")

★ **PRO TIP**

For another unique and subtly spiced variation, substitute an equal amount of garam masala for the five-spice powder.

FILLING

170 g / 3 large eggs

106 g / ½ cup packed light brown sugar

99 g / ½ cup granulated sugar

5 g / 1 teaspoon vanilla extract

6 g / 2 teaspoons Chinese five-spice powder

2 g / ½ teaspoon fine sea salt

439 g / 2 cups canned pumpkin puree

242 g / 1 cup half-and-half

One 9-inch piecrust made with All-Buttah Pie Dough (page 188; mixed for a mealy crust), parbaked, brushed with egg wash, and cooled completely (see page 191)

Whipped cream, for serving (optional)

I'm crazy for grapefruit in any form. This pie is a burst of glorious, fresh-squeezed grapefruit juice made into a curd, plopped inside a buttery crust, and topped with a heaping mound of meringue.

Makes one 9-inch single-crust pie

DIFFICULTY: Medium

MAKE AHEAD AND STORAGE: The pie, sans meringue, can be made ahead and refrigerated, tightly covered, for up to 1 day. Once the meringue is added, it's best to serve the pie the same day.

Grapefruit Meringue Pie

1. Make the filling: In a medium saucepan, melt the butter over medium heat. In a small bowl, whisk together the sugar and cornstarch, then add the cornstarch mixture to the pan, along with the grapefruit juice and egg yolks. Turn the heat down to low and cook, stirring constantly with a silicone spatula (be sure to get into the edges of the pot), until the curd thickens and comes to a first boil (a single large bubble comes up to the surface in the center), 3 to 4 minutes.

2. Strain the curd through a fine-mesh strainer into the cooled piecrust. Cover the pie with plastic wrap pressed directly against the surface of the curd and refrigerate until well chilled, at least 1 hour.

3. Make the meringue: In the bowl of a stand mixer fitted with the whisk attachment (or in a large bowl, using a hand mixer), whip the egg whites with the cream of tartar on medium-high speed until they reach soft peaks. Still on medium-high speed, gradually add the sugar in a slow, steady stream and continue whipping until the meringue holds medium peaks.

4. Dollop the meringue onto the center of the chilled pie. Use a small offset spatula to push the meringue out toward the edges, but maintain a mound in the middle. A few swirls always look nice too. Use a kitchen torch to toast the meringue all over.

⟶

FILLING

170 g / 6 oz / 12 tablespoons unsalted butter

198 g / 1 cup granulated sugar

35 g / ⅓ cup cornstarch

302 g / 1¼ cups freshly squeezed grapefruit juice (from about 3 grapefruits)

269 g / 10 large egg yolks

One 9-inch single piecrust made with All-Buttah Pie Dough (page 188; mixed for a mealy crust), blind-baked, brushed with egg wash, and cooled completely (see page 191)

MERINGUE

179 g / 6 large egg whites

Scant 1 g / ¼ teaspoon cream of tartar

99 g / ½ cup granulated sugar

Glazing the parbaked crust with egg wash before the final bake helps protect it from sopping up moisture from the filling. Toasting the meringue with a torch instead of in the oven help keeps it better adhered to the curd—no slippery meringue here! Because heat is only applied to the outside, rather than placing the whole pie under the broiler, the curd stays chilled and the meringue adheres better.

For this recipe, I use the easiest type of meringue, often known as "French" or "common" meringue, which is made simply by whipping egg whites and adding sugar. The meringue will not be fully cooked, and if you're skeeved out by the idea of uncooked egg whites, you can make an Italian meringue instead (follow the instructions for buttercream on page 158, leaving out the butter and lemon curd). Or just use pasteurized egg whites (sold in cartons in the dairy case) for the simple meringue, and you'll be good to go!

Variation

Lemon-Licorice Meringue Pie: Replace the grapefruit juice with lemon juice. For the meringue, stir 24 g / 2 tablespoons activated charcoal into the sugar, and once the meringue reaches soft peaks, add 5 g / 1¼ teaspoons anise extract or 12 g / 1 tablespoon licorice root powder. The charcoal is optional, but it gives the meringue a naturally licoricey color. (Both the charcoal and licorice root powder are available in the vitamin and supplements section of many large supermarkets and health food stores.)

I set out to create an apple pie sweetened only with apples. After a few tests, I ended up adding a little brown sugar to the mix for balance, but if you like things a little less sweet, you can leave it out. This filling is sweet-tart, but with a rich creaminess to it, because it's finished with butter. I use Honeycrisp apples, which hold up very well in baking, resulting in a filling that's tender but still has a little bite. This pie has everything: a bright, intense apple flavor; a hint of caramelly sweetness; a little bit of salt to tie it all together; and a tender, flaky crust.

Makes one 9-inch double-crust pie

DIFFICULTY: Medium

MAKE AHEAD AND STORAGE: The pie can be baked up to 1 day ahead (any longer, and the crisp texture of the crust suffers because it absorbs too much moisture from the filling) and stored, loosely covered, at room temperature.

Cider-Caramel Apple Pie

1. Roll out one disk of dough and fit it into a 9-inch pie pan (see page 190 for more details). Roll out the second disk as directed on page 190 and place on a parchment-lined baking sheet. Chill the crusts while you prepare the caramel and filling.

2. Make the caramel: In a large wide pot, bring the cider to a boil over medium heat and boil, without stirring, until the cider reduces to a sauce with the consistency of thin caramel, 45 to 60 minutes (the timing will depend on the size of your pot; check the progress every 15 minutes or so to start, and more frequently once it begins to thicken).

3. Stir the butter, salt, and vanilla into the caramel, then pour the mixture into a heatproof bowl to cool slightly, about 15 minutes.

4. Make the filling: Place the apples in a large bowl. In a small bowl, stir the brown sugar, flour, and cinnamon together. Add the mixture to the apples and toss to coat. Add the cooled caramel and toss well to combine.

5. Arrange the filling in the chilled piecrust: If you place the apples in overlapping concentric circles, like a rosette, there will be fewer air pockets between the fruit, reducing the chance of the top crust collapsing after baking. Once you reach the upper edge of the pie pan, begin to make the circles smaller to mound the filling higher in the center to give the baked pie the domed look.

All-Buttah Pie Dough for a double crust (page 188; mixed for a flaky crust), divided in half, shaped into 2 disks, and chilled

CARAMEL

1.81 kg / ½ gallon apple cider

57 g / 2 oz / 4 tablespoons unsalted butter

2 g / ½ teaspoon fine sea salt

5 g / 1 teaspoon vanilla extract

FILLING

1.36 kg / 8 large Honeycrisp apples (or another good baking apple), peeled and thinly sliced

212 g / 1 cup packed light brown sugar

40 g / ⅓ cup all-purpose flour

3 g / 1 teaspoon ground cinnamon

→

6. Roll up the top crust onto the rolling pin and gently unfurl it over the filling. Press the edges of the top and bottom crusts gently together to seal, then trim the excess dough away, leaving a ½-inch overhang. Tuck the overhang under itself all the way around the pie.

7. Crimp the edges of the crust as desired (see page 173). I refrigerate the pie for 20 to 30 minutes.

8. Preheat the oven to 425°F / 218°C, preferably with a baking stone on the bottom rack.

9. Brush the top crust with the egg wash and sprinkle generously with turbinado sugar. Use a small sharp knife to cut a few small vents in the crust. Bake the pie on the stone or bottom rack until the crust is deeply golden and the filling is bubbling up through the vents, 40 to 50 minutes. If the crust begins to brown too quickly, reduce the oven temperature to 375°F / 190°C and/or tent the crust or edges with foil. Cool the pie for at least 30 minutes before serving.

※ **WHY IT WORKS**

Reduced fruit juice makes a wonderful caramel-like sauce. The process is very similar to making traditional caramel, though a great deal of water must evaporate in order for the juice to reduce to mostly sugar.

★ **PRO TIP**

You may be tempted to make the cider caramel ahead of time, and you can, with one caveat. Because apples are so high in pectin, the caramel will firm up—whether left at room temperature or chilled—and make a sort of clumpy sauce resembling jelly. To use it, rewarm it in the microwave in 15-second bursts, stirring occasionally, just until fluid. It shouldn't be hot when you add it to the apples, but a bit warm is OK.

Egg wash: 57 g / 1 large egg, beaten with 15 g / 1 tablespoon water and a small pinch of fine sea salt

Turbinado or coarse sugar, for sprinkling

Variations

Molasses Apple Pie: Use a single crust, parbaked, brushed with egg wash, and cooled (see page 191). Substitute this filling: In a large pot, combine 170 g / ½ cup molasses, 53 g / ¼ cup packed dark brown sugar, 81 g / ⅓ cup apple cider, and 2 g / ½ teaspoon fine sea salt and bring to a simmer over medium heat. Add 1.36 kg / 8 large Honeycrisp apples (or another good baking apple), peeled, cored, and thinly sliced, and cook, stirring frequently, until the fruit is just barely tender, 7 to 9 minutes. Add 57 g / 2 oz / 4 tablespoons cold butter, cubed, and stir until melted and well combined. Cool the filling to room temperature, then proceed with the recipe, topping the filling with Streusel (page 109) instead of a top crust. Bake at 425°F / 218°C until the streusel and bottom crust are golden brown, 35 to 40 minutes.

Apple Butter Pie: Substitute this filling: In a medium bowl, whisk together 1.02 kg / 3 cups store-bought or homemade apple butter, 66 g / ⅓ cup granulated sugar, and 227 g / 4 large eggs until well combined. Pour into the chilled bottom crust, then proceed as directed. Reduce the baking time to 40 to 45 minutes.

To make your own apple butter: In a large pot, combine 1.81 kg / 12 large Honeycrisp apples, peeled, cored, and chopped, 181 g / ¾ cup apple cider, 266 g / 1¼ cups packed light brown sugar, 3 g / 1 teaspoon ground cinnamon, 1 g / ½ teaspoon ground ginger, 1 g / ½ teaspoon ground allspice, scant 1 g / ¼ teaspoon ground cloves, and scant 1 g / ¼ teaspoon freshly grated nutmeg. Bring the mixture to a simmer over medium-high heat. Reduce the heat to medium-low, cover the pot, and cook, stirring occasionally, until the apples are very tender and the mixture is thick and no longer liquid, 20 to 25 minutes. Use a blender or food processor to puree the mixture until relatively smooth. Cool to room temperature before using.

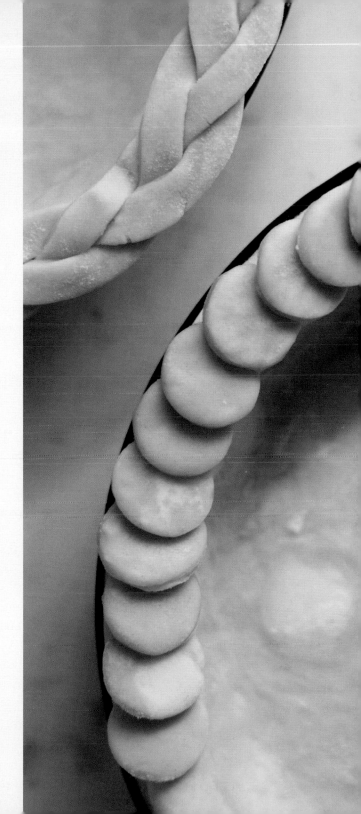

I was introduced to this pie by a friend who hails from upstate New York, where it's one of many dishes that celebrate the grape harvest. The first time I made it, I knew: This is my very favorite pie. Its flaky, buttery crust encases lots of juicy grapes, with barely anything else added, so all the fresh flavor shines through. I like to do a fat lattice for this pie, but you can do any type of top crust.

Makes one 9-inch double-crust pie

DIFFICULTY: Medium

MAKE AHEAD AND STORAGE: The pie can be baked up to 1 day ahead (any longer, and the crisp texture of the crust suffers, absorbing too much moisture from the filling). Store loosely covered at room temperature.

Concord Grape Pie

1. Roll out one disk of dough and fit it into a 9-inch pie pan (see page 190 for more details). Roll out the second disk as directed on page 190 and place on a parchment-lined baking sheet. Chill the crusts while you prepare the filling.

2. Make the filling: Squeeze the pulp from the grapes into a large bowl, releasing it from the skins. Reserve the skins in another bowl. Transfer the pulp to a medium saucepan, bring to a simmer over low heat, and simmer until the grapes have broken down and released their juices, about 10 minutes. Strain the mixture into the bowl with the skins, pressing firmly to extract all of the juice. Cool completely.

3. Whisk the granulated sugar, cornstarch, and salt together in a small bowl. Stir the sugar mixture into the cooled grape juice, then stir in the vanilla. Pour the filling into the chilled bottom crust. Refrigerate the pie for 20 to 30 minutes or freeze for 10 to 15 minutes.

4. Preheat the oven to 425°F / 218°C, preferably with a baking stone on the bottom rack.

5. Use the chilled top crust to make a Fat Lattice (fattice; see page 180). Trim away the excess dough from the lattice and/or fold it under the edge of the bottom crust. Crimp the edges with a fork (or as desired; see page 173). Chill the pie for 10 to 15 minutes in the freezer or 20 to 30 minutes in the refrigerator.

All-Buttah Pie Dough for a double crust (page 188; mixed for a flaky crust), divided in half, shaped into 2 disks, and chilled

FILLING

1.13 kg / 2½ pounds / 8 cups Concord grapes

198 g / 1 cup granulated sugar

28 g / ¼ cup cornstarch

Scant 1 g / ¼ teaspoon fine sea salt

2 g / ½ teaspoon vanilla extract

Egg wash: 57 g / 1 large egg, beaten with 15 g / 1 tablespoon water and a small pinch of fine sea salt

Turbinado or coarse sugar, for sprinkling

→

6. Brush the top and edges of the crust with the egg wash and sprinkle generously with turbinado sugar. Bake the pie on the stone or bottom rack until the crust is golden brown and the filling bubbles up through the lattice, 40 to 45 minutes; watch closely toward the end of the baking time, and if the crust is browning too quickly, reduce the temperature to 375°F / 190°C.

7. Cool the pie completely (or very nearly so) before serving—this one is really juicy, so cooling is crucial to sliceability.

❊ **WHY IT WORKS**

This pie relies on plenty of cornstarch to help thicken it—the grapes hold a lot of juice, and without enough starch, the pie can be a juicy disaster. Unlike many fruits favored for pie, grapes have a relatively low pectin content, which means the primary thickening power needs to come from another ingredient, not from the fruit.

★ **PRO TIP**

Concord grapes have a teasingly short season, but I'll be damned if I let that control how often I can make this delicious pie. I partially prep batches of the filling when the grapes are in season and freeze them for year-round use. Prepare the grapes as directed in step 2, then transfer the cooled mixture to a 1-quart canning jar, seal tightly, and freeze. When you're ready to use, thaw and proceed with the recipe.

There's something very special about the combination of sweet peaches, bourbon, and savory rosemary. I like to top this pie with a tightly woven lattice, but you can just make a classic double-crust pie.

Makes one 9-inch double-crust pie

DIFFICULTY: Medium

MAKE AHEAD AND STORAGE: This pie can be baked up to 1 day ahead and stored, loosely covered, at room temperature (any longer, and the crisp texture of the crust suffers, absorbing too much moisture from the filling).

Bourbon-Rosemary Peach Pie

1. Roll out one disk of dough and fit it into a 9-inch pie pan (see page 190 for more details). Roll out the second disk as directed on page 190 and place on a parchment-lined baking sheet. Chill the crusts while you prepare the filling.

2. Make the filling: Put the peaches in a medium heatproof bowl. In a medium saucepan, bring the bourbon (see Pro Tips) to a boil over medium heat and boil until reduced to 60 g / ¼ cup, 6 to 8 minutes. Add the rosemary and simmer for 1 minute, then take the pan off the heat and let steep for 15 minutes.

3. Remove and discard the rosemary sprigs, return the pan to the stove, and bring the bourbon to a simmer over medium heat. Stir in the brown sugar and simmer until the mixture is thick, 3 to 4 minutes. Take the pan off the heat and stir in the butter and salt.

4. Put the cornstarch in a small heatproof bowl and pour in a few tablespoons of the bourbon mixture, whisking constantly. Pour the slurry back into the bourbon mixture, whisking well to combine, and bring the mixture to a simmer. Simmer for 1 minute.

⟶

All-Buttah Pie Dough for a double crust (page 188; mixed for a flaky crust), divided in half, shaped into 2 disks, and chilled

FILLING

907 g / 4 large peaches, pitted and cut into thick slices (see Pro Tips)

242 g / 1 cup bourbon

6 g / 2 sprigs fresh rosemary

159 g / ¾ cup packed dark brown sugar

28 g / 1 oz / 2 tablespoons unsalted butter

1 g / ¼ teaspoon fine sea salt

27 g / 3 tablespoons cornstarch

Egg wash: 57 g / 1 large egg, beaten with 15 g / 1 tablespoon water and a small pinch of fine sea salt

Turbinado or coarse sugar, for sprinkling

5. Pour the bourbon mixture over the peaches, tossing gently to coat the fruit.

6. Arrange the filling in the chilled piecrust: If you place the slices in overlapping concentric circles, like a rosette, there will be fewer air pockets, reducing the chance of the top crust collapsing after baking. Once you reach the upper rim of the pie pan, begin to make smaller circles to mound the filling slightly higher in the center to give the baked pie the classic domed look. Pour any juices over the surface of the fruit.

7. Transfer the prepared top crust to the filled pie—you can use it as a solid top crust (see page 190) or make a lattice top (see page 177). Press the edges of the top and bottom crust gently together to seal, then trim the excess dough away, leaving a ½-inch overhang. Tuck the overhang under

itself all the way around the pie. Crimp the edges of the pie as desired (see page 173). Chill the pie for 20 to 30 minutes in the refrigerator or for 10 to 15 minutes in the freezer.

8. Preheat the oven to 425°F / 218°C, preferably with a baking stone on the bottom rack.

9. Lightly brush the top and edges of the piecrust with the egg wash. Sprinkle generously with turbinado sugar.

10. Bake the pie on the stone or bottom rack until the crust is deeply golden and the filling bubbles up through the vents in the top crust or the lattice, 45 to 50 minutes. If the crust begins to brown too quickly, reduce the oven temperature to 375°F / 190°C and/or tent the pie with aluminum foil. Cool the pie for at least 30 minutes before serving.

✳ **WHY IT WORKS**

Reducing the bourbon gives you all the boozy flavor without making a soupy pie. As with all fruit pies, the level of juiciness depends on the ripeness of the fruit. The cornstarch helps thicken the juices during baking, but it needs to come to a boil to have the proper thickening effect (and "cook out" any pasty flavor), so that bubbling of the juices at the end is important.

★ **PRO TIPS**

I don't peel my peaches, plums, or nectarines—I love the texture of their skins in baked goods and the beautiful color they lend as well. But if you're not a fan, feel free to peel.

If you have really juicy peaches, drain the juices from the slices and add the juice to the bourbon when it's reducing—that way you make the most of that peachy flavor without watering down your pie.

Makes one 10-inch double-crust tart

DIFFICULTY: Easy

MAKE AHEAD AND STORAGE: The tart is best eaten the same day it's baked, but it can be stored airtight or wrapped tightly in plastic wrap at room temperature for up to 2 days.

Free-form tarts are wonderful: Crisp bottom crust! Flexible shaping! No special equipment required! This double-crusted tart pairs perfectly a smooth, creamy almond filling with a subtly tangy cream cheese crust.

Almond Cream Tart

1. Make the almond cream: In the bowl of a stand mixer fitted with the paddle attachment (or in a large bowl, using a hand mixer), combine the butter, granulated sugar, orange zest, and lemon zest. Scrape the seeds from the vanilla bean and add to the bowl (use the pod for vanilla sugar; see Pro Tip, page 97). Beat on medium-low speed until the mixture is light and fluffy, 4 to 5 minutes.

2. Add the eggs one at a time, mixing on medium speed until each one is fully incorporated before adding the next. Scrape the bowl well. Add the almond extract, if using, and the vanilla extract, if using, and mix to combine.

3. In a medium bowl, mix the almond flour, all-purpose flour, and salt. Add the mixture to the mixer and mix on low speed until fully incorporated. Set aside.

4. Line two baking sheets with parchment paper. On a lightly floured surface, roll out one disk of dough to a ¼-inch-thick circle about 11 inches in diameter. Roll up the dough onto the rolling pin and unfurl onto one of the prepared baking sheets. Transfer to the refrigerator and chill for at least 20 to 30 minutes. Roll out the second disk of dough the same way, transfer to the second baking sheet, and refrigerate.

5. Take the first chilled crust out of the refrigerator and scoop the almond cream onto the center. Spread the cream out to about 1½ inches from the edge all the way around, keeping it mounded in the center.

ALMOND CREAM

113 g / 4 oz / 8 tablespoons unsalted butter, at room temperature

99 g / ½ cup granulated sugar

6 g / 1 tablespoon finely grated orange zest

6 g / 1 tablespoon finely grated lemon zest

½ vanilla bean, split lengthwise (or 7.5 g / 1½ teaspoons vanilla extract)

113 g / 2 large eggs

1 g / ¼ teaspoon almond extract (optional)

95 g / 1 cup almond flour

15 g / 2 tablespoons all-purpose flour

2 g / ½ teaspoon fine sea salt

→

6. Lightly brush the exposed edges of the bottom crust with water. Remove the second crust from the refrigerator, roll it up onto the rolling pin, and carefully unfurl it over the bottom crust, centering it over the filling. Press the edges gently to seal all the way around, then use a paring knife to trim away any rough edges. Crimp the edges as desired (see page 173). Chill the tart in the fridge for 20 to 30 minutes or in the freezer for 10 to 15 minutes.

7. Preheat the oven to 425°F / 218°C, preferably with a baking stone on the bottom rack.

8. Lightly brush the top crust with the egg wash and sprinkle generously with pearl sugar, if desired. Cut steam vents into the top crust with a sharp paring knife—a few short lines or a small X.

9. Bake the tart on the stone or bottom rack until the crust is evenly golden brown, 35 to 45 minutes. Cool for at least 15 minutes before serving, warm or at room temperature.

❊ **WHY IT WORKS**

Free-form tarts can be filled with just about anything—fresh fruit, custard, or curd. You can also get creative with the shape—round, square, or rectangular—anything goes! The almond cream filling in this recipe is equally versatile—it makes a good filling for Danish or other pastries (see pages 312 and 299). You can even tweak it to use other nuts—see my filling for the Pistachio Pithiviers on page 308.

★ **PRO TIP**

Pearl sugar is a large-crystal white sugar. It can be used as a finishing sugar on all kinds of desserts. It has a crisp texture and looks very pretty. You can buy it at baking supply stores or specialty markets, or online.

Double recipe Cream Cheese Pie Dough (page 192; mixed for a mealy crust), divided in half, shaped into 2 disks, and chilled

Egg wash: 57 g / 1 large egg, beaten with 15 g / 1 tablespoon water and a small pinch of fine sea salt

Pearl sugar or coarse sanding sugar, for sprinkling (optional)

It's not fair to call such a beautiful tart a "scrap tart," but that's the name that applies. The first time I made it, I was using up leftovers from several bags of nuts. I've since come up with all sorts of more intentional combinations, and it's great with nearly any nut. The phyllo crust is oh-so-crisp—and great for when you're not up for a full-on piecrust.

Makes one 10-inch tart

DIFFICULTY: Easy

MAKE AHEAD AND STORAGE: The tart can be made up to 1 day ahead and kept in an airtight container at room temperature. Leftovers will keep for up to 3 days more.

Any-Nut Tart in Phyllo Crust

1. Preheat the oven to 375°F / 190°C, preferably with a baking stone on the bottom rack. Lightly grease a 10-inch tart pan and place it on a foil-lined baking sheet.

2. Make the crust: Unfold the phyllo sheets and cover them with damp paper towels. In a small bowl, whisk together the granulated sugar and cinnamon. Place one sheet of phyllo on your work surface (keep the remaining sheets covered) and brush it all over with butter. Evenly sprinkle on a heaping teaspoon of the cinnamon sugar. Place another sheet of phyllo on top, arranging it slightly askew so that the corners of the 2 sheets do not match up, and brush with butter. Sprinkle with cinnamon sugar. Repeat with the remaining phyllo, butter, and

sugar. The finished "crust" should look like a sunflower, with multiple corners poking out from the mismatched sheets of phyllo.

3. Carefully transfer the phyllo to the prepared tart pan. Press the layered phyllo sheets into the bottom of the pan and up the sides to completely cover it; work around the edges with your fingers, scrunching the layered phyllo together to create a ruffled effect. Set aside.

4. Make the filling: In a medium bowl, whisk together the butter, brown sugar, honey, salt, and vanilla. Add the eggs one at a time, whisking until each one is fully incorporated before adding the next.

⟶

CRUST

8 sheets phyllo dough (about 14 by 18 inches), thawed

37 g / 3 tablespoons granulated sugar

1 g / ½ teaspoon ground cinnamon

113 g / 4 oz / 8 tablespoons unsalted butter, melted

FILLING

71 g / 2.5 oz / 5 tablespoons unsalted butter, melted

213 g / 1 cup packed light brown sugar

191 g / ½ cup honey

2 g / ½ teaspoon fine sea salt

5 g / 1 teaspoon vanilla extract

170 g / 3 large eggs

255 g / 2 cups whole or roughly chopped nuts (such as cashews, peanuts, pistachios, pecans, or pine nuts, or a combo)

5. Place the nuts in the crust, spreading them out with your hands to settle them in evenly. Slowly pour the custard over the nuts.

6. Bake the tart on the stone or bottom rack until the filling is set at the edges but slightly jiggly in the center, 33 to 36 minutes; the nuts should look lightly golden and the crust should be evenly browned. Cool completely.

❄ WHY IT WORKS

Much like a traditional nut pie (think pecan), this tart uses a simple custard to enrobe the nuts. The egg proteins coagulate in the oven, so the custard sets into a creamy filling. Overbaking the tart will result in a tough or rubbery filling—bake it until the custard is just barely set so it stays silky smooth.

★ PRO TIP

Paper-thin phyllo can sometimes brown too quickly. Keep a close eye on the crust throughout the baking time, and at the first sign of overbrowning, loosely tent the tart with aluminum foil. This protects the edges while keeping the oven hot enough that the bottom of the tart gets nice and crisp.

With homemade orange concentrate and lemon juice, this tart is a balance of sweet and sour, and it's beautiful to boot. While you can keep it simple (and trust me, it will still wow), I sometimes get fancy with the finishing and make a mascarpone topping with candied orange slices.

Makes one 10-inch tart

DIFFICULTY: Medium

MAKE AHEAD AND STORAGE: The tart will keep, tightly wrapped in plastic wrap, in the refrigerator for up to 3 days.

Orange Tart

1. Preheat the oven to 325°F / 162°C, preferably with a baking stone on the bottom rack.

2. Make the filling: In a medium saucepan, bring the orange juice to a simmer over medium heat and simmer, uncovered, until reduced by half. Transfer to a medium bowl and stir in the lemon juice. Let cool to room temperature.

3. Add the eggs, egg yolks, granulated sugar, and mascarpone to the juice mixture and whisk to combine.

4. Pour the filling into the crust and bake just until the custard is set around the edges but still jiggly in the center, 35 to 40 minutes. Cool completely. If making the optional garnish, reduce the oven temperature to 225°F / 107°C.

5. Make the optional garnish, if desired: Line a baking sheet with a silicone mat. Put the powdered sugar in a medium shallow bowl. Dip each orange slice in the powdered sugar to coat and place on the mat, spacing the slices at least ⅛ inch apart.

6. Bake the oranges until they are dried and slightly shriveled, 1½ to 2 hours.

7. In the bowl of a stand mixer fitted with the whisk attachment (or in a medium bowl, using a hand mixer), whip the mascarpone, orange zest, and granulated sugar on medium-high speed until light and fluffy, 2 to 3 minutes. Add the cream and whip to medium peaks.

8. Spread the mascarpone mixture over the tart, or use a piping bag to pipe it around the edges. Finish with the candied orange slices.

FILLING

605 g / 2½ cups freshly squeezed orange juice (see Pro Tips; from about 5 oranges)

60 g / ¼ cup freshly squeezed lemon juice

170 g / 3 large eggs

135 g / 5 large egg yolks

198 g / 1 cup granulated sugar

227 g / 1 cup mascarpone cheese

One 10-inch tart crust made with Tart Dough (page 193), parbaked and cooled completely (see page 194)

OPTIONAL GARNISH

57 g / ½ cup powdered sugar

1 orange, thinly sliced into rounds, seeds removed

113 g / ½ cup mascarpone cheese

6 g / 1 tablespoon finely grated orange zest

49 g / 2 tablespoons granulated sugar

121 g / ½ cup heavy cream

❊ WHY IT WORKS

Rose Levy Beranbaum taught me that tart crusts behave much better if you freeze them overnight and bake right from the freezer. While this step isn't totally necessary for this recipe, overnight freezing before baking makes a huge difference (see more info on preparing tart crusts on page 194)—I've never had a shrunken crust when I've followed her advice!

★ PRO TIPS

If you don't have time to reduce the OJ, just use less (302 g / 1¼ cups) to start and skip to step 3. Because orange juice isn't as deeply colored as the rind of the fruit, the custard in this tart is yellowish rather than orange. If you want to pop up the color, you can use duck eggs—their yolks are much darker, and they are also really delicious—or add a drop or two of red food coloring to tint the filling.

These tarts feature a press-in crust with a simple panna cotta–style filling, and they are finished with raspberry jam and chocolate. You can spread, pipe, or drizzle on the jam and chocolate, but I like to use a pastry brush or small spoon to make "splatter tarts" (see Pro Tip).

Sweet Cream Tartlets

1. Press each piece of dough into a 3¾-inch tartlet pan: Start with the sides and work your way to the middle, patting gently to even the dough to about ⅛ inch thick all over and letting the excess dough push up above the edges of the pan. Trim the dough by holding a paring knife flush against the edge of each pan and cutting away the excess smoothly, leaving a clean edge. Prick the dough all over with a fork. Freeze the crusts until firm, 15 to 20 minutes.

2. Preheat the oven to 400°F / 204°C, preferably with a baking stone on the bottom rack.

3. Transfer the tartlet pans to a baking sheet and bake on the stone or bottom rack until the crusts appear dry on the surface and the edges are firm, 15 to 18 minutes. If the dough puffs up noticeably during baking, prick it with a fork to deflate. When the tart shells are fully baked, you can also slam the tray down on the counter once or twice to help flatten the crusts.

4. Cool the crusts completely, then invert the pans over a baking sheet and tap them gently to unmold the crusts onto the baking sheet; turn them right side up.

⟶

1 recipe Chocolate Press-In Tart Dough (page 197), divided into 8 equal pieces (50 g / 3½ tablespoons each)

57 g / 2 oz bittersweet chocolate (I use 60% cacao), chopped, melted, and cooled slightly

FILLING

81 g / ⅓ cup cool water

12 g / 1 tablespoon powdered gelatin

484 g / 2 cups heavy cream

66 g / ⅓ cup granulated sugar

5 g / 1 teaspoon vanilla extract

TOPPING

113 g / ⅓ cup seedless raspberry jam

57 g / 2 oz bittersweet chocolate (I use 60% cacao), chopped, melted, and cooled slightly

5. Spoon a heaping tablespoon of melted chocolate into the base of each cooled shell and spread it into an even layer that coats the base. Set aside to allow the chocolate to set completely.

6. **Make the filling:** Pour the water into a shallow cup and sprinkle the gelatin evenly over it. Let soak for 5 minutes.

7. In a small saucepan, heat 242 g / 1 cup of the heavy cream and the sugar over medium heat, stirring, until the cream is hot and the sugar is dissolved. Add the gelatin and stir until it is fully melted.

8. Pour the hot cream mixture into a medium bowl. Stir in the remaining 242 g / 1 cup cream and the vanilla.

9. Pour the custard into the cooled tart shells, filling them to just below the edges. Transfer the tarts to the refrigerator and chill until the custard is set, 20 to 30 minutes.

10. In a small heatproof bowl, microwave the jam until thinned and fluid, 30 to 45 seconds. Use a small spoon to drizzle the jam over the chilled tarts, then do the same with the cooled melted chocolate, or make "splatter tartlets"; see Pro Tip. Refrigerate the tarts until ready to serve.

❋ **WHY IT WORKS**

Panna cotta (the name is Italian for "cooked cream") is a delicious dessert all on its own, and it makes a killer filling for pies and tarts. Made with milk, cream, or a combo, the silky-smooth custard is set with gelatin. This method makes the surface set beautifully smooth—which makes the panna cotta the perfect base for pretty finishes.

★ **PRO TIP**

To splatter on the jam and chocolate, I use a silicone pastry brush with thick bristles. Line your work surface with parchment paper, then dip the pastry brush into the jam. Flick the brush over the tarts, and the jam will splatter randomly. Clean the brush, then do the same with the chocolate.

These little tartlets are a great example of how a simple tweak can make a basic recipe entirely new. An easy press-in crust is filled with a lightly thickened lemon curd flecked with plenty of poppy seeds. I love the texture of the poppy seeds in this ultra-creamy filling.

Makes eight 3¾-inch tartlets

DIFFICULTY: Easy

MAKE AHEAD AND STORAGE: The lemon curd can be made ahead, covered tightly, and refrigerated for up to 5 days. The tartlets can be made up to 2 days ahead and refrigerated in an airtight container, but add the garnish close to serving time.

Lemon–Poppy Seed Tartlets

1. Make the filling: In a medium saucepan, melt 113 g / 4 oz / 8 tablespoons of the butter over medium heat. In a small bowl, whisk together the sugar and cornstarch. Add the cornstarch mixture to the pan, along with the lemon zest, lemon juice, salt, and egg yolks. Turn the heat down to low and cook, stirring constantly with a silicone spatula (be sure to get into the edges of the pot), until the curd thickens and comes to a first boil (a single large bubble comes up to the surface in the center), 3 to 4 minutes.

2. Take the pan off the heat and stir in the remaining 57 g / 2 oz / 4 tablespoons butter until it melts. Strain the curd into a shallow dish and cover it with plastic wrap pressed directly against the surface of the curd. Refrigerate until thoroughly chilled, at least 2 hours.

3. Press each piece of dough into a 3¾-inch tartlet pan (see Pro Tip). Start with the sides and work your way to the middle, patting gently to even the dough to about ⅛ inch thick all over and letting the excess dough push up above the edges of each pan. Trim the dough by holding a paring knife flush against the edge of the pan and cutting away the excess smoothly, leaving a clean edge. Prick the dough all over with a fork. Freeze the crusts until firm, 15 to 20 minutes.

FILLING

170 g / 6 oz / 12 tablespoons unsalted butter

198 g / 1 cup granulated sugar

20 g / 3 tablespoons cornstarch

6 g / 1 tablespoon finely grated lemon zest

302 g / 1¼ cups freshly squeezed lemon juice (from about 5 lemons)

1 g / ¼ teaspoon fine sea salt

269 g / 10 large egg yolks

18 g / 2 tablespoons poppy seeds

1 recipe Press-In Tart Dough (page 196), divided into 8 equal pieces (43 g / 3 tablespoons)

⟶

4. Meanwhile, preheat the oven to 400°F / 204°C, preferably with a baking stone on the bottom rack.

5. Transfer the pans to a baking sheet and bake on the stone or bottom rack until the crusts appear dry on the surface and the edges are evenly pale golden, 15 to 18 minutes. If the dough puffs up noticeably during baking, prick it with a fork. When you take the baking sheet out of the oven after baking, you can slam it down on the counter once or twice to help flatten the crusts. Cool the crusts completely, then invert the pans and tap them to unmold the crusts onto the baking sheet; turn them right side up.

6. Stir the poppy seeds into the chilled curd. Spoon the curd into the cooled crusts (about 50 g / ¼ cup per crust).

7. **Make the optional garnish, if desired:** In the bowl of a stand mixer fitted with the whisk attachment (or in a medium bowl, using a hand mixer), whip the cream and sugar to medium peaks. Dollop the cream onto the tarts using a spoon or a disposable pastry bag fitted with a medium plain tip. Grate some lemon zest over the cream and sprinkle a few poppy seeds on top of each one.

❄ **WHY IT WORKS**

This press-in tart crust isn't flaky at all—the butter and sugar are creamed together before the flour is added, which means the dough stays tender and mealy during baking. And the mealier a crust is, the less likely it will be to puff up in the oven. That means you can skip the pie weights here—the crust will stay basically flat with no extra help.

★ **PRO TIP**

Press-in crusts have a tendency to cling to grooves and ridges, making them harder to unmold. Pans with curves are OK, just make sure they're smooth and rounded so the crusts will be easy to unmold.

OPTIONAL GARNISHES

181 g / ¾ cup heavy cream

25 g / 2 tablespoons granulated sugar

1 medium lemon

Poppy seeds

CHAPTER 4

Pastries

This chapter is full of so much goodness—of all different kinds. The term "pastry" encompasses many things, from simple muffins and scones to yeast-risen pastries and flaky croissants. They're the things that make you a baker, and from the easy to complex, they're a ton of fun.

Like most of my favorite sweets, they're versatile. You can use the doughs in different ways, you can combine or swap out fillings, and you can manipulate the pastries into different shapes.

WHY MY BENCH KNIFE MAY BE MY FAVORITE TOOL

My trusty bench knife (also called a bench or pastry scraper) is one of the most used tools in my kitchen. A bench knife has a metal blade attached to a sturdy handle; the blade is usually 4 to 5 inches long and sharp, but not as sharp as a chef's knife—perfect for cutting through dough. I use it to portion bread, pie, tart, and pastry dough, and it's my favorite tool for cutting everything from cinnamon rolls to butter cubes. It's also handy for shaping. I also use it to keep certain doughs squared off at the edges, which is especially important for lamination. And when I'm finished working, a few scrapes with my bench knife get all the flour or scraps of dough off my work surface—yet another reason I love this tool!

MIXING INFO

The recipes in this chapter involve a wide variety of familiar mixing methods, from creaming (muffins) to foaming (pavlova) to cut-in (biscuits). But certain techniques specific to pastries deserve special attention: the "straight-dough method," used for brioche, and the lamination method for croissants and Danishes.

STRAIGHT-DOUGH METHOD

The straight-dough method is used to make yeast-risen doughs and is so named because the ingredients are combined all at once in the stand mixer. It's the basis for my insanely versatile brioche dough (page 286) and for all sorts of baked goods. For this type of dough, you just combine the ingredients as directed in the recipe and mix to the proper level of gluten development. The process does require a decent amount of time, because you have to wait while the yeast does its work. If you're anything like me, though, after the first bite of whatever you make with the dough, you'll decide that the time was totally worth it.

* First things first: I use instant yeast, available in grocery stores or online, for all of my yeast-raised doughs. This yeast should be combined directly with the flour. (When you're using any other kind, it must be combined with water before being added to the other ingredients.)

* Mixing the dough generally means starting at low speed, mixing for a certain period of time, and then increasing the speed to medium or high and continuing until you achieve the proper stage of gluten development. When combining the ingredients, how

vigorously and how long you mix them depends on what stage of gluten development is desired. There are three primary types of gluten development: short, improved, and intense. Brioche, the main bread dough in this book, has intense development.

✢ A dough with intense gluten development looks very smooth and uniform. When you pull it apart with your hands, it will stretch almost endlessly, forming a "gluten window"—a portion of dough so thin you can nearly see through it.

✢ After the dough is mixed, it must go through a series of steps specific to bread baking:

1. **Bulk fermentation:** The dough is allowed to rise (a process known as fermentation); this builds flavor and structure.

2. **Preshaping:** The dough is shaped into loaves or individual breads, such as rolls, which are usually rounds or ovals.

3. **Resting:** The dough gets a 10- to 20-minute rest. This helps it relax before the final shaping.

4. **Shaping:** The dough is given its final shape and/or placed in the pan(s) or mold(s) it will be baked in.

5. **Proofing:** The dough is set in a warm place for the final stage of fermentation, known as proofing, loosely covered with greased plastic wrap or a slightly damp towel. When you press properly proofed dough with your finger, it will leave a distinct indentation that will slowly disappear. The dough is ready to be baked!

SLOWING DOWN (RETARDING) FERMENTATION

Fermentation refers to the development of flavor and structure in a dough, which is what causes it to rise. The yeast feeds on sugars from the complex carbohydrates (starch) in the dough, releasing bubbles that expand it. In baking lingo, the word "retardation" refers to a slowdown in the fermentation process, which takes place in a chilled environment. Refrigerated dough rises more slowly—the fermentation process still happens, but at a drastically reduced rate. Dough can be refrigerated after mixing, after bulk fermentation, or, if you aren't ready to bake it, after shaping.

There are a few reasons why you may want to retard fermentation:

FLAVOR: As the yeast digests the sugars in the dough, the dough develops flavor—both from the action itself and from the natural bacteria in the dough and the surrounding environment. Most yeast-risen doughs can benefit from a slower rise. If you're retarding dough to build flavor, it's best to refrigerate the dough right after mixing, for at least 8 hours. Bring it back to room temperature before proceeding.

CONVENIENCE: I love making doughnuts for breakfast, but I don't necessarily want to wake up at 4 a.m. to make that happen. If I retard the dough, I can make it the day before, so it's ready and waiting for me in the morning. Refrigerate the dough just after mixing, for 8 hours or more. Then bring it back to room temperature before proceeding with the recipe.

TIMING: Occasionally the dough you mixed is rising too quickly for you to deal with it. Think of Thanksgiving— you're juggling a turkey, side dishes, and a pie, plus your rolls. No problem—transfer the dough to the fridge to slow the process down and it will still be ready to go when you've caught up!

LAMINATION METHOD

"Lamination" refers to a method of folding dough over
itself that results in flaky, layered pastries, from palmiers to croissants. Some laminated doughs are yeast-
risen and some aren't, but the folding technique is the
same for both. A block of butter is sealed inside the
dough, which is then rolled out and folded multiple
times. Each roll-out and folding creates layers of butter within the dough. Then, when the dough is baked,
the moisture in the butter evaporates, creating steam,
which physically leavens the dough and creates lots
and lots of flaky layers.

immediately begin to sizzle (little bubbles will form all around it) and then rise to the surface. If the test dough browns too quickly, turn the heat off and let the oil cool a bit. Too-hot oil will make a doughnut that may look perfect on the outside but is doughy or even raw inside. Too-cold oil means oil will be absorbed into the doughnut or other pastry, making it greasy on your hands—and in your mouth!

MY ADVICE: My favorite method for draining doughnuts and beignets is simple: several layers of paper towels on a baking sheet. When the top layer gets saturated, toss it and use the dry ones underneath. Some folks opt for a wire rack set on top of paper towels to absorb the grease. Either way is fine. Be sure to use a spider (skimmer) or slotted spoon to remove the fried pastry from the oil to drain them as you lift them out.

FRYING

If you're going to make beignets (page 281) or doughnuts (page 283), you're going to need to know your way around a pot of hot oil. First off: It's easiest to fry when you have a decent amount of oil. Yes, you can skimp a bit and get OK results, but if you can, use at least 4 inches of oil in a deep heavy pot. I fry pastries at 325° to 350°F / 162° to 177°C—you can attach a deep-frying or candy thermometer to your pot to help you determine if the oil is up to temp. Or you can do what I do: Throw a scrap piece of dough (from whatever you're about to fry) into the pot as a tester. It should

CUTTING BISCUITS, SCONES, AND OTHER PASTRIES

Whether you're cutting biscuits, doughnuts, or puff pastry, the same rules apply:

Dip the cutter in flour to help prevent sticking and make a cleaner edge. Place the cutter on the dough and press down firmly in one smooth motion; try not to twist the cutter, which can smoosh the dough down and affect the height of the final rise. I love my set of round metal cutters, which range in size from ½ inch to 3 inches in circumference, but in a pinch, anything round will work, like the rim of a glass.

SHAPING PASTRIES

This chapter has several recipes that make a large amount of dough. That's because when I make something complicated like puff pastry, I want to get a lot out of it! Most of the doughs in this chapter can be prepared ahead and kept in the refrigerator or freezer for extended periods. So if you prepare the brioche dough, for example, you can use it for a few recipes, shaping it in different ways.

You can use the same dough (and filling) to create five different-shaped pastries. Many of the shaping techniques that follow can be used for both individual pastries and larger ones. Some are as simple as cutting the dough into a shape and using your hands to add the final touches. I love my pastry wheel and use it often for the recipes in this chapter. A pastry wheel is a round sharp blade with a handle that rotates as you push it through the dough, cutting it perfectly in an easy, smooth motion. If you don't have one, you can always use a sharp knife, a pizza wheel, if you have one, or even, in some cases, scissors.

Turnovers: To make turnovers, cut the dough into squares (which will make a pastry shaped like an equilateral triangle) or rectangles (which will make a more exaggerated right-triangle shape). Center the filling on the dough, then fold one corner over to meet its opposite. Press the edges to seal, and crimp if desired.

Closed Square: Start with a square piece of dough. Pipe or scoop the filling, if using, onto the center of the square (this shape also looks good on its own). Working with one corner at a time, fold the corner toward the center of the dough and press gently to seal (see Kolaches, page 293). If you're using a filling, it may ooze out a little at the edges—which I love!

Foldover Diamond: Cut the dough into squares. Pipe or scoop the filling onto the center of the square, then fold one of the corners over toward the center and press gently to seal. Then fold over the opposite corner and seal—the filling may ooze toward the other corners, and that looks great!

Filled Square: This shape is a little bit like a free-form tart. Cut the dough into rectangles or circles. Cut a narrow strip away from each of the four edges or all around the circumference. Place the strips on top of the edges of the base dough and press to seal, forming a wall of dough around the empty center. Trim the edges as needed. Pipe or scoop the filling onto the center.

Pinwheel: Cut the dough into squares. Use a bench knife (bench scraper), knife, or pastry wheel to cut a slit in the dough at one corner, at least 1 inch deep (longer cuts will make a more exaggerated pinwheel look). Fold the piece of dough over to the right, toward the center of the square, and press gently to seal. Repeat at each corner, making the pinwheel shape. Pipe or scoop the filling onto the center.

Easy Braid: Braiding is a great technique that works well with both small and large pastries. See Almond Danish Bread (page 299) for a simple way to encase filling in a beautifully braided pastry.

Twist: I love this method for making twisted pastries that lie flat on the baking sheet and don't unfurl. You can leave them as is, or place a filling on top (fresh fruit works especially nicely). Start with long, thin rectangular strips of dough (about 5 inches by 1 inch, for example). Use a pastry wheel to cut a slit lengthwise down the center of each piece, leaving both ends intact. Hold one end in each hand and loop the right end through the center slit twice. Then do the same with the other end. This will twist the pastry but keep the ends flat.

PIPING PASTRIES

Some batters, like pâte à choux and meringue, can be piped into shapes.

I like my pastries to be similar in size and shape, so I often draw guidelines onto parchment paper to help me when I'm piping. Use a dark pen or marker to draw the shape, then flip the parchment over so the ink won't touch whatever you pipe onto it.

MY ADVICE: When piping pâte à choux, it's very common for the batter to form a "tail" as you finish piping. Never fear! Dip your finger in water and touch it gently to the surface, and it will smooth right out, making the finished shape perfectly round, with a prettier result after baking.

When piping meringue, you need to work relatively quickly, as it will lose volume as you work. If the meringue starts to get runny toward the end of piping a batch, it will be more difficult to work with.

MAKING IT PRETTY

There's nothing more gorgeous than a towering, flaky biscuit or a pile of freshly glazed doughnuts. Here are some of my favorite tips for making your pastries beautiful.

Glaze with egg wash: A coating of egg wash makes pastry brown better and more evenly, plus it adds a lovely sheen to the surface. I brush it on anywhere and everywhere: pastries, pie dough, even certain cookies!

My basic egg wash is 57 g / 1 large egg whisked with 15 g / 1 tablespoon water and a small pinch of salt (see page 168). Depending on your preference for browning and sheen, though, you can also glaze with just egg white, just egg yolk, melted butter, or cream. Here's a rundown on the different results for each of these options:

* **Egg white only:** Makes a nice sheen on the surface but doesn't promote browning.

* **Egg yolk only:** Promotes browning, but the finished look will be rather matte rather than having a sheen.

* **Melted butter:** Can help promote browning, but it can run off the surface relatively quickly; I usually wait to brush it on items just before they're done baking and/or right when they've come out of the oven.

* **Cream:** Provides a little browning and a slight sheen, but it's not comparable to the results with egg wash.

Sprinkle with sugar: A sprinkling of sugar is one of my favorite ways to dress up a pastry—I do it with almost every one of these recipes. I like turbinado sugar because of its caramel color and flavor, but sanding sugar, superfine sugar, and pearl sugar are all great options, as is vanilla sugar. If you're working with a wet batter, as for cream puffs, you can apply the sugar directly to the pastry before baking. If the item is on the drier side (like many doughs), first brush on an egg wash, melted butter, or cream (see opposite) to help the sugar stick.

DETERMINING DONENESS

It can be trickier to gauge the doneness of pastries than of other baked goods. It's especially tough with yeast-risen products—they may look perfect and golden on the outside, but who knows what's going on inside? The best way to find out is to insert an instant-read thermometer into the thickest part of it (yup—just like you'd do with a piece of meat). The target temperature for baked pastry doughs is around 190°F. If your pastry is very golden brown on the outside but still has a low internal temperature, tent with foil, decrease the oven temperature by 25°F, and continue baking until the pastry reaches the right internal temp.

MY ADVICE: One of the most common problems beginning bakers have is that they are so afraid of overbaking that they underbake instead. Don't fear browning: It leads to the texture you find in baked goods at the best pastry shops. Golden brown means crispy and crunchy; pale means a soggy and chewy dough or pastry.

I landed my first job in a bakery when I was sixteen. I would come in after school and make huge batches of scone mix to help the morning baker. After I graduated from high school, I became the principal baker—and spent the summer waking up at 2 a.m. Even though I had to go to bed at 7 p.m., I felt like the coolest kid in town. The bakery offered a bunch of different flavors of scones, and I could never decide on a favorite (see Note).

Makes about 18 scones

DIFFICULTY: Easy

MAKE AHEAD AND STORAGE: You can make and cut or scoop the dough, wrap the pieces in plastic wrap, and refrigerate for up to 12 hours before baking. Unwrap and bake directly from the refrigerator. The baked scones are best eaten fresh from the oven, but they will keep airtight for up to 4 days. Reheat leftover scones by splitting them in half and toasting in a little butter on a hot griddle or in a cast-iron pan.

Any-Fruit or -Nut Scones

1. Preheat the oven to 400°F / 204°C, with racks in the upper and lower thirds. Line two baking sheets with parchment paper.

2. In a large bowl, whisk together the flour, granulated sugar, baking powder, and salt. Add the butter and toss to coat the cubes with flour. Cut the butter into the flour by rubbing it between your forefingers and thumbs until the butter pieces are between the size of peas and walnut halves. Add the fruit/nuts and toss gently to combine.

3. Make a well in the center of the dry ingredients and pour in the cream. Toss the mixture with your fingers to combine, then knead gently to ensure everything is evenly moistened.

4. Scoop ¼-cup mounds of the dough onto the prepared baking sheets (I do this by hand because I like them to look craggy, but you can use a #16 / ¼-cup scoop), leaving at least 1½ inches between them. Brush the tops of the scones with the egg wash and sprinkle generously with turbinado sugar.

5. Bake the scones, switching the sheets from front to back and top to bottom at the halfway mark, for 20 to 22 minutes, until the tops and edges are golden brown. The scones can be served warm or at room temperature.

361 g / 3 cups all-purpose flour

132 g / ⅔ cup granulated sugar

12 g / 1 tablespoon baking powder

1 g / ¼ teaspoon fine sea salt

142 g / 5 oz / 10 tablespoons cold unsalted butter, cut into ½-inch cubes

340 to 425 g / 2 to 2½ cups fruit and/ or nuts (your choice; see Note for some of my faves)

242 g / 1 cup heavy cream

Egg wash: 57 g / 1 large egg, beaten with 15 g / 1 tablespoon water and a small pinch of fine sea salt

Turbinado or coarse sugar, for sprinkling

Some of my favorite scone flavors
are simple:

Just Fruit: Raspberry! Cherry! Peach!
(Small fruits can be used whole, larger
ones I chop or slice into bite-size pieces.)

Just Nuts: Toasted almonds! Pistachios!
Candied pecans!

But I also like combos, including:

Black-and-Blue: Equal parts blackberries
and blueberries.

Apricot Oat: Decrease the amount of
flour to 248 g / 2½ cups, add 1 cup old-
fashioned oats, and use dried apricots.

Chocolate–Macadamia Nut: Equal parts
nuts and chopped chocolate.

Apple Cinnamon: Add 2 g / 1 teaspoon
ground cinnamon to the dry ingredients
and use chopped apples.

(More) Traditional Scones: Decrease
the amount of cream to 181 g / ¾ cup.
In step 4, divide the dough into 4 equal
pieces. Shape each piece into a disk
about 6 inches across and cut each one
into 4 wedges. Transfer the wedges to the
baking sheets, spacing them about 1 inch
apart. Brush with the egg wash and sprinkle with turbinado sugar. Bake for 18 to
20 minutes. (*Makes about 16 scones.*)

❄ **WHY IT WORKS**

In the grand tradition of recipes made
with the cut-in method (for more on
this method, see page 167), scones are
tender on the inside and lightly crisp on
the outside. Generally speaking, the main
difference between a scone and a biscuit
is the liquid used to bind the ingredients.
Using cream rather than buttermilk gives
scones a tighter, denser, and oh-so-rich
crumb.

★ **PRO TIP**

I like my fruit scones almost marbled with
fruit, which means that if the fruit is really
juicy, I don't mind if it breaks down a bit
during mixing. But if you want to keep the
fruit more intact, here's how: Make the
dough without adding the fruit, then divide it into 3 pieces, sprinkle a third of the
fruit onto each piece, and gently work the
3 pieces together, then shape and bake.

These biscuits are my go-to when I need to make something to take to a friend or neighbor. Slathered in gravy, they've gotten me through many a brunch. And they've appeared in piles in the middle of the table at fried chicken dinners. Anytime is a good time for biscuits—making them seems like the accomplishment of bread, without any rising time, plus you get to do it with your hands and feel super homemade-y. Whatever you do, eat them warm and fresh—biscuits aren't made for holding.

Makes 12 biscuits

DIFFICULTY: Easy

MAKE AHEAD AND STORAGE: The biscuits are best fresh from the oven, but the dough can be made and shaped up to 12 hours ahead and refrigerated, covered with plastic wrap. Unwrap and bake directly from the refrigerator.

Buttermilk Biscuits

1. Preheat the oven to 400°F / 204°C, with a rack in the middle. Line a baking sheet with parchment paper.

2. In a large bowl, whisk together the flour, baking powder, and salt. Add the butter and toss to coat the cubes with flour. Cut the butter into the flour by rubbing it between your forefingers and thumbs until the butter pieces are between the size of peas and walnut halves.

3. Make a well in the center of the dry ingredients and pour in the buttermilk. Toss the mixture with your fingers to begin to combine, then knead gently to ensure everything is evenly incorporated.

4. Turn the dough out onto a lightly floured surface and press it out to about 1¼ inches thick. Shape into a rough square. Using a 2½-inch ring or biscuit cutter, cut out biscuits, pressing the cutter straight down (so you will get tall, straight-sided biscuits) rather than twisting it (which can pinch the edges of the dough together and prevent a good rise). Transfer the biscuits to the prepared baking sheet, leaving about 1½ inches between them. Gently bunch up the scraps and repeat the process.

5. Transfer the baking sheet to the freezer for 5 to 7 minutes or to the refrigerator for 15 to 17 minutes to chill the dough, which helps ensure a higher rise.

6. Brush the tops of the chilled biscuits with the egg wash and bake for 17 to 20 minutes, until they have risen and the tops are very golden. Serve hot or warm.

602 g / 5 cups all-purpose flour

24 g / 2 tablespoons baking powder

4 g / 1 teaspoon fine sea salt

170 g / 6 oz / 12 tablespoons cold unsalted butter, cut into ½-inch cubes

484 g / 2 cups cold buttermilk

Egg wash: 57 g / 1 large egg, beaten with 15 g / 1 tablespoon water and a small pinch of fine sea salt

❄ WHY IT WORKS

Buttermilk biscuits get a little bit of flake-inducing steam action from the presence of butter. As with pie dough and puff pastry, the moisture in the butter evaporates in the oven, creating steam, which acts as a physical leavener, pushing the dough up and creating flaky layers. Additional lift comes from baking powder, a chemical leavener, which helps ensure tall, light biscuits every time.

★ PRO TIP

Just like other doughs made with the cut-in method (pie dough!), biscuit dough benefits greatly from chilling before baking. This allows the butter to chill again, as the mixing and shaping processes can often warm it up. The colder the butter inside the dough is when it hits the oven, the taller and lighter your biscuits will be.

Crème fraîche makes a great substitute for the buttermilk in my classic biscuit recipe, and the result is a light and airy biscuit, not a flaky one, with a subtle tang. I serve these sweet biscuits for snacks or as a dessert with fruit and whipped cream. The photo is on page 262.

Makes 12 biscuits

DIFFICULTY: Easy

MAKE AHEAD AND STORAGE: The biscuits are best eaten fresh from the oven, but the dough can be shaped up to 12 hours ahead and refrigerated, covered with plastic wrap. Unwrap and bake directly from the refrigerator.

Crème Fraîche Biscuits

1. Preheat the oven to 400°F / 204°C, with a rack in the middle. Line a baking sheet with parchment paper.

2. In a food processor, pulse together the flour, granulated sugar, baking powder, and salt. Add the butter and pulse until it's well incorporated—the mixture should look like coarse meal. Add the crème fraîche and pulse just until the dough comes together—do not overmix!

3. Turn the dough out onto a lightly floured surface and press it into a rectangle about 1¼ inches thick (no need to be precise). Use a pastry wheel or knife to cut the dough into 12 equal squares and transfer to the prepared baking sheet, leaving about 1 inch between them.

4. Transfer the baking sheet to the freezer for 5 to 7 minutes or the refrigerator for 15 to 17 minutes to chill the dough, which helps ensure a higher rise.

5. Brush the tops of the chilled biscuits with the egg wash and sprinkle generously with turbinado sugar. Bake for 17 to 20 minutes, until the biscuits are tall and the tops are very golden. Serve warm.

★ PRO TIP

If you like, you can cut these biscuits into rounds with a 2½- to 3-inch biscuit cutter. Be sure to flour the cutter, and try to use one swift downward motion with minimal twisting, for the cleanest cuts and best rise. You can reuse the dough scraps once, but keep kneading to a minimum—just press the dough into the proper thickness and go!

361 g / 3 cups all-purpose flour

149 g / ¾ cup granulated sugar

12 g / 1 tablespoon baking powder

2 g / ½ teaspoon fine sea salt

113 g / 4 oz / 8 tablespoons cold unsalted butter, cut into ½-inch cubes

226 g / 1 cup crème fraîche

Egg wash: 57 g / 1 large egg, beaten with 15 g / 1 tablespoon water and a small pinch of fine sea salt

Turbinado or coarse sugar, for sprinkling

❋ WHY IT WORKS

The crème fraîche plays the role of the typical buttermilk in a biscuit recipe—it provides fat for richness, liquid for binding, and acid that helps activate the baking powder.

To me, strawberries are downright sacred. I wouldn't say they are my favorite fruit, but every year, the first one to hit my lips (preferably while I'm standing in the field where I've just picked it) is almost always the best thing I've ever eaten. The berries in the dough make these biscuits taste a bit like there's jam baked right inside.

Makes 12 biscuits

DIFFICULTY: Easy

MAKE AHEAD AND STORAGE: The biscuits are best fresh from the oven, but the dough can be made and shaped up to 12 hours ahead and refrigerated, covered with plastic wrap. Unwrap and bake directly from the refrigerator.

Strawberry Cream Biscuits

1. Preheat the oven to 400°F / 204°C, with a rack in the middle. Line a baking sheet with parchment paper.

2. In a large bowl, whisk together the flour, granulated sugar, baking powder, and salt. Add the butter and toss to coat the cubes with flour. Cut the butter into the flour by rubbing it between your forefingers and thumbs until the pieces are between the size of peas and walnut halves.

3. Make a well in the center of the dry ingredients and pour in the cream and vanilla. Toss the mixture with your fingers to begin to combine, then knead gently to ensure everything is evenly incorporated.

4. Turn the dough out onto a lightly floured surface, and press it into a rectangle about 1 inch thick (no need to be precise). Scatter the strawberries evenly over the dough, then fold the dough over onto itself a few times.

5. Reflour your work surface and press the dough out to about 1¼ inches thick. Using a 2½-inch ring or biscuit cutter, cut out biscuits, pressing the cutter straight down (so you will get tall, straight-sided biscuits) rather than twisting it (which can pinch the edges of the dough together and prevent a good rise). Transfer the biscuits to the prepared baking sheet, leaving 1½ inches between them. Gently bunch up the scraps and repeat the process.

601 g / 5 cups all-purpose flour

99 g / ½ cup granulated sugar

24 g / 2 tablespoons baking powder

2 g / ½ teaspoon fine sea salt

170 g / 6 oz / 12 tablespoons cold unsalted butter, cut into ½-inch cubes

302 g / 1¼ cups cold heavy cream

5 g / 1 teaspoon vanilla extract

302 g / 2 cups sliced strawberries (from ½ pint)

Egg wash: 57 g / 1 large egg, beaten with 15 g / 1 tablespoon water and a small pinch of fine sea salt

Turbinado or coarse sugar, for sprinkling

⟶

6. Transfer the baking sheet tray to the freezer for 5 to 7 minutes or to the refrigerator for 15 to 17 minutes to chill the dough, which helps ensure a higher rise.

7. Brush the tops of the chilled biscuits with the egg wash and sprinkle generously with turbinado sugar. Bake for 22 to 26 minutes, until the biscuits are tall and the tops are very golden. Serve warm.

❋ WHY IT WORKS

Laying the strawberry slices on the dough and folding it over them is a great way to incorporate the fruit without overmixing, which would add more liquid (from the juices) to the dough while simultaneously making it tough.

★ PRO TIP

Instead of mixing the berries into the dough, you can sandwich them inside the individual biscuits: Divide the dough into 12 equal pieces. Pat each piece out to a rectangle about ½ inch thick, arrange a few strawberry slices over one half of the dough, and fold the other half over itself. Press the edges to seal, transfer to the prepared baking sheet, and proceed with the recipe.

From top: Crème Fraîche Biscuits and Strawberry Cream Biscuits (page 261)

This is a slightly tweaked version of a recipe my mom used to bake on the weekends. The dough was lightly sweet, and she added dried fruit or nuts to some of it for the grownups, and chocolate chips to the rest for my brother and me. It's a recipe I've clung to ever since I moved away from home. I make these biscuits when I'm feeling homesick, and I always suddenly feel better. They're damn good and super-easy.

Drop Biscuits

Makes 12 biscuits

DIFFICULTY: Easy

MAKE AHEAD AND STORAGE: The biscuits are best eaten the day they are made, preferably fresh from the oven.

1. Preheat the oven to 375°F / 190°C, with racks in the upper and lower thirds. Line two baking sheets with parchment paper.

2. In a food processor, pulse together the flour, brown sugar, baking powder, baking soda, and salt. Add the butter and pulse until it's well incorporated—the mixture should look like coarse meal.

3. In a container with a spout (such as a 2-cup liquid measure), whisk together the buttermilk, egg, and vanilla. Pour the mixture into the food processor and pulse just until the dough comes together.

4. Scoop the dough onto the prepared baking sheets using your hands or a #16 / ¼-cup scoop, staggering the biscuits and leaving at least 1½ inches between them, as they will spread a bit in the oven. Sprinkle the tops of the biscuits with a little turbinado sugar.

5. Bake the biscuits until lightly browned underneath and evenly golden on the surface, 15 to 18 minutes. Serve warm.

❋ WHY IT WORKS
What's in a name? My mama calls these scones, and I call them drop biscuits—and really, we're both right. The butter in this recipe is mixed in more thoroughly than in any of my other biscuit recipes, so they're cakey, not flaky. Also, biscuits are usually made with buttermilk, while scones are made with cream. These are easy to shape and (bonus!) impossible to mess up.

241 g / 2 cups all-purpose flour

71 g / ⅓ cup packed light brown sugar

6 g / 1½ teaspoons baking powder

3 g / ½ teaspoon baking soda

2 g / ½ teaspoon fine sea salt

85 g / 3 oz / 6 tablespoons cold unsalted butter, cut into ½-inch cubes

121 g / ½ cup buttermilk

57 g / 1 large egg

5 g / 1 teaspoon vanilla extract

Turbinado or coarse sugar, for sprinkling

★ PRO TIP
I usually make these biscuits plain and enjoy them with a little salted butter. But when I really need a pick me up, I add 170 g / 6 oz chopped bittersweet chocolate to the dough at the end and sprinkle the surface of each biscuit with flaky salt before baking. Serve hot or warm.

Nothing beats a lightly sweet biscuit-topped cobbler. I want plenty of juicy fruit, sure, but there had better be enough topping that I get some in every bite. For me, individual cobblers are the way to go—that way, people don't have to share their biscuits.

Makes 8 individual cobblers

DIFFICULTY: Easy

MAKE AHEAD AND STORAGE: The cobbler is best the day it's baked, preferably still warm from the oven. Store leftovers tightly covered in the fridge—or try blending them into a milk shake!

Mini Cherry Cobblers

1. Preheat the oven to 375°F / 190°C, with a rack in the middle. Line a baking sheet with parchment paper and place eight 6-ounce round or oval baking dishes on it.

2. In a small bowl, whisk together the granulated sugar and flour. In a large bowl, toss the cherries with the lemon juice, then add the sugar mixture and toss to coat the fruit. Divide the cherries evenly among the baking dishes.

3. Divide the biscuit dough into 8 equal pieces. Crumble a piece of dough evenly over the surface of each dish of fruit. Brush the topping with the egg wash and sprinkle with turbinado sugar.

4. Bake the cobblers until the topping is golden brown (the fruit may bubble up around the edges a bit), 30 to 35 minutes. Cool for 5 to 10 minutes before serving.

❋ **WHY IT WORKS**

This is a great example of repurposing a favorite recipe for another use. The dough is crumbled over the fruit to provide even coverage, instead of being scooped or rolled out and cut into shapes. Bonus: This is much easier too! You can also use other biscuit doughs here (the Crème Fraîche Biscuit dough on page 260 is really good crumbled over cranberries or rhubarb).

★ **PRO TIP**

If you want to make a single large cobbler, use a 9-by-13-inch baking pan and increase the baking time to 45 to 50 minutes.

66 g / ⅓ cup granulated sugar

30 g / ¼ cup all-purpose flour

907 g / 2 pounds (about 6 heaping cups) cherries, thawed if frozen, halved and pitted

10 g / 2 teaspoons freshly squeezed lemon juice

1 recipe Drop Biscuit dough (page 263)

Egg wash: 57 g / 1 large egg, beaten with 15 g / 1 tablespoon water and a small pinch of fine sea salt

Turbinado or coarse sugar, for sprinkling

These muffins are chock-full of the nuts and spices I love in baklava, but the best part is the phyllo shells that hold them—soaked with honey butter, they are sticky-crispy good.

Baklava Muffins

Makes 12 muffins

DIFFICULTY: Easy

MAKE AHEAD AND STORAGE: The muffins can be stored airtight at room temperature for up to 2 days.

1. Preheat the oven to 350°F / 175°C, with a rack in the middle. Grease a 12-cup muffin pan.

2. **Make the shells:** In a small saucepan, melt the butter over medium heat. Stir in the honey and lemon zest and take the pan off the heat.

3. Unfold the phyllo sheets and cover them with damp paper towels. Lay one sheet of phyllo on a work surface (keep the remaining sheets covered). Brush the sheet evenly with the butter mixture. Top with another sheet of phyllo and brush with butter. Repeat with the remaining phyllo, using all but a few tablespoons of the butter mixture.

4. Use a pastry wheel or knife to cut the stack of phyllo into 12 equal rectangles. Press each rectangle into a muffin cup. Crumple the edges a bit so the phyllo doesn't lie flat but instead looks like ruffles around the edges of the muffin cups.

5. Bake the shells until they just begin to turn golden brown, 5 to 7 minutes. Cool completely.

6. **Make the muffins:** In the bowl of a stand mixer fitted with the paddle attachment (or in a large bowl, using a hand mixer), cream the butter and granulated honey on medium-low speed until light and fluffy, 4 to 5 minutes. Add the eggs one a time, mixing until each is fully incorporated before adding the next. Scrape the bowl well. Add the vanilla and almond extracts and mix to combine.

SHELLS

113 g / 4 oz / 8 tablespoons unsalted butter

85 g / ¼ cup honey

6 g / 1 tablespoon finely grated lemon zest

5 sheets phyllo dough (about 14 by 18 inches), thawed

MUFFINS

113 g / 4 oz / 8 tablespoons unsalted butter, at room temperature

120 g / 1 cup granulated honey (see Note)

99 g / 2 large eggs

5 g / 1 teaspoon vanilla extract

1 g / ¼ teaspoon almond extract

241 g / 2 cups all-purpose flour

8 g / 2 teaspoons baking powder

3 g / ¾ teaspoon fine sea salt

⟶

7. In a medium bowl, whisk the flour, baking powder, salt, cinnamon, cardamom, and cloves to combine. Add one third of the mixture to the butter mixture and mix to combine. Add half of the buttermilk and mix to combine. Repeat with another third of the flour and the remaining buttermilk, and then mix in the remaining flour.

8. In a medium bowl, stir together the nuts. Remove 50 g / ⅓ cup of the mixed nuts and set aside. Stir the remaining nuts into the batter.

9. Scoop the batter evenly into the cooled shells (I use a #16 / ¼-cup scoop, but you can also just eyeball it). Use the reserved butter mixture to brush the tops of the muffins, then sprinkle a few teaspoons of the reserved nuts on top of each one.

10. Bake the muffins until the phyllo is very crisp and golden and a toothpick inserted into the center comes out clean, 22 to 25 minutes. Cool for 10 to 15 minutes in the pan, then turn out onto a wire rack, turn right side up, and cool completely.

❋ **NOTE**

You can find granulated honey in many grocery and health food stores—check the health foods aisle or the sweeteners in the baking aisle; it's also sometimes sold with the sugar substitutes for coffee or tea. Or you can order it online. Note that some granulated honey is pure honey, and some is a blend of honey and sugar—both work in this recipe, but the sugar-honey combo doesn't have as intense a honey flavor.

❀ **WHY IT WORKS**

Parbaking the phyllo cups helps ensure the bottoms of the muffins are still crispy when the muffins are done. Granulated honey is a wonderful relatively new product—the flavor isn't as intense as most liquid honey, and since it sweetens without adding liquid, it can be used in many places you'd normally use granulated or brown sugar.

★ **PRO TIP**

If the phyllo dough is your favorite part, you can add a little extra. Double the amounts for the dough and the melted butter, and build a second stack of phyllo as directed. Cut it crosswise into 12 equal strips, about 1 inch wide. After you've formed the phyllo cups, arrange a strip shaped into a circle on top of each one; the dough should easily adhere to the top edges of each cup because of all the butter. For a crinkly finish, crumple the strips up a bit.

2 g / 1 teaspoon ground cinnamon

1 g / ½ teaspoon ground cardamom

Scant 1 g / ¼ teaspoon ground cloves

121 g / ½ cup buttermilk, at room temperature

128 g / 1 cup coarsely chopped pine nuts

128 g / 1 cup coarsely chopped pistachios

64 g / ½ cup coarsely chopped walnuts

A crepe cake isn't really a cake at all, but a stack of crepes sandwiched together with filling, creating a sliceable wonder! It's towering and impressive but, unlike a layer cake, requires minimal effort. If you're looking for shortcuts, you can use the jam or marmalade of your choice in place of the curd in the filling, but I love the tang from the grapefruit.

Makes 1 cake

DIFFICULTY: Medium

MAKE AHEAD AND STORAGE: The batter and cooled crepes can be refrigerated for up to 2 days, tightly wrapped in plastic wrap. The grapefruit curd can be refrigerated for up to 1 week. The assembled cake should be served the same day. Refrigerate leftovers wrapped tightly for up to 2 days.

Grapefruit Crepe Cake

1. Make the crepes: In a large bowl, whisk the milk, eggs, butter, water, liqueur, and vanilla extract to combine. Add the flour and salt and whisk to combine. If the batter looks lumpy, press it through a fine sieve into another bowl.

2. Spray a crepe pan or medium nonstick skillet with nonstick spray and set it over medium heat. When the pan is hot (sprinkle a few drops of water into the pan—if they immediately sizzle and evaporate, you're good to go), use a 4-ounce scoop, ladle, or measuring cup to pour batter into the pan, using a circular motion to cover the bottom of the pan. Working quickly, lift the pan off the burner and swirl it to spread the batter evenly. Cook the crepe until the edges look lacy and golden, 2 to 3 minutes.

3. Use a silicone spatula to loosen the edges of the crepe, then vigorously shake the pan back and forth to loosen the bottom so that the crepe slides freely around the pan. Use a spatula to carefully flip the crepe and cook the other side until lightly golden, 30 seconds to 1 minute. Transfer the crepe to a plate and top with a piece of parchment or waxed paper. Repeat with the remaining batter.

4. Make the filling: In the bowl of a stand mixer fitted with the whisk attachment (or in a large bowl, using a hand mixer), whip the cream, powdered sugar, and vanilla on medium-high speed until the cream reaches soft peaks. Transfer approximately 1 cup of the cream to a small bowl and reserve in the refrigerator.

CREPES

363 g / 1½ cups whole milk

170 g / 3 large eggs

85 g / 3 oz / 6 tablespoons unsalted butter, melted

60 g / ¼ cup water

30 g / 2 tablespoons Cointreau or other orange-flavored liqueur

5 g / 1 teaspoon vanilla extract

151 g / 1¼ cups all-purpose flour

1 g / ¼ teaspoon fine sea salt

Nonstick spray, for the pan

⟶

5. Add the grapefruit curd to the remaining cream and continue whipping until it reaches medium peaks.

6. Assemble the cake: Place a crepe on a cake stand or serving platter (see Pro Tips). Top with 2 heaping tablespoons of the curd whipped cream, spreading it evenly. Top with another crepe and press gently to anchor it to the filling. Continue layering the remaining crepes and filling in the same manner, but leave the top crepe uncovered.

7. Pile the reserved whipped cream on top of the cake and garnish with grapefruit slices or segments, if desired. Dust the whole thing with powdered sugar before slicing and serving.

❄ **WHY IT WORKS**
You can make crepe cakes with different fillings, such as ganache or frosting, but make sure the filling is stiff enough to stand up to being stacked (fillings that are loose will ooze out of the sides, be absorbed into the crepes, and make the whole thing soggy).

★ **PRO TIPS**
The number of crepes this recipe makes will vary according to the size of pan you use—I use a 6-inch skillet and usually end up with 25 to 30 crepes.

Be sure to assemble the crepe cake on the stand or platter you will serve it on—it's not easy to move once it's finished!

FILLING

484 g / 2 cups heavy cream

57 g / ½ cup powdered sugar

2.5 g / ½ teaspoon vanilla extract

357 g / 1½ cups Grapefruit Curd (page 339)

Grapefruit slices or segments, for garnish (optional)

Powdered sugar, for dusting

If you've ever tasted a canelé, a classic rum-flavored French pastry, you know what lust is. They have a delicate flavor, a crispy exterior, and an incredibly custardy interior, but they can be hard to get just right. They're traditionally prepared in copper molds lined with edible wax. My version uses silicone molds, which are much easier to deal with (and cheaper).

Note that the batter must be refrigerated overnight.

Makes 16 canelés (yield may vary, depending on the size of your mold)

DIFFICULTY: Hard

MAKE AHEAD AND STORAGE: The canelés are best served the day they are made, but you can keep them airtight at room temperature for up to 1 day.

Canelés

1. The day before you want to make the canelés, combine the milk, cream, butter, and 50 g / ¼ cup of the sugar in a medium saucepan and bring to a simmer over medium heat.

2. Meanwhile, in a large heatproof bowl, whisk together the remaining 198 g / 1 cup sugar and the flour to combine. When the milk is about to simmer, add the eggs, yolks, rum, and vanilla to the bowl and whisk to combine.

3. Pour the hot milk mixture into the bowl in a slow, steady stream, whisking constantly just until the batter is smooth; take care not to incorporate too much air.

4. Strain the batter into a storage container, cover tightly, and refrigerate overnight or for up to 24 hours.

5. The next day, set the batter out to warm to room temperature for 1 hour—you can work with it in batches.

6. Preheat the oven to 450°F / 232°C, with a rack in the middle.

7. Rub the cups of a silicone canelé pan generously with softened butter (see Pro Tips). Place the pan on a baking sheet and heat in the oven for 3 to 4 minutes. Meanwhile, transfer the batter to a container with a spout (such as a large liquid measure).

8. When the pan is hot, pour the batter into the molds, filling each three-quarters full. Immediately return the pan to the oven and bake until the canelés puff up and begin to brown, 30 to 32 minutes.

484 g / 2 cups whole milk

60 g / ¼ cup heavy cream

28 g / 1 oz / 2 tablespoons unsalted butter

248 g / 1¼ cups granulated sugar

150 g / 1¼ cups all-purpose flour

113 g / 2 large eggs

54 g / 2 large egg yolks

30 g / 2 tablespoons dark rum

15 g / 1 tablespoon vanilla extract

Softened unsalted butter, for greasing the pan

9. Reduce the oven temperature to 400°F / 204°C and bake the canelés for 30 to 32 minutes more—the surface should be very golden.

10. Remove the pan from the oven. Use a small offset spatula to loosen each pastry from the mold and flip it over in the mold (this will help brown the pastries evenly all over). Return the canelés to the oven and bake until the tops are very golden, 12 to 15 minutes more.

11. Let the canelés cool completely in the pan before unmolding.

❋ **WHY IT WORKS**
The batter has a strong enough structure from eggs and flour to set the exterior but a high enough moisture content to keep the interior soft and custardy, even after the long baking time, which is crucial to the caramelized exteriors.

★ **PRO TIPS**
My pan has 8 cups that each hold 75 g / ⅓ cup batter. If your molds are larger, you'll need to increase the baking time—it may take experimentation to get it just right.

Resist the urge to open the oven door during baking other than when called for in the recipe—the canelés are more likely to bake properly with consistent temperatures and minimal fussing.

Goodness, do I love meringue! I love it when it's soft and pillowy (and even more when it's toasted), and I love it when it's crisp and lightly chewy. It's so versatile—there are so many things you can do with it: Top a pie! Pipe it out for cookies! My favorite way to use it is baked into pavlova, a crisp meringue base topped with whipped cream and fruit. I make mine in individual portions, here filled with fresh blackberries. These are a great summer dessert.

Makes 4 individual pavlovas

DIFFICULTY: Medium

MAKE AHEAD AND STORAGE: Although the pavlovas are best served the same day, the meringues and topping/filling can be prepared up to 5 hours ahead. Don't assemble until you're ready to serve.

Blackberry Pavlovas

1. Preheat the oven to 250°F / 121°C, with a rack in the middle. Line a baking sheet with parchment paper; see Pro Tip.

2. Make the meringues: In the bowl of a stand mixer fitted with the whisk attachment (or in a large bowl, using a hand mixer), whip the egg whites and cream of tartar on medium speed until lightly foamy, then raise the speed to high and whip until white and frothy, 1 to 2 minutes. With the machine running, gradually add the sugar in a slow, steady stream and continue whipping until the meringue reaches medium peaks, 3 to 4 minutes more.

3. *To make simple, classic rounds* to be *topped* with the whipped cream and fruit, spoon the meringue into 4 equal mounds on the prepared baking sheet, leaving at least 3 inches between them. Use a small offset spatula to spread each one into an even circle about 1 inch thick. No need to worry about smoothness—swirls and ripples look great here!

To make tall hollow shells to be *filled* with the whipped cream and fruit, transfer about half of the meringue to a disposable pastry bag and cut a ¾-inch opening from the tip. Pipe 4 flat 4-inch-wide rounds onto the prepared baking sheets, leaving at least 3 inches between them. Refill the pastry bag with the remaining meringue and pipe 3 or 4 rings (one on top of the other) onto the outer edge of each round to create a wall. If you like, you can then create vertical ridges by smoothing the sides of the walls in upward motions with

MERINGUE

179 g / 6 large egg whites

1 g / ¼ teaspoon cream of tartar

248 g / 1¼ cups granulated sugar

TOPPING/FILLING

304 g / 2 cups blackberries

10 g / 2 teaspoons freshly squeezed lemon juice

74 g / 6 tablespoons granulated sugar, plus more to taste

302 g / 1¼ cups heavy cream

½ vanilla bean, split lengthwise

an offset spatula. You can also use any leftover meringue to pipe little decorative circles/balls onto the tops of the walls, if desired.

4. Transfer the meringues to the oven, turn the temperature down to 200°F / 93°C, and bake for 40 to 45 minutes, until the meringues begin to look dry on the surface but have no color; if they begin to brown, decrease the oven temperature to 175°F / 79°C. Turn the oven off and leave the meringues in it to cool completely; this helps dry them out so they are crisp.

5. **Make the topping/filling:** In a medium bowl, toss the blackberries, lemon juice, and 37 g / 3 tablespoons of the sugar to combine. Let macerate for 10 to 15 minutes.

6. In the bowl of a stand mixer fitted with the whisk attachment (or in a large bowl, using a hand mixer), whip the cream on medium-high speed until soft peaks form. Scrape the seeds from the vanilla bean (save the pod to use in vanilla sugar; see Pro Tip, page 97) and add to the cream, then add the remaining 37 g / 3 table-spoons sugar and whip to medium peaks.

7. To serve, top or fill each meringue with one quarter of the whipped cream and top with one quarter of the berries. Drizzle any berry juice remaining in the bowl over the pavlovas and serve immediately.

❋ **WHY IT WORKS**

Meringue is one of the most fascinating examples of the many things eggs—and specifically egg whites—can do. Egg whites beaten into a foam can expand to up to eight times their original volume. At the beginning of whipping, the whisk breaks up the whites, causing the protein strands to begin to loosen. As the proteins are agitated further, they begin to form bonds with one another, creating long, continuous strands with large air bubbles, which increase the volume of the whites. Meringue isn't baked so much as it's dried out under low heat, making it crisp—and an excellent base for whipped cream and berries.

★ **PRO TIP**

If you want to make sure your meringues are even, you can use a large round cutter or small plate, about 4 inches in diameter, to trace circles onto the parchment paper. Use a dark pen or marker, then turn the paper over so the ink doesn't come into contact with the meringues. Use the circles as a guide when you portion or pipe out the meringue.

Makes about 12 cream puffs

DIFFICULTY: Medium

MAKE AHEAD AND STORAGE: Although
the filled cream puffs should be served
immediately after glazing, all the components can be made ahead. The unfilled
puffs can be stored airtight at room
temperature for up to 3 days—recrisp
in a 350°F / 175°C oven if necessary
before filling. The diplomat cream and
the optional glaze will keep for up to
5 days—the diplomat cream refrigerated, the glaze at room temperature. The
filled puffs will keep refrigerated airtight
for up to 1 day.

The shells of these cream puffs, made with incredibly versatile pâte à choux (éclairs! crullers!) are golden brown and oh-so-crisp, providing a glorious contrast with the creamy filling. I like to drizzle them with fruit glaze, but chocolate sauce is killer too—or you can do both, you saucy thing, you.

Cream Puffs

1. **Make the pâte à choux:** In a medium saucepan, bring the water, milk, butter, and salt to a boil over medium-low heat. Add the flour all at once, stirring constantly with a wooden spoon, then reduce the heat to low and cook, stirring constantly, until the mixture becomes a slightly sticky paste and forms a ball around the spoon and there's a film of starch on the bottom of the pan, 2 to 3 minutes.

2. Transfer the paste to the bowl of a stand mixer fitted with the paddle attachment (or use a large bowl and a hand mixer). Mix on low speed for 30 seconds to 1 minute to help cool the paste.

3. Whisk the 5 eggs together in a liquid measuring cup. With the mixer running on medium speed, add the eggs in a slow, steady stream and continue mixing until fully incorporated, 4 to 6 minutes.

4. Test the consistency of the batter by dipping the paddle (or a beater) into the batter and lifting it up. The batter should form a V shape that eventually breaks away from the batter in the bottom of the bowl. If the dough is too stiff or pulls away too quickly,

PÂTE À CHOUX

121 g / ½ cup water

121 g / ½ cup whole milk

57 g / 2 oz / 4 tablespoons unsalted butter

4 g / 1 teaspoon fine sea salt

181 g / 1½ cups bread flour

284 g / 5 large eggs, plus 57 or 113 g / 1 or 2 more eggs if needed

Egg wash: 57 g / 1 large egg, beaten with 15 g / 1 tablespoon water and a small pinch of fine sea salt

⟶

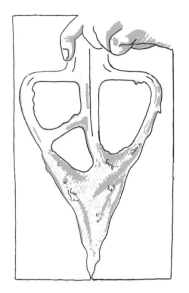

whisk another egg and then, with the mixer on medium speed, pour in the egg in a slow, steady stream, mixing until incorporated, about 1 minute. Do the test again and add the other egg if needed, mixing until you get the V. Transfer the batter to a disposable pastry bag (or zip-top bag) fitted with a large plain tip, such as #804 (see page 93), or cut a ¾-inch opening at the tip.

5. Line two baking sheets with parchment paper. Hold the pastry bag straight up and down above one of the baking sheets and pipe 2-inch mounds of pâte à choux onto the baking sheet, spaced 1 inch apart. As each round nears the correct size,

release the pressure on the bag and twist it slightly to finish. If the tops of the puffs have little points or divots, dip your finger in water and press gently to smooth them out—this will keep the cream puffs round and pretty. Let the puffs rest on the baking sheets until the batter forms a skin, 20 to 30 minutes.

6. Preheat the oven to 400°F / 204°C, with racks in the upper and lower thirds.

7. Brush the cream puffs with the egg wash and bake until evenly golden brown and very crisp (when you tap them with a fingertip, they should feel firm and sound hollow), 24 to 26 minutes. Cool completely.

8. **Fill the puffs:** There are two ways you can do this: You can just cut them in half and fill them (easy), or fill them from underneath (a little trickier). If you cut them in half, scoop the diplomat cream, or pipe it (a decorative star tip makes for a cool look), into the bottoms of the puffs.

If you want to pipe in the cream from underneath, transfer the diplomat cream to a pastry bag fitted with a medium ½-inch plain tip (such as #12) or a Bismarck tip (see page 93),

FILLING AND OPTIONAL FINISH

1 recipe Diplomat Cream (page 341)

1 recipe Berry Glaze (page 58)

or use a disposable piping bag or heavy-duty zip-top bag and cut a ½-inch-wide opening at the tip/corner. Insert the tip into the center of the underside of a cream puff and apply pressure until the puff feels heavy and full. Repeat with the remaining puffs.

9. Chill the filled cream puffs for 30 minutes if you want to glaze them.

10. To glaze the puffs (optional): Drizzle about 1 tablespoon of glaze over each chilled puff and let set for 10 minutes—it will firm up slightly.

11. Serve the puffs or keep refrigerated until ready to serve.

✳ **WHY IT WORKS**

Pâte à choux contains a proportionally high level of moisture, much like popover or pancake batter, but baked pâte à choux has a crisp exterior and a firm structure, in part because the flour absorbs much of the moisture. That's why I opt for bread flour here—it has a higher protein content and absorbs a greater amount of moisture during mixing and gelatinizes the starch, a crucial step in making pâte à choux. Then, during baking, more moisture is released in the form of steam, which creates one large air bubble that expands and expands until the structure sets, leaving a hollow interior.

★ **PRO TIP**

If you like, use a dark pen or a marker to trace 2-inch circles onto the parchment paper, then flip the paper over so you'll have guides when you pipe the cream puffs.

I love yeast-risen doughnuts, but I adore this beignet recipe, which takes you from zero to doughnuts in 45 minutes or less. The batter is simple to whip up and it cooks fast. When I make these for a houseful of guests, the aroma is enough to wake everyone up. The beignets disappear just as quickly as they appeared, accompanied by sighs of satisfaction.

Makes about 55 beignets

DIFFICULTY: Easy

MAKE AHEAD AND STORAGE: The beignet batter can be made up to 1 day ahead and stored in an airtight container in the refrigerator. The beignets are best served hot, or at least within a few hours of being made.

Ricotta Beignets

1. Cover a baking sheet with several layers of paper towels.

2. In a large bowl, whisk the ricotta to loosen it slightly. Add the eggs and egg yolk and whisk to combine. Add the granulated sugar and orange zest and whisk to combine. Scrape the seeds from the vanilla bean and add the seeds to the bowl (use the pod for vanilla sugar; see Pro Tip, page 97) and whisk to combine. Add the flour, baking powder, and salt and whisk just to combine—do not overmix. The batter can be used immediately or refrigerated overnight (see Pro Tip).

3. In a medium pot, heat about 4 inches of oil over medium heat. You can either attach a deep-fry or candy thermometer to the pot and heat until it reads around 325°F / 162°C or just use a little bit of batter to test the oil temperature: If the batter immediately sizzles and rises to the surface, the oil is ready; if the batter begins to brown immediately, the oil is too hot—remove it from the heat and let it cool somewhat, then try the test again.

4. Working in batches so you don't overcrowd the pot, drop tablespoons of dough (I use a #60 / 1-tablespoon scoop, but you can just wing it) into the hot oil and fry, turning occasionally, until the beignets are golden brown on both sides, 3 to 4 minutes. Use a slotted spoon or a spider to lift the beignets out of the oil and set them on the paper towels to drain.

5. Transfer the warm beignets to a serving platter. Sift powdered sugar generously over them and serve immediately.

489 g / 2 cups ricotta cheese (whole-milk is best), at room temperature

170 g / 3 large eggs, at room temperature

27 g / 1 large egg yolk, at room temperature

66 g / ⅓ cup granulated sugar

½ vanilla bean, split lengthwise

6 g / 1 tablespoon finely grated orange zest

210 g / 1¾ cups all-purpose flour

12 g / 1 tablespoon baking powder

1 g / ¼ teaspoon fine sea salt

About 967 g / 4 cups vegetable oil for deep-frying

Powdered sugar, for finishing

⟶

❋ WHY IT WORKS

While the flour provides structure and the eggs keep things bound together, the ricotta is the true base of this batter, giving it a slightly tangy flavor and a tender texture. The right fry temp is key: You want the beignets to brown slowly enough that they cook all the way through—if the oil is too hot, they'll look golden but be uncooked in the middle.

★ PRO TIP

If you make the batter ahead and refrigerate it (see Make Ahead, page 281), it's best to bring it to room temperature before frying (adding cold batter to the oil will cause the frying temperature to fluctuate drastically). But if you are pressed for time, just let the batter sit at room temperature for 15 to 20 minutes, which is about how long it will take to heat the oil.

For most of my life, my grandma lived in a house that was originally built by my great-great-great-grandparents. When she was a kid, her grandma lived there. For hundreds of years, that house was "Grandma's house" to generations of my family. One day, my grandma gave me an old yellow recipe box filled with handwritten cards, including this one. It's been my doughnut recipe ever since.

Note that the dough should rest in the refrigerator overnight—but see Pro Tips for a work-around.

Makes 2 dozen doughnuts

DIFFICULTY: Medium

MAKE AHEAD AND STORAGE: The dough can be refrigerated for up to 15 hours. The doughnuts are best eaten the same day they're fried.

Yeast Doughnuts

1. In the bowl of a stand mixer fitted with the dough hook (or in a large bowl, using a hand mixer), mix the flour, sugar, cinnamon, nutmeg, salt, and yeast on low speed to combine. Add the milk and melted butter and mix on low speed to combine, 2 to 3 minutes. Add the eggs, mixing until incorporated. Scrape the bowl well. Turn the speed up to medium and mix until the dough begins to pull away from the sides of the bowl, 3 to 4 minutes (it will be a bit sticky).

2. Transfer the dough to a large greased bowl, cover with plastic wrap, and refrigerate overnight (see Pro Tips).

3. **Shape the doughnuts:** Take the bowl out of the refrigerator and let the dough sit at room temperature for 15 to 20 minutes. Line two baking sheets with parchment paper and lightly flour the paper.

4. Divide the dough in half. On a lightly floured work surface, roll one half out to about 1 inch thick. Cut into doughnuts using a floured doughnut cutter. (Alternatively, you can use two round cutters, a 2½- to 3-inch one to cut the doughnuts and a ½-inch one to cut out the holes.) Transfer the doughnuts to the prepared baking sheet, spacing them at least 1 inch apart. Roll out the second piece of dough and cut out more doughnuts.

5. Once all the doughnuts are cut, cover them loosely with greased plastic wrap or a slightly damp towel.

723 g / 6 cups all-purpose flour

66 g / ⅓ cup granulated sugar

1 g / ½ teaspoon ground cinnamon

Scant 1 g / ¼ teaspoon freshly grated nutmeg

4 g / 1 teaspoon fine sea salt

10 g / 1 tablespoon instant dry yeast

363 g / 1½ cups whole milk

57 g / 2 oz / 4 tablespoons unsalted butter, melted

113 g / 2 large eggs, at room temperature

About 967 g / 4 cups vegetable oil, for deep-frying

398 g / 2 cups granulated sugar

6 g / 1 tablespoon ground cinnamon

⟶

Let rise in a warm place until nearly doubled in size, 30 to 45 minutes. You can knead the scraps together to reroll once or twice.

6. Pour at least 4 inches of oil into a large heavy-bottomed pot set over medium heat. Bring the oil to about 350°F / 175°C. You can use a deep-fry or candy thermometer to monitor the temperature, or you can just do what my great-grandma did (and I do!) and throw a piece of scrap dough into the oil as a test. If it begins to bubble and rise to the surface, the oil is ready; but if it very quickly turns brown, the oil is too hot—remove from the heat and let cool slightly.

7. Meanwhile, whisk together the sugar and cinnamon in a large bowl. Line a baking sheet or platter with several layers of paper towels.

8. When the oil is hot, drop in the doughnuts a few at a time and fry, turning once, until golden brown, 4 to 5 minutes. Transfer to the paper towels to drain. Fry the doughnut holes until golden brown, 1 to 2 minutes.

9. While the doughnuts are still warm, toss them in the cinnamon sugar (if you wait until they cool, the sugar won't stick as well).

Variations

Basic Glazed Doughnuts: Mix 113 g / 1 cup powdered sugar, 45 g / 3 tablespoons heavy cream or milk (enough to make a runny glaze; add 45 g / 3 tablespoons to start, then add more if desired), and 2.5 g / ½ teaspoon vanilla extract, if desired. The thinner the glaze, the more fully it will coat the doughnut (in a thin layer); the thicker the glaze, the more it will stay on just the top of the doughnuts. Pour the thin glaze over the doughnuts or dunk the doughnuts into the thick glaze to coat the tops.

Chocolate-Glazed Doughnuts: Mix 113 g / 1 cup powdered sugar, 10 g / 2 tablespoons unsweetened cocoa powder (dark, if you can get it), and 60 g / 4 tablespoons milk or cream (add 60 g / 4 tablespoons to start, then add more if desired; see Basic Glazed Doughnuts). Glaze as directed above.

Fruit-Glazed Doughnuts: Make the glaze on page 106, using any kind of fruit. Glaze as directed above.

Coconut-Glazed Doughnuts: Mix 113 g / 1 cup powdered sugar, 60 g / ¼ cup coconut milk (add 60 g / 4 tablespoons to start, then add more if desired; see Basic Glazed Doughnuts), and 2.5 g / ½ teaspoon vanilla extract, if desired. Glaze as directed above. If desired, press the freshly glazed doughnuts into toasted coconut flakes.

※ **WHY IT WORKS**
The high moisture content that makes the dough a bit sticky is what's largely responsible for the doughnuts' light and fluffy texture. You can add a little more flour to make the dough easier to work with, but too much can weigh things down.

★ **PRO TIPS**
If you'd like to make the dough and fry up the doughnuts on the same day, warm the milk to 100° to 105°F / 38° to 41°C before adding it to the dough. Then let the dough rise at room temperature until doubled in size, 60 to 90 minutes.

Instead of cutting the dough into regular doughnuts, I sometimes use a pizza cutter to cut the dough into 2-inch squares (no hole in the middle)—these are especially good for filled doughnuts. Increase the frying time by 1 to 2 minutes. (This makes about 2½ dozen doughnuts.) If you want to fill them (whipped cream, jam, fruit curd!), you'll need about 470 g / 2 cups. Let cool for 5 to 10 minutes before using a piping bag fitted with a round tip. Use the tip to make a hole in the side or bottom, then fill the doughnuts.

Every baker should have a good brioche recipe. Why? Because it's the most buttery bread ever. It's great baked on its own, shaped into rolls, as here, or loaves, but the dough can also be shaped into all kinds of different pastries (see pages 288 to 300), and even used as a delicious free-form tart crust (see page 288). I like to make the dough a day ahead and let it rise slowly in the fridge: That way, it's both easier to handle and develops better flavor. But there is a shortcut option for same-day baking (see Pro Tips).

Makes 24 rolls

DIFFICULTY: Medium

MAKE AHEAD AND STORAGE: The dough can be refrigerated for up to 18 hours. For longer storage, press the dough out into a 1-inch-thick rectangle, wrap tightly in plastic wrap, and freeze for up to 3 months; thaw in the refrigerator overnight. The brioche rolls are best the same day, but the baked and cooled rolls can be frozen, tightly wrapped, for up to 1 month. To thaw, tightly wrap the rolls in foil and heat in a 300°F / 148°C oven for 12 to 17 minutes.

Brioche Rolls

1. **Make the brioche dough:** In the bowl of a stand mixer fitted with the dough hook, mix the flour, granulated sugar, and salt on low speed to combine. Add the yeast and mix to combine, 10 to 15 seconds more. Add the eggs and milk and mix for 4 minutes. The dough should form a sticky, shaggy ball around the hook.

2. Increase the speed to medium and slowly add the butter 1 tablespoon at a time, being careful to incorporate each addition before adding the next; the entire process should take about 3 minutes. (If you add the butter too quickly, it can create a greasy disaster in the bowl, so pace it out.) Scrape the bowl down once or twice to make sure everything is homogeneous. (This mixing period is called *intense* mixing—and it is! Don't be alarmed if the mixing is noisy or difficult in the early to mid stages, it will come together.) Then knead the dough until it is smooth and uniform, 1 minute more.

3. Grease a large bowl with nonstick spray. Transfer the dough to the bowl, cover the bowl with plastic wrap, and refrigerate for at least 12 hours.

4. **The next day, make the rolls:** Grease 24 brioche à tête molds or the cavities of two muffin pans (if you only have one muffin pan, you can work with half the dough, and keep

BRIOCHE DOUGH (MAKES 1.36 KG / 3 POUNDS)

623 g / 5 cups plus 3 tablespoons bread flour

99 g / ½ cup granulated sugar

12 g / 1 tablespoon fine sea salt

10 g / 1 tablespoon instant yeast

283 g / 5 large cold eggs, lightly whisked

242 g / 1 cup whole milk

397 g / 14 oz unsalted butter, at room temperature

Nonstick spray, or oil, for greasing the bowl

Egg wash: 57 g / 1 large egg, beaten with 15 g / 1 tablespoon water and a small pinch of fine sea salt

Pearl sugar, for sprinkling (optional)

the rest refrigerated until you're ready to shape and bake it).

5. Divide the dough into 24 equal portions (each about 71 g). The dough can get sticky and difficult to work with if left out too long, so I refrigerate most of the pieces and work with only a few at a time.

6. To shape each piece, roll one piece into a log shape and visually divide it into thirds. Cut off one third of the dough and roll it into a tight ball. Roll the remaining dough into a larger ball. Place the larger ball into a prepared mold or muffin cup. Press your thumb gently into the center of the ball to create a slight dent and place the smaller ball of dough on top. If using brioche à tête molds, transfer the mold to a baking sheet. Repeat with the remaining dough. Cover the rolls with greased plastic wrap and let rise for 45 minutes.

7. Preheat the oven to 375°F / 190°C. Brush the brioche with the egg wash and, if desired, sprinkle with pearl sugar. Bake until the brioche is very golden brown, 25 to 28 minutes.

❋ **WHY IT WORKS**

Brioche is the ultimate enriched bread— it's loaded with eggs, milk, sugar, and plenty of butter. Enriched doughs generally rise less than other bread doughs, so a slow rise in the refrigerator means better flavor.

★ **PRO TIPS**

It's best to divide and shape the dough straight from the fridge. If you have trouble, you can even pop individual pieces in the freezer for a few minutes to make handling easier.

If you'd like to use the dough the same day you make it, use warm milk (105° to 110°F / 41° to 43°C) and let the dough rise at room temperature until doubled in size, 60 to 90 minutes. Press the dough into an even layer on a baking sheet, cover with plastic wrap pressed snugly against the surface, and refrigerate for 30 minutes or freeze for 10 to 15 minutes before proceeding.

Light and buttery, brioche makes a lovely base for fruit in baked pastries—so why not a tart? You can use any fruit or nut here, but this version, with thin slices of apples and plenty of cinnamon, is a fall favorite. If you like, you can fold the edges of the crust over the fruit, like a galette.

Makes 1 big tart

DIFFICULTY: Medium

MAKE AHEAD AND STORAGE: This tart is best the same day it's made. Store any leftovers in an airtight container at room temperature for up to 2 days.

Brioche Apple Tart

1. Use the butter to generously grease an 18-by-13-inch baking sheet, including the rim.

2. On a lightly floured surface, roll out the dough to a ½-inch-thick rectangle a little larger than the pan (about 1 inch on all sides), so that the dough will come up the sides of the pan.

3. Roll up the dough around the rolling pin and transfer the dough to the prepared baking sheet. Use a pastry wheel to trim the edges so they are flush with the edges of the pan. Cover the baking sheet with greased plastic wrap (I use nonstick spray) and let the dough rise in a warm place for 30 to 35 minutes.

4. Preheat the oven to 350°F / 175°C, with a rack in the middle.

5. Meanwhile, peel, quarter, and core the apples, then slice crosswise ⅛ to ¼ inch thick (see Pro Tip).

6. In a small bowl, whisk together the brown sugar and cinnamon. Uncover the dough and sprinkle it evenly with half the cinnamon sugar. Arrange the apple slices across the dough (see Pro Tip). Sprinkle the remaining cinnamon sugar evenly over the apples. Finish with the salt.

7. Bake the tart until the edges of the crust are golden brown, the apples are tender when pierced with the tip of a paring knife, and the sugar has caramelized, 32 to 36 minutes. Cool the tart for at least 15 minutes before slicing and serving, warm or at room temperature.

28 g / 1 oz / 2 tablespoons unsalted butter, at room temperature

1 recipe Brioche Dough (page 286), cold

1.13 kg / about 6 medium Honeycrisp apples (or another good baking apple)

106 g / ½ cup packed light brown sugar

2 g / 1 teaspoon ground cinnamon

Flaky sea salt, for sprinkling

❊ WHY IT WORKS

I call this a tart because it resembles one, but with a yeast-risen dough as the base, you could almost as easily call it a sweet bread. A "tart crust" made from brioche dough is buttery, soft, and chewy, and if you roll the dough out thin, it becomes lightly crisp on the bottom when it bakes. Thicker and more substantial than a traditional tart crust, it's less delicate but just as delicious. I like this crust for its ability to stand up to plenty of fruit topping, and it's far simpler to shape than a regular tart crust.

★ PRO TIP

I core my apples in a way that makes them easier to slice: I use a sharp knife to quarter the apples, then I core each quarter individually by laying it on the cutting board on one of its cut sides, holding the knife at a 45-degree angle, and cutting out the core in a single motion. The apples then have a flat base (where the core was), so they can lie flat on the cutting board, which makes it easy to slice and arrange them in my favorite style: fans. To do this, place each apple quarter on the side where the core was, so the rounded side is facing up.

Thinly slice the apple crosswise, holding the slices together as you go. Keep the apple quarters together until you're ready to fan them out on the dough. (Leaving the quarters together makes it simpler to make tight, pretty fans.)

Every good baker should know how to make pull-apart bread. It isn't difficult, and it always looks amazing. I use all kinds of fillings—nut butters, chocolate, or (my fave) fruit preserves. Fig jam is a great pairing because it adds subtle sweetness and some texture to the loaves.

Makes two 9-by-5-inch loaves

DIFFICULTY: Medium

MAKE AHEAD AND STORAGE: The loaves can be assembled, covered with greased plastic wrap, and refrigerated for up to 12 hours; bring to room temperature before baking. This bread is best served the same day, but baked loaves can be frozen, tightly wrapped in plastic wrap, for up to 3 months.

Figgy Pull-Apart Bread

1. Grease two 9-by-5-inch loaf pans. Line the pans with parchment paper, leaving an overhang on the two longer sides (see page 27). Generously grease the parchment with the butter.

2. Divide the dough into 2 equal pieces. On a lightly floured surface, roll each piece of dough out to a ½-inch thickness. (It's easiest to work with one piece at a time, keeping the second piece in the freezer until ready to use.) Use a 3-inch round cutter (or a drinking glass) to cut 12 rounds from the first piece of dough. Top each round of dough with 1 table-spoon of the jam, spreading it evenly over the whole surface. Fold each round in half, jam side in, forming a half-moon shape. Stand 12 of the dough pieces up in a row running the length of one of the loaf pans, with the straight sides of the half-moons against the bottom of the pan and the rounded sides up. Repeat with the second piece of dough.

3. Cover the pans with greased plastic wrap and let the dough rise in a warm place until nearly doubled in size, 60 to 90 minutes.

4. Preheat the oven to 350°F / 175°C, with a rack in the middle.

5. Brush the dough with the egg wash and sprinkle evenly with turbinado sugar. Bake the loaves until they are evenly golden brown and an instant-read thermometer stuck into the thickest part of the loaf (you can aim it between segments so the hole

28 g / 1 oz / 2 tablespoons unsalted butter, at room temperature

1 recipe Brioche Dough (page 286), cold

510 g / 1½ cups fig jam

Egg wash: 57 g / 1 large egg, beaten with 15 g / 1 tablespoon water and a small pinch of fine sea salt

Turbinado or coarse sugar, for sprinkling

doesn't show) registers 190°F / 88°C, 40 to 45 minutes. (If the loaves appear to be browning too quickly, tent them with foil.)

6. Cool the loaves in the pans for 15 minutes, then use the parchment overhangs to lift the breads out and transfer to a wire rack to cool a bit more. The bread is best served slightly warm.

❊ WHY IT WORKS

Pull-apart bread is a classic, and it's a great way to pair a flavorful filling with versatile brioche dough. Because brioche is heavily enriched (thanks to the butter, milk, and eggs), it stays soft even after baking to a perfect golden brown, making it easy to pull apart. Plus, the dough itself has so much flavor that you don't need to add much to it—in this case, just a swipe of jam!

★ PRO TIP

If you want to make just one loaf, you can freeze the remaining dough (see Make Ahead and Storage on page 286) for another loaf, or something else altogether.

My mom's side of the family hails from Hungary, and every year around the holidays she makes *kalacs,* a huge, gorgeous loaf spiraled with filling. These little pastries, called *kolaches,* feature a buttery dough base and a spiced poppy seed filling. This is one of my favorite ways to shape filled pastries—it allows you to use plenty of filling, all wrapped up in a neat package.

Makes 12 pastries

DIFFICULTY: Medium

MAKE AHEAD AND STORAGE: These pastries are best the same day they are made, but you can keep them in an airtight container at room temperature for up to 2 days.

Poppy Seed Kolaches

1. Make the filling: In a medium saucepan, bring the milk, honey, poppy seeds, dates, cinnamon, and salt to a simmer over medium heat and simmer, stirring occasionally, until the mixture is thick, 6 to 8 minutes. Stir in the vanilla and set aside to cool to room temperature.

2. Line two baking sheets with parchment paper.

3. On a lightly floured surface, roll the dough out to a ½-inch thickness (about 12 by 16 inches). Cut into 4-inch squares—you should get 12 pieces. Transfer to the prepared baking sheets, leaving at least 2½ inches between them.

4. Scoop 28 g / 2 tablespoons of the filling into the center of each square,

lightly pressing the mound of filling with the back of the spoon to flatten it slightly. Bring two opposite corners of each square together in the center and press to seal; when you press on the dough, the filling should ooze outward a little bit, almost to the edges. Repeat the process with the remaining opposite corners.

5. Cover the sheets with greased plastic wrap and let the pastries rise in a warm place until nearly doubled in size, 35 to 45 minutes.

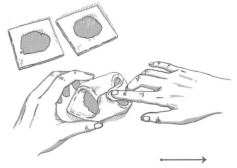

FILLING

121 g / ½ cup whole milk

121 g / ⅓ cup honey

142 g / 1 cup poppy seeds

74 g / ½ cup chopped dates

1 g / ½ teaspoon ground cinnamon

1 g / ¼ teaspoon fine sea salt

2.5 g / ½ teaspoon vanilla extract

½ recipe Brioche Dough (page 286), cold

Egg wash: 57 g / 1 large egg, beaten with 15 g / 1 tablespoon water and a small pinch of fine sea salt

6. Preheat the oven to 375°F / 190°C, with racks in the upper and lower thirds.

7. Brush the pastries with the egg wash. Bake until evenly golden brown, 30 to 35 minutes, rotating the sheets from front to back and top to bottom at the halfway mark. Cool for at least 15 minutes before serving.

❋ **WHY IT WORKS**

This shape, which I call a closed square (see page 253), is great for pastries with filling, especially when you want a decent amount inside. But you can use other shaping methods to make this same pastry—pinwheel, foldover diamond, and filled square all would work great too; see page 253.

★ **PRO TIP**

You can make the filling with 170 g / 1½ cups walnuts, pecans, or almonds, finely chopped, instead of the poppy seeds.

Laminated brioche combines the lightness of a croissant with the dense richness of brioche. The traditional lamination process is time-consuming, so I came up with a shortcut that's just as delicious. My cheater's version produces the characteristic layers a little more quickly and simply by using melted butter instead of the usual cold butter block. The maple sugar sprinkled between the layers gets caramelized as the rolls bake. I love to serve these for the holidays.

Makes 16 rolls

DIFFICULTY: Medium

MAKE AHEAD AND STORAGE: The rolls are best the same day they are made, but you can keep them in an airtight container at room temperature for up to 2 days.

Faux-Laminated Maple Sugar Brioche Rolls

1. On a lightly floured surface, roll the dough out to a ½-inch-thick rectangle, about 20 by 12 inches. Brush the surface of the dough evenly with melted butter and sprinkle 2 tablespoons / 20 g of the maple sugar evenly over it. Position the dough so that one of the long sides is facing you. Fold the left edge over toward the center, about three quarters of the way over the dough. Fold the right edge one quarter of the way over the dough and make sure it meets and touches the left edge (see page 297). The dough will now look somewhat like an open book with an off-center spine. Fold the larger side over the smaller side. You will now have 4 layers of dough. Transfer the dough to a parchment-lined baking sheet.

If the dough feels warm, cover it with plastic wrap and refrigerate for 10 to 15 minutes. If it's still cool to the touch and easy to work with, proceed with the next steps.

2. Roll out the dough again to a rectangle about 20 by 12 inches, brush it with melted butter, and sprinkle it with another 2 tablespoons / 20 g of the maple sugar. Position the dough so that one of the long sides is facing you. Fold the left edge of the dough one third of the way over the dough. Do the same with the right edge of the dough, resting it on top of the piece you just folded over, as though you were folding a letter to fit into a business envelope. You will now have 3 layers of dough. If the dough

1 recipe Brioche Dough (page 286), cold

170 g / 6 oz / 12 tablespoons unsalted butter, melted

78 g / ½ cup maple sugar, plus more for sprinkling, if desired

is warming up and becoming less easy to work with, transfer it back to the baking sheet, cover it with plastic wrap, and refrigerate for 10 to 15 minutes.

3. Repeat step 1 so you have 4 layers again. If the dough feels warm or sticky at any point during this process, refrigerate it for 10 to 15 minutes before proceeding.

4. Repeat step 2 so you have 3 layers again. If the dough feels warm or sticky at any point during this process, refrigerate it for 10 to 15 minutes before proceeding. Wrap the finished dough in plastic wrap and refrigerate for 10 to 15 minutes.

5. Lightly grease 16 muffin cups (see Pro Tip).

6. On a lightly floured surface, roll out the dough one more time to a ½-inch-thick rectangle, about 20 by 12 inches. Cut the dough lengthwise into 16 equal strips. Tightly roll each strip up into a spiral and place it spiral side up in a cup in one of the prepared muffin pans. Cover the pan with greased plastic wrap and let the rolls rise until they appear puffy, 30 to 45 minutes.

7. Preheat the oven to 375°F / 190°C, with racks in the upper and lower thirds.

8. Sprinkle the chilled rolls with more maple sugar, if desired. Bake, rotating the sheets from front to back and top to bottom at the halfway mark, until the rolls are evenly golden brown all over and the internal temperature registers 190°F / 88°C on an instant-

read thermometer, 25 to 33 minutes. Cool for 15 minutes in the pan, then invert onto a wire rack to cool completely.

❋ **WHY IT WORKS**
The brioche dough already has plenty of butter in it, but the thin coats of melted butter help create separate layers—and give the sugar something to stick to. Because the dough is not made with an internal butter block (see page 301), it's much less important to get the temperatures exactly right. You can refrigerate the dough at any point if you feel you need to, but otherwise you can pretty much zoom through all the rolling and folding steps.

★ **PRO TIP**
This recipe requires two muffin pans, though you don't fill both fully. I fill the outer cups of the pans, and leave the center cavities empty—this helps the rolls bake evenly.

These buttery braided brioche loaves are stuffed with almond cream. They freeze well, so you can make one for now and one for later! And no one needs to know that the impressive-looking braiding is so easy.

Makes 2 loaves

DIFFICULTY: Medium

MAKE AHEAD AND STORAGE: This bread is best eaten the same day it's made, but you can keep it in an airtight container at room temperature for up to 3 days. You can freeze the un-iced baked loaves—wrapped tightly in plastic wrap and then in aluminum foil—for up to 3 months.

Almond Danish Bread

1. Line two baking sheets with parchment paper.

2. Roll one piece of the dough out to a ½-inch-thick rectangle, about 10 by 14 inches. Trim the edges of the dough with a knife or pastry wheel to even them, then transfer the dough to one of the baking sheets. Repeat with the second piece of dough and transfer it to the second baking sheet. Put one of the sheets in the refrigerator while you work with the other.

3. Pipe or scoop half the almond cream into a line down the length of the dough, spreading it evenly but leaving 3 inches of exposed dough on the left and right sides. Use a bench knife (bench scraper), knife, or pastry wheel to cut horizontal 1-inch-wide slits down both of the long sides of

the dough; you should end up with 12 or 13 strips on each side. Starting at the top right, fold the first strand diagonally over the filling; it should reach the other side of the filling. Fold the first strand on the top left side over in the same way, crossing over the first strand and making an X where the dough strips meet each

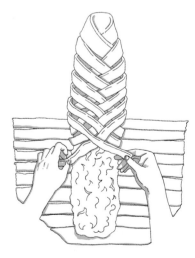

1 recipe Brioche Dough (page 286), cold

1 recipe Almond Cream (page 233), cold

6 g / 2 teaspoons ground cinnamon

Egg wash: 57 g / 1 large egg, beaten with 15 g / 1 tablespoon water and a small pinch of fine sea salt

Turbinado or coarse sugar, for sprinkling

85 g / ¼ cup apricot jam

21 g / ¼ cup sliced almonds

OPTIONAL ICING

113 g / 1 cup powdered sugar

45 g / 3 tablespoons heavy cream, plus more if needed

2.5 g / ½ teaspoon vanilla extract

other. Repeat to crisscross the strands all the way down the loaf. Pinch the excess dough at the ends on both the top and the bottom to make sure they're well sealed. If you like, you can tuck the dough over or under itself to make a cleaner edge, or just leave it as is—both work.

4. Repeat with the second piece of dough.

5. Cover the loaves with greased plastic wrap and let rise at room temperature for 40 to 45 minutes, until noticeably puffy.

6. Preheat the oven to 350°F / 175°C, with racks in the upper and lower thirds.

7. Brush the loaves with the egg wash and sprinkle generously with turbinado sugar. Bake until the loaves are evenly golden brown, 40 to 45 minutes.

8. At the end of baking time, warm the jam to loosen it slightly.

9. Brush each baked loaf with jam and sprinkle with the almonds. Cool completely.

10. **Glaze the loaves, if desired:** Whisk together the powdered sugar, cream, and vanilla in a medium bowl to combine. If the glaze seems too thick, add more cream in 14-g / 1-tablespoon increments as necessary to reach the desired consistency. Drizzle or pipe the icing on top of the cooled loaves and let set for at least 5 minutes before slicing.

❊ **WHY IT WORKS**
It can be difficult to shape brioche into intricate designs because the enrichments—butter, milk, and eggs—keep the dough soft. This shaping method is relatively quick to complete. And the crisscrossed strips hold the filling, which is also quite rich and can spread easily, in place.

★ **PRO TIP**
This style of braiding works great for individual pastries too, and it's great for cream cheese and fruit fillings. To make smaller pastries, cut the dough into 3-by-5-inch pieces and use 1 to 2 tablespoons of filling for each one, leaving a 1-inch edge of dough on each side. Cut the slits ½ inch apart, and crisscross the strips as directed on page 299. This technique will make about 18 individual pastries—reduce the baking time to 18 to 22 minutes.

Puff pastry is made using the technique of lamination, which creates gorgeous crisp, flaky layers (more about this on page 251). I fell in love with the process when I was working in a hotel kitchen one summer. The process is laborious but strangely calming—and the results are insanely satisfying! If you're too intimidated to give it a go, you can use store-bought puff pastry for most of the recipes in this book that call for it, but making your own is a really fun weekend project.

Makes about 1.36 kg / 3 pounds dough

DIFFICULTY: Hard

MAKE AHEAD AND STORAGE: The dough can be tightly wrapped in plastic wrap and refrigerated for up to 3 days or frozen for up to 3 months (wrap them individually); thaw overnight in the fridge.

Puff Pastry

1. Make the butter block: I use a baking sheet as a visual guide when I make puff pastry and roll the dough out to slightly larger than the baking sheet, so I don't need to use a ruler. Cut a 13-by-18-inch piece of parchment paper and place it on your work surface with one of the short ends facing you.

2. In a medium bowl, blend the butter and flour together with a wooden spoon or silicone spatula. Scoop the mixture onto the lower third of the parchment paper and use an offset spatula to spread it into a rectangle 6 by 9 inches and ½ inch thick. Use the blade of the spatula to help keep the edges squared off while you work. (See page 303 for more about forming a butter block.) Fold the upper part of the parchment down over the butter block—you can use the paper to help you square off the edges. Transfer the wrapped butter block to the refrigerator.

3. Make the dough: In the bowl of a stand mixer fitted with the dough hook, mix the bread flour, all-purpose flour, and salt to combine. Add the butter and mix on low speed until it is fully incorporated and the mixture looks a little crumbly, about 1 minute. Add the water and mix until the dough comes together, 4 minutes. Increase the speed to high and mix for 1 to 2 minutes more, until the dough is smooth.

4. Turn the dough out onto a large sheet of plastic wrap and use your hands to form it into a rough rectangular shape. Wrap tightly in the plastic and chill for 30 to 40 minutes. (This lets the dough rest and also

BUTTER BLOCK

453 g / 1 lb unsalted butter, at room temperature

71 g / ⅔ cup bread flour

DOUGH

397 g / 3⅓ cups bread flour

198 g / 1⅔ cups all-purpose flour

6 g / 1½ teaspoons fine sea salt

113 g / 4 oz / 8 tablespoons unsalted butter, at room temperature

287 g / 1 cup plus 3 tablespoons cool water

allows it to come to a temperature and texture similar to the butter block.)

5. When the dough and the butter block are both chilled but still flexible (60° to 70°F / 16° to 21°C), it's time to lock the butter into the dough: On a lightly floured surface, roll the dough out to a rectangle 12 by 10 inches and ⅔ inch thick. If necessary, turn the rectangle so that one of the shorter ends is facing you.

6. Peel the paper back from the top of the butter block, leaving it on the paper so that you can use it to help you to guide it onto the dough: Invert it onto the bottom half of the dough, positioning it so that there is a ½- to ¾-inch margin of dough around the sides and bottom of the butter block. Fold the top of the dough down over the butter block so that it meets the opposite edge of the dough. Press the edges of the dough together firmly all the way around to seal, then fold the excess dough at the bottom and edges under itself. You should now have a firm but pliable rectangular package of dough (about 6 by 10 inches) enveloping the butter block. If the dough and/or butter block are too soft to proceed with rolling and folding, cover the dough with plastic wrap, place it on a

parchment-lined baking sheet, and chill it for about 30 minutes.

7. Line a baking sheet with parchment paper. On a lightly floured surface, roll the dough out to a rectangle 13 by 19 inches and ½ inch thick. If you're having a hard time rolling the dough, it's probably too cold. Let stand at room temperature for 10 to 15 minutes. On the other hand, if bits of butter are breaking through the surface and getting all melty and

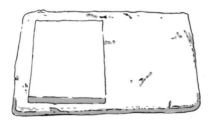

Locking in the butter

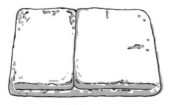

4-fold, part 1

4-fold, part 2

squishy, it's too warm; return it to the refrigerator to firm up.

8. There are two kinds of folds used for making puff pastry: the 4-fold and the 3-fold. You will be making a 4-fold, a 3-fold, a 4-fold, and a final 3-fold. (If this sounds confusing, it will all make sense soon!) For the first 4-fold, position the dough so that one of the long sides is facing you. Fold the left edge about three quarters of the way over the dough. Fold the right edge one quarter of the way over the dough so it meets the left edge. The dough will now look somewhat like an open book with an off-center spine.

⟶

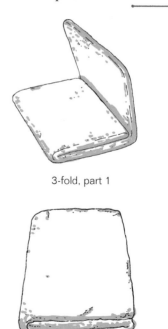

3-fold, part 1

3-fold, part 2

TIPS FOR WORKING WITH LAMINATED DOUGHS

- It's crucial that both the dough and the butter block be at the correct temperature and consistency for all the rolling and folding stages. The dough should be chilled but not overly firm. If the dough or the butter is too cold, it may crack and not form strong layers. If either is too warm, they may mash together, preventing those layers from forming. Ideally the dough and butter should be at 60° to 70°F / 15° to 21°C. Eventually you'll be able to gauge the dough's temperature and consistency with your hands, but when you're just getting started, I recommend using an instant-read thermometer.

- Make the butter block first. To shape it precisely, draw a 6-by-9-inch rectangle on a piece of parchment paper, flip the paper over, and use a spatula to spread the smooth butter into the same size as the rectangle. Square off the edges with a bench knife (bench scraper).

- The dough should be roughly twice as large as the butter block. So I don't have to constantly measure, I gauge the size by having a large sheet pan (13 by 18 inches) on hand, and I roll out the dough so it is large enough to fit snugly inside the pan.

- Each time you roll out the dough, take a moment to square off the edges by pushing against them with the bench knife to encourage straight sides and sharp corners. The more effectively you do this, the better formed your layers will be. With rounded edges, the edges of the dough won't match up when you fold, and your layers will be compromised.

- As you fold, brush off any excess flour on the surface of the dough. Any flour you use during rolling and folding will be incorporated into the dough, and if too much gets worked in, you will be looking at a tougher end product.

Rolling and squaring
chocolate puff pastry

Variations

Yeasted Puff Pastry Dough: Make the butter block as directed. For the dough, omit the all-purpose flour and use a total of 567 g / 4¾ cups bread flour. Decrease the butter to 71 g / 2.5 oz / 5 tablespoons plus 1 teaspoon and replace the water with 360 g / 1⅔ cups whole milk. Add 14 g / 1 tablespoon plus 1 teaspoon instant yeast and 66 g / ⅓ cup granulated sugar with the salt. Mix all the ingredients on low speed for 3 minutes, (not 4), then mix on medium-high speed for 3 minutes. Transfer the dough to a greased bowl, cover with plastic wrap, and refrigerate overnight. If necessary, let the dough soften at room temperature for 15 to 20 minutes before locking in the butter block, then proceed as directed.

Chocolate Puff Pastry Dough: Replace 43 g / ⅓ cup of the flour in the butter block with 43 g / ½ cup unsweetened cocoa powder. Replace 43 g / ⅓ cup of the flour in the dough with 28 g / ⅓ cup unsweetened cocoa powder.

9. Fold the larger side over the shorter side. You will now have 4 layers of dough. Transfer the dough to the parchment-lined baking sheet. Brush all excess flour off the surface of the dough. Cover the baking sheet with plastic wrap and refrigerate the dough for about 30 minutes—you want the dough to relax and return to the ideal temperature.

10. **Now make the first 3-fold:** On a lightly floured surface, roll the chilled dough out again to a rectangle 13 by 19 inches and ½ inch thick. With one of the long sides facing you, fold the left edge one third of the way over the dough. Then do the same with the right edge, folding it one third of the way over so that it rests on top of the piece you just folded. You will now have 3 layers of dough. Brush away the excess flour. Return the dough to the baking sheet, cover, and refrigerate for another 30 minutes.

11. Repeat steps 8 and 9 to make another 4-fold. Return the dough to the baking sheet, cover, and refrigerate for about 30 minutes.

12. You're almost done! Repeat step 10 to make another 3-fold. Return the dough to the baking sheet, cover, and refrigerate for about 30 minutes.

13. The dough is ready to be rolled and shaped as directed in the individual recipes. Or wrap the dough and refrigerate or freeze until ready to use.

❋ **WHY IT WORKS**

The folding (also known as "turns") forms multiple layers of butter and dough. Then, when the heat of the oven hits the puff pastry, the moisture in the butter begins to evaporate, creating steam, which pushes the pastry upward. Lots of flaky layers are the result.

★ **PRO TIPS**

I use a bench knife (bench scraper) to help keep the edges straight and the corners squared off as I work on a dough like this. It's important to keep the dough as squared off as possible, because that will help the edges to meet evenly when you complete a fold. And that ensures cleaner layers in the finished puff pastry. If the edges of the finished dough are rounded, they won't meet up, and there will be gaps in the layering.

If you're freezing the dough, it's great to first roll it out into three or four ½-inch-thick sheets, which are quick and easy to thaw whenever you're ready to use them—just like the store-bought ones!

Palmiers are made by shaping and cutting puff pastry in a way that maximizes its many layers. The results look a bit like a heart. Then the palmiers are coated in sugar and baked to crisp and caramelized perfection. And if you're going to try your hand at making puff pastry, why not make it chocolate?

Makes about 30 palmiers

DIFFICULTY: Hard

MAKE AHEAD AND STORAGE: The shaped palmiers can be refrigerated, tightly covered, for up to 3 days; bake directly from the refrigerator. They can also be frozen; see Pro Tip.

Chocolate Palmiers

1. Preheat the oven to 400°F / 204°C, with racks in the upper and lower thirds. Line two baking sheets with parchment paper.

2. Cut the dough into 2 equal pieces. Keep one half refrigerated while you work with the other piece. On a lightly floured surface, roll out the dough to a rectangle nearly—but not quite—15 by 10 inches and ½ inch thick.

3. Sprinkle 37 g / 3 tablespoons of the sugar on your work surface and place the dough on top. Sprinkle another 37 g / 3 tablespoons sugar over the surface of the dough. Roll out to a rectangle 15 by 10 inches and ½ inch thick, squaring the dough off at the edges with a bench knife while you work to keep them sharp and straight. Then, if the edges are rough or wavy, trim them to even them.

4. Fold the two long sides over to meet exactly in the center of the dough. Then fold in half along the center seam, forming a log. Repeat with the second piece of dough.

5. Spread the remaining sugar on a small plate. Use a sharp knife to slice the log of dough into ½-inch-thick pieces. Dip both sides of each piece into the sugar and transfer to the prepared baking sheets, leaving ½ inch between them.

6. Bake the palmiers for 10 to 12 minutes. Remove the baking sheets from the oven and flip each palmier over. Bake for 10 to 12 minutes more, until both sides are caramelized and crisp. Transfer to a wire rack to cool.

1 recipe Chocolate Puff Pastry (page 305)

149 g / ¾ cup granulated sugar, plus more as needed

❋ **WHY IT WORKS**

Palmiers add the wonders of a sugary coating to the flaky layers created by lamination. As the sugar caramelizes slowly in the oven, it creates the perfect texture and not-too-sweet pastry.

★ **PRO TIP**

The shaped palmiers freeze well. Freeze them on parchment-lined baking sheets until firm, then transfer to zip-top freezer bags and freeze for up to 3 months. Bake them straight from the freezer—just increase the baking time by 3 to 5 minutes, and if they're browning too quickly, decrease the oven temperature to 375°F / 190°F.

A pithiviers is made with two rounds of puff pastry sandwiched with a creamy nut filling (classically an almond frangipane). The surface is scored with a knife before baking to create a design, which can range from simple to elaborate. File this under the list of impressive-looking things you can make with puff pastry.

Makes one 10-inch pithiviers

DIFFICULTY: Hard

MAKE AHEAD AND STORAGE: The pithiviers is best the day it's baked, but you can keep it in an airtight container at room temperature for up to 1 day.

Pistachio Pithiviers

1. Preheat the oven to 400°F / 204°C, with a rack in the middle. Line a baking sheet with parchment paper.

2. **Make the filling:** In the bowl of a stand mixer fitted with the paddle attachment (or in a large bowl, using a hand mixer), cream the butter, sugar, and lemon zest on medium-low speed until light and fluffy, 4 to 5 minutes. Add the egg and mix on low speed to combine. Scrape the bowl well, then add the egg yolk and vanilla and mix to combine. Scrape the bowl well.

3. In a medium bowl, stir together the pistachios, all-purpose flour, almond flour, salt, and cinnamon. Add the mixture to the butter mixture and mix on low speed until fully combined. Set aside.

4. On a lightly floured surface, roll out half of the dough into a circle ½ inch thick. Transfer the dough to the prepared baking sheet and use a pastry wheel or knife to cut out a 10-inch circle (use a 10-inch cake pan or plate as a guide).

5. Scoop the filling onto the center of the dough and spread it out, leaving about a ½-inch border all the way around the edges. (I like to mound the filling a little more in the center to give the finished pastry a rounded look, but you can keep it flat if you prefer.)

6. Roll out the second piece of puff pastry the same way that you did the first. Roll it up onto your rolling pin, then unfurl it over the filling. Trim the dough into a circle, flush with the edges of the bottom piece. Press the edges of the dough gently together to seal. Crimp the edges with your finger or a fork, if you like.

FILLING

113 g / 4 oz / 8 tablespoons unsalted butter, at room temperature

99 g / ½ cup granulated sugar

6 g / 2 teaspoons finely grated lemon zest

57 g / 1 large egg

27 g / 1 large egg yolk

5 g / 1 teaspoon vanilla extract

89 g / ¾ cup shelled pistachios, finely chopped

40 g / ⅓ cup all-purpose flour

33 g / ⅓ cup finely ground almond flour

3 g / ¾ teaspoon fine sea salt

Scant 1 g / ¼ teaspoon ground cinnamon

½ recipe Puff Pastry Dough (page 301), divided into 2 equal pieces

Egg wash: 57 g / 1 large egg, beaten with 1 tablespoon water and a small pinch of fine sea salt

Granulated sugar, for sprinkling

7. Brush the egg wash all over the dough. If you like, for a traditional look, use a sharp paring knife to score a pattern in the surface of the dough; see Pro Tip. Sprinkle sugar over the pithiviers and bake until very golden brown all over, 22 to 25 minutes. Cool for at least 10 minutes before serving.

❋ WHY IT WORKS

The shallow score marks on the top of a pithiviers are purely decorative. Sometimes you hardly see them before baking, but when the puff pastry hits the heat of the oven and begins to puff up, the scored marks expand slightly, leaving visible indentations in the baked dough. These stay pale, while the rest of the surface turns golden brown from the egg wash.

♠ PRO TIP

To score the pithiviers, you can cut parallel lines, evenly spaced, on the surface of the dough, then draw little diagonal lines between them. Or you can make crescent-shaped scores, starting in the center and working outward to create the look of a flower. Or, if you're worried about it looking uneven, just go for random scores. But be sure not to cut all the way through the dough; you want to barely etch the surface. Pithiviers also look great as minis; cut the dough into 3½-inch rounds, and use about 3 g / 2 tablespoons filling per pastry.

I've always loved the classic combination of lemon and ricotta. Add a crispy, crunchy crust to the mix, and I'm sold. These turnovers are wonderful—you can go all out and make everything yourself, or you can take shortcuts with store-bought puff pastry (see Pro Tip) and/or lemon curd.

Makes 14 turnovers

DIFFICULTY: Hard

MAKE AHEAD AND STORAGE: The unbaked turnovers can be refrigerated on a parchment-lined baking sheet, covered with plastic wrap, for up to 1 day or frozen for up to 3 months; thaw overnight in the fridge before baking. The puff pastry can be refrigerated for up to 3 days or frozen for up to 3 months; thaw in the fridge. Roll out the puff pastry as directed, then place it on a parchment-lined baking sheet. You can stack multiple layers with a piece of parchment in between each. Wrap the tray tightly in plastic wrap. Once baked, these are best eaten the same day.

Lemon Ricotta Turnovers

1. Preheat the oven to 400°F / 204°C, with racks in the upper and lower thirds. Line two baking sheets with parchment paper.

2. Make the turnovers: In a medium bowl, mix together the ricotta, lemon curd, and lemon zest until relatively smooth.

3. On a lightly floured surface, roll the dough out to a ¼-inch-thick rectangle, about 8 by 28 inches (you can divide the dough into 2 pieces and work in batches if it's easier). Cut the dough into fourteen 4-inch squares.

4. Transfer the squares to the prepared baking sheets. Scoop 21 g / 1½ tablespoons of the filling onto each square, placing the mounds slightly off center. Brush the two edges of the dough closer to the filling with water, then fold the dough over to encase the filling and form a triangle. Use your fingers or a fork to press or crimp the edges to seal.

5. Brush the turnovers with the egg wash. Bake until evenly golden brown, 17 to 20 minutes.

TURNOVERS

227 g / 1 cup ricotta

85 g / ⅓ cup Lemon Curd (page 338)

6 g / 1 tablespoon finely grated lemon zest

½ recipe Puff Pastry Dough (page 301)

Egg wash: 57 g / 1 large egg, beaten with 15 g / 1 tablespoon water and a small pinch of fine sea salt

⟶

OPTIONAL GLAZE

113 g / 1 cup powdered sugar

6 g / 1 tablespoon finely grated lemon zest

15 g / 1 tablespoon freshly squeezed lemon juice

30 g / 2 tablespoons whole milk, plus more if needed

6. Meanwhile, make the glaze, if using: In a medium bowl, whisk together the powdered sugar, lemon zest and juice, and milk. If necessary, add additional milk so the glaze can be easily drizzled.

7. Cool the baked turnovers for at least 15 minutes before serving. If glazing, let them cool for at least 30 minutes, or the glaze will melt away (not a bad thing if you're not looking for a sharp look—if you want it to be more like doughnut glaze, go right ahead and do it while they're warm). Drizzle the glaze using a spoon, or transfer it to a disposable pastry bag or zip-top bag, cut a ¼-inch opening from the tip/corner, and use that for drizzling (see page 86).

❋ **WHY IT WORKS**

Turnovers are made for improvising. Got puff pastry (or even scraps of pie dough)? Then raid your fridge and find a filling—the classic combo of crispy, flaky crust encasing filling works with almost anything.

★ **PRO TIP**

You can make these using store-bought puff pastry. Or you can even make them with a triple recipe of All-Buttah Pie Dough (page 188)—begin at step 3.

Danish pastries are wonderful: They can be adjusted to suit your mood—you can raid your fridge for potential fillings based on what you have. This recipe is perfect for riffing on—the cream cheese base will work with nearly any kind of fruit, but I especially love it with sour cherries. If you're not up to making your own puff pastry, you can use store-bought, but it won't have the same yeasty flavor.

Makes 10 pastries

DIFFICULTY: Medium

MAKE AHEAD AND STORAGE: These pastries are best the day they are made, but you can store leftovers airtight at room temperature for up to 2 days.

Cherry-Cheese Danish

1. Line two baking sheets with parchment paper.

2. On a lightly floured surface, roll the dough out to a ¼-inch-thick rectangle about 8 by 20 inches. Cut into ten 4-inch squares. Transfer the squares to the prepared baking sheets. Cover with greased plastic wrap and let rise at room temperature until nearly doubled in size, 35 to 45 minutes.

3. Preheat the oven to 400°F / 204°C, with racks in the upper and lower thirds.

4. In the bowl of a stand mixer fitted with the paddle attachment (or in a large bowl, using a hand mixer), cream the cream cheese and granulated sugar on medium-low speed until light and fluffy, 3 to 4 minutes.

Add the egg and mix well on medium speed. Scrape down the bowl, then add the vanilla and cinnamon and mix to combine.

5. Scoop 28 g / 2 tablespoons of the cream cheese filling onto the center of each pastry square, then spread it a bit so it covers most of the surface, leaving about ¼ inch uncovered on all sides. Top the filling on each pastry with 34 g / scant ¼ cup of the cherries.

6. Brush the edges of the dough with the egg wash. Sprinkle 4 g / 1 teaspoon of the turbinado sugar on top of the cherries on each pastry. Bake the pastries until the dough is evenly golden brown, 20 to 25 minutes. Cool for at least 10 minutes before serving.

½ recipe Yeasted Puff Pastry Dough (page 305)

227 g / 8 ounces cream cheese, at room temperature

99 g / ½ cup granulated sugar

57 g / 1 large egg

5 g / 1 teaspoon vanilla extract

1 g / ¼ teaspoon ground cinnamon

340 g / 2 cups pitted sour cherries

Egg wash: 57 g / 1 large egg, beaten with 15 g / 1 tablespoon water and a small pinch of fine sea salt

41 g / 3 tablespoons plus 1 teaspoon turbinado or coarse sugar

✳ WHY IT WORKS

Yeasted puff pastry is the ideal dough for Danish. Light and crisp, it's a blank canvas for fillings of all sorts—fresh or dried fruit, chocolate, or nuts, to name a few.

★ PRO TIP

Experiment with Danish shapes (see page 253). Some shapes require you to cut the dough in a way that will leave scraps behind. Cut the scraps of dough into bite-size pieces and toss them in cinnamon sugar, then group them into rounds on a parchment-lined baking sheet (a single layer of dough about 3 inches in diameter works for me. Drop 16 g / 1 tablespoon of cream cheese filling onto the center of each round. Bake at 400°F / 204°C until golden and crisp, 15 to 20 minutes.

From top: Spiced Croissants (page 314), Cherry-Cheese Danish, Lemon Ricotta Turnovers (page 310)

These croissants have a nontraditional twist that makes them perfect for fall. Warm spices are made into a paste and spread onto the dough before it's shaped. They're like an amazing cinnamon roll–croissant hybrid, and you should eat them warm.

Makes 20 croissants (24 if you use the extra half triangles of dough)

DIFFICULTY: Hard

MAKE AHEAD AND STORAGE: The shaped croissants can be refrigerated on the baking sheets, tightly covered, for up to 12 hours. Or freeze until firm, then toss into a zip-top bag and freeze for up 3 months; thaw in the refrigerator. Whether they are refrigerated or frozen, let rise as directed in the recipe before baking. The baked croissants are best the same day.

Spiced Croissants

1. Line two baking sheets with parchment paper.

2. **Make the filling:** In a small bowl, mix the butter, brown sugar, flour, cinnamon, ginger, cloves, and vanilla into a spreadable paste.

3. Divide the dough into 4 equal pieces; refrigerate all but one piece of the dough. On a lightly floured surface, roll one piece of dough out to a rectangle about 9 by 12 inches and ¼ inch thick. Use a knife or pastry wheel to square off the edges. Cut the piece of dough crosswise into 5 triangles with a base about 4 inches wide (see page 317). You'll end up with 2 half pieces, which you can either match up and press gently together to make an additional croissant (it will be a bit wonky but still delish) or save to make Danishes (see Pro Tip, page 313).

4. Cut a ½-inch slit in the center of the base of each triangle (see figure 1, page 317). Place one triangle on a clean work surface. Spread 1 tablespoon of the spice paste evenly across the dough. Lift up the dough and stretch the triangle by pulling the top and base gently to elongate it a bit. Lay the dough back down on the surface, with the base of the triangle facing you. Roll up the dough—first lift the points of the base of the triangle up on either side of the slit you cut, then fold them over so both pieces

FILLING

113 g / 4 oz / 8 tablespoons unsalted butter, at room temperature

106 g / ½ cup packed light brown sugar

30 g / ¼ cup all-purpose flour

4 g / 2 teaspoons ground cinnamon

2 g / 1 teaspoon ground ginger

1 g / ½ teaspoon ground cloves

5 g / 1 teaspoon vanilla extract

1 recipe Yeasted Puff Pastry Dough (page 305)

Egg wash: 57 g / 1 large egg, beaten with 15 g / 1 tablespoon water and a small pinch of fine sea salt

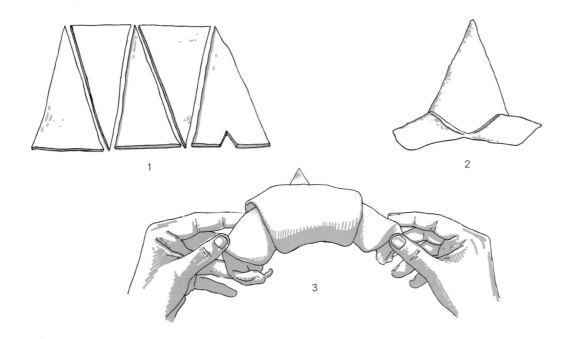

1

2

3

rest on the work surface, on either side of the remaining triangle. Roll the rest of the dough up toward the point of the triangle (2). When you finish, the point should be on the bottom. Move the outside ends toward each other a bit to bend the pastry into a crescent shape (3). Transfer the croissant to a prepared baking sheet. Repeat with the remaining triangles, leaving 2 inches between the croissants on the baking sheets. Then roll out, fill, and shape the remaining 3 pieces of dough.

5. Cover the baking sheets with greased plastic wrap and let the pastries rise at room temperature until nearly doubled in size, 35 to 45 minutes.

6. Preheat the oven to 400°F / 204°C, with racks in the upper and lower thirds.

7. Brush the croissants with the egg wash. Bake until they're evenly golden brown, 18 to 20 minutes, switching the sheets from front to back and top to bottom at the halfway mark. If you're unsure about whether the croissants are done, take the internal temperature—it should register around 185°F / 85°C. Cool for at least 5 minutes before serving.

✳ WHY IT WORKS

The inside of a proper croissant should have a honeycomb texture. When a filling is added to a laminated dough like this, it can disrupt this texture, leaving a pocket of air around the filling. Spreading a thin layer of filling evenly over the surface of the dough minimizes this effect, resulting in a croissant with the classic interior.

★ PRO TIP

You can get creative with the filling you spread onto the dough: Nut butter, jam, and curd will all produce nice results.

CHAPTER 5

Custards & Creams

I didn't learn the true value of a good custard until I worked in a bakery. These recipes are real workhorses—they're delicious on their own, but many of them can be combined with other elements to make other even more amazing desserts. After all, what's a cream puff without the cream? What's a mousse cake without the mousse? What's a custard pie without the custard? And what's anything, really, without a healthy dollop of whipped cream on top?!

Not only are these recipes versatile, they're the epitome of flexible. There are a lot of ways to add your own tweaks to the recipes to create different flavors. Even the methods are easily varied. And almost any custard can be made ahead of time, which means using it as a component in another dessert becomes even easier.

SUGAR + STARCH = NO CLUMPING!

Many custards are thickened with starch—flour, cornstarch, or tapioca starch. Starch has a nasty habit of clumping when it's combined with other ingredients, especially liquid. The liquid envelops the starch, and if the starch is bonded to other starches, it can form pockets that don't get incorporated. In theory, whisking vigorously prevents this, but sometimes the starch lumps are very small and are missed, resulting in a grainy custard.

To prevent this, here's a simple trick: Always whisk your starch with your sugar (or a portion of the sugar). This disperses the starch throughout the sugar, and since the sugar granules will begin to dissolve when combined with liquid, the starch will be evenly dispersed throughout the custard too.

BASIC METHODS

Baked Custard: This method can be as simple as whisking the ingredients to combine and pouring them into the baking vessel. It can also refer to a technique that begins with heating the liquid with a portion of the sugar. The remaining sugar and eggs are whisked to combine, and the warm liquid is slowly poured into them. The warm custard is then poured into baking dishes and baked until set. Commonly used for bread pudding, crème brûlée, crème caramel, and flan.

Cold-Set Custard: The liquid is warmed to dissolve the sugar and infuse it with any flavoring. Then melted gelatin is added and the mixture is poured into molds and refrigerated to set. Commonly used to make panna cotta.

Stirred Custard: This technique sometimes involves the addition of starch, such as cornstarch, to thicken it. The liquid is heated with a portion of the sugar. Then the remaining sugar, starch (if any), and eggs are mixed to combine and the warm liquid is slowly poured into them. The mixture is returned to the saucepan and cooked, stirring constantly, until it thickens. Commonly used to make crème anglaise, pastry cream, and pudding.

Mousse: A flavorful base (e.g., crème anglaise, melted chocolate, curd) is lightened with whipped eggs, whipped egg yolks, whipped egg whites, or whipped cream, or a combination.

GUIDELINES FOR CUSTARDS

☼ Be sure to use a large enough saucepan or bowl for cooking or mixing your custard. When cooking a custard on the stovetop, use a saucepan large enough to allow for the liquid to expand as it heats. (This will help prevent disaster, as cream loves to boil over!) When combining the ingredients in a bowl, allow plenty of room for folding, especially if you're working with aerated ingredients (see page 324), which have a lot of volume and are easiest to mix if you've got plenty of room.

☼ Add the sugar to the eggs (or yolks) just before you add the other ingredients. Custard recipes typically call for whole eggs or egg yolks to be combined with sugar for the base; this mixture is called a "liaison." It should not be mixed ahead, because sugar is hygroscopic, meaning it readily absorbs moisture (as is the case when an open box of brown sugar turns clumpy on you). It will begin to pull moisture from the eggs if it sits, causing them to coagulate and making the resulting custard grainy.

☼ Temper ingredients before combining them. In the custard world, the word "temper" means to gradually add a portion of one ingredient or mixture to another in order to bring the two to the same temperature in a controlled way. If you add an egg-and-sugar mixture directly to a saucepan of hot milk, it's likely to cook unevenly and may even scramble. You can prevent this by gradually whisking a portion of the hot liquid—usually about a quarter of it—into the egg mixture to gently bring the eggs to a warmer temperature. This will allow the custard to set slowly and evenly, which is key to a smooth texture!

☼ Look for the "first boil." A lot of recipes, particularly stovetop custards like pudding and pastry cream, call for the custard to be cooked to "first boil." The term refers to a true boil, which happens only when the whole mixture is thoroughly heated. Small bubbles may appear around the edge of the pan earlier, but you want to keep going until a large bubble (or a few) appears in the very center of the pan, bursting through the thickened custard.

TYPES OF CUSTARDS AND CREAMS

There are many types of custards—some are just multiple kinds combined!

Bavarian Cream: A gelatin-set custard made with a crème anglaise base and lightened with whipped cream. Similar to mousse, but the base is always crème anglaise.

Chantilly Cream: Whipped cream sweetened with sugar and flavored with vanilla.

Chiboust: Pastry cream lightened with meringue—I like a 1:2 ratio of cream to meringue. The texture is light and fluffy, much like a mousse.

Cream: A basic custard that is usually boiled and thickened with egg yolks along with starch (think pastry cream).

Crème Anglaise: Also known as vanilla sauce, a versatile boiled custard thickened with yolks and, often, a small amount of starch. Traditionally flavored with vanilla, anglaise is *nappe* in texture (see photo at right), which is a French term that means it's thick enough to coat the back of the spoon, and a line will remain when you run your finger through the sauce on the spoon.

Crème Brûlée: A rich yolk-thickened custard that is baked and cooled, then topped with sugar that is brûléed (literally, "burnt," with a kitchen torch) to create a hard caramel layer on the surface. The custard is smoother and more liquid than in crème caramel or flan.

Crème Caramel: A rich yolk-thickened custard baked on top of a layer of caramel. When the custard is inverted to unmold, the caramel is both a concentrated layer of flavor on the surface and a sauce for serving. The custard is essentially the same as flan and more solid than crème brûlée.

Cremeux: From the French word for "creamy," a dense boiled cream thickened with egg yolks and often starch as well. Similar in texture to pudding.

Curd: Fruit juice combined with sugar and thickened with egg yolks, often finished with butter. Thick and spreadable.

Diplomat Cream: Pastry cream lightened with whipped cream. Thick but light and airy in texture.

Flan: As with crème caramel, sugar is melted into a caramel and poured into the baking dish(es), then a rich yolk-thickened custard is poured on top and baked. When the custard is unmolded, the caramel is both a layer of flavor on the surface and a sauce for serving. The texture is more solid than crème brûlée. Essentially the same as crème caramel.

Mousse: Classically a base of egg yolks, sugar, and flavoring lightened with whipped cream, meringue, or both. The base can also be a prepared custard such as crème anglaise, a cream, a pudding, or a curd. Rich but light and airy.

Mousseline: Pastry cream combined with butter or buttercream. Smooth and very rich.

SHAKE AND JIGGLE: DETERMINING DONENESS

Learning the art of the "shake test" is essential to mastering all kinds of baked custards, from crème brûlée and cheesecake to the filling for your favorite custard pie. When the custard goes into the oven, it's liquid. Take note of the way it ripples when you give the dish or pan a gentle shake. Toward the end of the baking time, the custard should no longer appear fluid, though it shouldn't be totally firm either. You still want to see subtle movement. The outer edges of the custard should appear smooth and set, but the center should still jiggle slightly—a little like Jell-O. Keep in mind that some baking dishes (like ceramic ramekins) will retain heat very efficiently, so you may want to remove them a minute or two earlier and allow for carryover cooking. The larger the baking vessel, the more carryover time there will be.

THREE TIPS FOR PERFECT MOUSSE

Be prepped and ready. Have all your tools and ingredients ready on your work surface. This is especially important if you're using gelatin, which will cause the mousse to begin to set up very quickly.

Pay attention to the temperature of the base. Recipes may differ depending on the type of mousse, but in general, the base should be slightly warm or at room temperature, not cold. If you're adding gelatin to the base, you don't want it to begin setting before you're finished mixing!

Prepare the aerators, and add them in order from most stable to least stable if using more than one. A mousse can use one or more of three aerators: whipped cream, egg yolks (which more often act as the base of the mousse), or egg whites. Cream can be whipped to soft peaks ahead and refrigerated; you can whisk it a few times by hand when you're ready to add it if you need it firmer. Egg yolks are more stable than egg whites, and they can be held for a few minutes before you add them to the mousse while you prepare other ingredients. Egg whites should be added to the mousse as soon as possible after whipping to ensure that they maintain maximum volume.

Panna Cotta: Milk and/or cream warmed with sugar and flavoring, then set with gelatin. The mixture is poured into molds or serving vessels and chilled until firm. The texture is firm but creamy.

Pastry Cream: A boiled cream thickened with egg yolks and often a starch as well. The texture is thicker and more substantial than crème anglaise.

Pâte à Bombe: The base of many custards, including some mousses. Egg yolks are combined with sugar and whipped over a water bath until pale and thick.

Pot de Crème: Eggs and/or egg yolks cooked with cream and/or milk, sugar, and flavoring, then poured into a baking vessel and baked until set. A rich, creamy texture with a slight skin on the surface and a smooth interior.

Pudding: Traditionally a boiled cream thickened with egg yolks and often a starch as well. Some versions are thickened with other ingredients, like rice or tapioca pearls. Similar to cremeux (see page 322).

Sabayon (also called *zabaglione* or *zabaione*): A mixture of egg yolks, sugar, and wine, traditionally Marsala. The mixture is heated in a double boiler and then whipped until light and thick. Often served as a sauce for fruit, typically warm.

Soufflé: A thick, flavored custard base (often pastry cream) lightened with egg whites and baked. The aerated whites expand in the oven, creating a light and airy sweet or savory dish.

Whipped Cream: Heavy cream whipped to soft, medium, or stiff peaks; often sweetened or flavored.

TYPES OF FROZEN CUSTARD-BASED DESSERTS AND ICES

Frozen Custard: Similar to ice cream (usually made with milk and/or cream), but with a higher percentage of egg yolks, making a richer base. Usually churned just before serving, giving it a soft, very creamy texture.

Frozen Soufflé: A mixture prepared like mousse that is poured into a mold and frozen until set. Even when frozen, it has a light, airy texture.

Frozen Yogurt: Made with milk containing added yogurt cultures, churned until frozen. Relatively soft, like soft-serve.

Gelato: Made with a higher ratio of sweetened milk and less cream (or none). Less air is incorporated during churning than for ice cream, so the result is very dense and rich.

Ice Cream: Made with sweetened cream and milk (more cream than milk). Contains no more than 50 percent air, so is somewhere between densely rich and light.

Sherbet: Most commonly a fruit-based frozen dessert, with dairy added for a light, creamy texture and flavor. Softer than ice cream, but not as loose as soft-serve.

Soft-Serve: The same base as ice cream, but churned shortly before serving for a softer texture.

INFUSING

Since all custards have a liquid component, infusing is a great way to add flavor. Classic flavorings include vanilla bean, tea, whole spices, and coffee. But you can also kick things up a notch—try infusing the fruit juice with fresh herbs, or throw in large pieces of citrus zest, along with a vanilla bean.

To infuse the liquid, pour it into a saucepan, immerse the flavoring ingredient in it, and bring to a gentle simmer over medium-low heat. Then remove from the heat, cover the pan, and infuse for 10 to 15 minutes. Strain the liquid to remove the flavoring ingredient (larger ingredients can just be fished out with a slotted spoon) and proceed with the recipe.

Sorbet: An often fruit-based frozen dessert made without dairy products.

MAKE IT PRETTY

Custards are fun to dress up. Many have to be served in glasses or dishes—and that's an opportunity to make things look really good with minimal effort. Buy a set of fancy dishes just for things like pudding or mousse—they'll look great with hardly any effort.

UNMOLDING CUSTARDS

Not all custards are meant to be unmolded (e.g., crème brûlée, pots de crème, soufflés), but others can be, like panna cotta, cheesecake, and some kinds of mousse. The standard way to do this is to lightly warm a small knife in warm water, wipe it dry, then gently run it around the edges of the dessert to release it. Place a plate on the top of the mold, invert the whole thing, and lift the mold away, leaving the custard on the plate.

WHEN AND WHY TO USE A WATER BATH

Recipes for baked custards often call for baking them in a water bath. Pour the custard into its mold(s), ramekin(s), or pan and put in a roasting pan. Then pour enough hot water (I usually put a kettle on when I begin the recipe) into the roasting pan to come halfway or so up the sides of the mold(s). The water surrounding the mold(s) protects the custard from the direct heat of the hot oven.

Baked custards set when the egg proteins coagulate. If the proteins are warmed slowly and gradually, they will come together into a silky-smooth custard (egg proteins coagulate at around 149°F / 65°C, and custards are usually baked at 325° to 375°F / 162° to 190°C). If the proteins are heated too quickly or subjected to high temperatures, they will coagulate and begin to contract. This can lead to custards that are overbaked at the edges and underbaked in the center, or that curdle, soufflé, or have cracks on the surface. A water bath helps regulate the temperature around the custard so that it cooks slowly and evenly.

Is it always necessary to use a water bath? No. But I do use one when I make crème brûlée or cheesecake—for different reasons. Crème brûlée is usually baked in shallow dishes, which can make it more likely to overcook; and a water bath ensures that cooks evenly and does not overbake (nothing worse than rubbery custard). Cheesecake, on the other hand, is baked in a deep pan, but I use a water bath to prevent the surface of the custard from cracking. I bake custard pies without a water bath—and without overcooking or cracking—the crust helps protect the filling. That will work for other baked custards, but the already lengthy baking time is even longer. Given the choice between a water bath and longer baking time, I usually opt for the water bath.

Or you can make your custards in disposable containers, like little plastic or paper cups, then just snip them open with scissors and peel them off when you're ready to serve. You can also use cupcake liners or freestanding baking cups (see Resources, page 369), which you can peel away.

Custards baked in springform pans are just as easy: Run a small knife around the edges, then release and remove the ring. You can serve on the bottom of the pan or run a large offset spatula all around the edges and invert to release the custard onto a serving plate.

PIPING MOUSSE AND CUSTARD

Piping mousses, puddings, and such into molds or serving dishes (instead of spooning them) reduces the chance of air bubbles forming, which isn't a huge deal but can interfere with the look. To pipe a custard into a mold, hold the bag straight up and start with the tip of the bag touching the bottom of the mold. Apply pressure and pipe, holding the bag straight up and letting the custard flow out, gradually lifting the bag up, until you've filled the mold to the level you like.

You can also pipe custards decoratively to achieve different effects. Most custards are on the soft side, so they won't hold a really strong shape, but you can pipe filling into pastries or between cake layers and make some nice looks.

BRÛLÉING

While this technique is most commonly used for crème brûlée (see page 322), you can brûlée other custards (and even custard pies). I use a kitchen torch, an

WHY STRAIN CUSTARD?

Some recipes tell you to strain custard to remove any bits of cooked egg that may have resulted from the addition of the liaison (the egg-and-sugar mixture; see page 321) to the liquid. I'm not against straining, but this reasoning is wrong. A custard with bits of egg will have a compromised flavor. What's the point of straining a custard if it's not going to taste good anyway?

Nonetheless, I do always strain custard, but for a different reason: to remove the chalazae. Chalazae are the ropelike strands of egg white that hold the yolk in place in the center of the egg. They're not noticeable in most preparations, but these pesky strands are impervious to cooking and don't break down in a custard base. Since I'm aiming for the ultimate in sinfully smooth, I strain the custard. Call it an insurance policy.

GETTING THE PERFECT TEXTURE

When it comes to making frozen desserts at home, a few things are worth noting:

Don't add too much sugar or booze: Both can inhibit freezing, resulting in very soft mixtures that may never freeze fully.

Don't skimp on chilling time: This goes for everything—the equipment you're using (like the bowl of an ice cream maker) and the dessert itself once you put it in the freezer. I always advise making frozen desserts one full day before you're planning to serve them. The wait is hard, but not as hard as watching your beautiful dessert melting before you can eat it!

Don't overfill the ice cream maker: Yes, this may mean you have to churn in batches (bummer!), but if you fill the machine more than two-thirds full, the ice cream will likely slosh out during churning. And as ice cream freezes, it expands—so too full can really be trouble!

inexpensive kitchen tool I fully believe is worth investing in, rather than the broiler. For best results, use superfine sugar, because it will melt faster under the heat, creating a lovely even layer—but regular granulated sugar works too. You can also grind granulated sugar in a spice grinder or food processor to make it slightly finer if you don't have superfine sugar.

You can sprinkle the sugar across the surface or spoon it on and tap it around while tilting the container to form an even layer. Be sure the layer is thin—if it's too thick, the sugar on top will melt and caramelize but leave a layer of uncooked sugar underneath.

Beginning on one side of the dessert, hold the kitchen torch a few inches above the surface and wave it back and forth instead of holding it still in one place. First the sugar will melt and then it will begin to bubble and brown. Continue to brûlée until the whole surface is evenly caramelized, then let cool for a few minutes before serving.

To brûlée under a broiler, apply the sugar to the surface the same way and place the vessel under the broiler, moving the dish around as necessary. Watch carefully, as broilers vary greatly (if yours has both a high and a low setting, opt for low). If you will be using the broiler, it's best to underbake the custard by 1 to 2 minutes so it doesn't overbake during broiling.

LAYERING

I often layer multiple colors and flavors in mousse or panna cotta. I usually start with a base-note flavor like vanilla, then use others, like caramel or chocolate (see the Black Bottom Crème Brûlée, page 345) for contrasting notes and colors. It's important to let each layer set before you add the next, or they'll run together.

SIFTING

When you have a custard with a lovely smooth surface, you can sift ingredients such as powdered sugar or cocoa powder across the whole surface, or just a portion of it, to achieve a super-pretty effect. Sometimes I use a piece of paper to cover up most of the custard and then sift onto the uncovered portion—the paper results in sharp lines (you can also move the paper and repeat the dusting to make stripes). If you're feeling fancy, you can hold a sturdy stencil over the surface and sift through it to make a pattern.

DRIZZLES AND SPLATTERS

Drizzles and splatters look great on the smooth surface of a custard. Follow the guidelines for drizzling on page 86. Or you can splatter by dipping a pastry brush into a relatively fluid glaze or ganache and flicking the brush over the dessert (see Sweet Cream Tartlets, page 240).

ICE CREAM: THE ULTIMATE EFFORTLESS DESSERT

Everyone loves ice cream. Even people who say it's not their favorite dessert go bananas and/or nuts (puns very much intended) when there are creamy homemade scoops to be had. You can do tons of fun things with ice cream:

Sandwich it between pairs of your favorite cookies for epic ice cream sandwiches. I like to use softer cookies; I strongly encourage you to try this with Flourless Cocoa Cookies (page 30).

Make milk shakes. If you're feeling fancy, make Salted Caramel Sauce (page 54) or Dulce de Leche (page 206) and swirl it all over the inside of the glass before you pour the milk shake in.

Make sundaes. Layer scoops of different kinds of ice cream with fresh fruit and drizzle ganache over the whole thing, then top with something crunchy, such as nuts, Caramel Corn (page 154), or homemade sprinkles (page 95).

Make floats. Buy fancy soda or just use seltzer water and flavoring. Sweet Cream Ice Cream (page 362) with spicy ginger beer rocks my world.

Make an ice cream cake. I save all kinds of scraps in my freezer and then, when I have enough, I use them to make ice cream cakes. Anything goes: cookie crumbs, cake scraps, bits of overripe fruit, etc. Layer the ingredients to create the ice cream cake, alternating layers of ice cream with something textural, like cake or cookie crumbs. I build ice cream cakes in springform pans (cake/cookies on the base and ice cream on top) or loaf pans (start with ice cream in the bottom, because that will become the top when you unmold it, and top with cake or cookies). It's best to line any pan with plastic wrap, as it prevents leaking during building and also makes it easier to unmold (use the excess plastic around the edges as handles to pull the cake out of the pan—or in the case of a springform, cleanly away from the base).

Serve anything à la mode—a slice of pie or tart, a warm brownie or blondie, or even a cupcake in lieu of frosting!

Reasons I'm obsessed with pudding: It's the ultimate comfort dessert; it can be made nearly anytime/anywhere because it's so fast and easy; it's fun to make with kids; and it's easy to adapt for different flavors, serving sizes, and whatnot. You can store the pudding in the refrigerator in a large bowl or divide it among individual dishes. And don't forget to eat what's left in the pan while it's still warm—just you and a spoon.

Makes 6 servings

DIFFICULTY: Easy

MAKE AHEAD AND STORAGE: The pudding can be refrigerated for up to 4 days.

Vanilla Pudding

1. Combine the milk, cream, salt, and 50 g / ¼ cup of the sugar in a medium saucepan. Scrape the seeds from the vanilla bean and add the seeds and pod to the pan. Bring the mixture to a simmer over medium heat.

2. Meanwhile, in a medium heatproof bowl, whisk together the remaining 99 g / ½ cup sugar and the corn-starch.

3. When the milk mixture has come to a simmer, turn the heat down to medium-low. Whisk the egg yolks into the sugar-and-cornstarch mixture, then pour in about one third of the hot milk mixture in a slow, steady stream, whisking constantly. Pour the yolk mixture into the pan and cook the pudding, stirring constantly with a silicone spatula and taking care

to scrape the bottom and sides of the pan, until the pudding gets very thick and comes to "first boil" (a large bubble will rise to the surface in the center), 3 to 4 minutes. Remove the pan from the heat, fish out the vanilla bean, and stir in the vanilla extract.

4. Pour the pudding into a large heat-proof bowl (shallow if you want it to cool quickly) or six 6-ounce ramekins, custard cups, or other individual serving dishes. Cover with plastic wrap pressed directly against the surface of the pudding to prevent a skin from forming (if you secretly love pudding skin, like a select few of us, skip this step).

5. Refrigerate the pudding until fully chilled, at least 2 hours, before serving.

725 g / 3 cups whole milk

121 g / ½ cup heavy cream

2 g / ½ teaspoon fine sea salt

149 g / ¾ cup granulated sugar

½ vanilla bean, split lengthwise

28 g / ¼ cup cornstarch

108 g / 4 large egg yolks, at room temperature

5 g / 1 teaspoon vanilla extract

→

Pudding falls under the classification of boiled, or stirred, custard—it's cooked on the stovetop to the proper thickness, then chilled. It's important to bring the mixture to a boil to activate the starch (in this case, cornstarch). Otherwise, an enzyme naturally occurring in the eggs will begin to consume the starch, which will make the pudding thin out as it sits in the fridge.

★ **PRO TIP**

Although pudding is traditionally served chilled, I've always loved it just made, when it's still warm. It makes a great (unusual) dessert for a dinner party—even as one component in a plated dessert. You can spread some warm pudding on each plate and top with a slice of pound cake and some fresh fruit. Or layer the same ingredients in a large bowl, preferably glass, to make a trifle!

Variations

Chocolate Pudding: Omit the vanilla bean. In step 2, whisk 8 g / 2 teaspoons instant espresso powder into the sugar/cornstarch mixture. When you add the vanilla extract, also stir in 170 g / 6 oz chopped bittersweet chocolate (I use 60% cacao) until fully melted and incorporated.

Salty Butterscotch Pudding: Omit the vanilla bean. Replace the granulated sugar with 160 g / ¾ cup packed dark brown sugar, increase the salt to 3 g / ¾ teaspoon, and increase the vanilla extract to 10 g / 2 teaspoons. Garnish the chilled pudding with a sprinkling of flaky salt, to taste.

I used to think classic mousse was a bit daunting, but it was the basis of so many things we learned to make in pastry school that it eventually became almost effortless. The real key is planning out the preparation of the various components, because once you have them all ready, it's really just a matter of mixing properly. Follow my tips, and soon you will think mousse is easy-peasy too!

Makes 6 servings

DIFFICULTY: Medium

MAKE AHEAD AND STORAGE: The crème anglaise can be made ahead, covered with plastic wrap pressed directly against the surface, and refrigerated for up to 5 days. The mousse can be tightly covered with plastic wrap and refrigerated for up to 3 days.

Vanilla Bean Mousse

1. Make the crème anglaise: Place a quart-sized canning jar (or similar-size vessel so the crème will cool down quickly) in a large bowl. Pile ice around the canning jar and pour enough water into the bowl to come three quarters of the way up the sides of the jar.

2. In a medium saucepan, combine the milk, cream, salt, and 50 g / ¼ cup of the sugar. Scrape the seeds from the vanilla bean and add the seeds and pod to the pan. Bring the mixture to a simmer over medium heat.

3. Meanwhile, in a medium heatproof bowl, whisk together the egg yolks and the remaining 62 g / ¼ cup plus 1 tablespoon sugar.

4. When the milk has come to a simmer, turn the heat down to medium-low. Pour one third of the hot milk mixture into the yolk mixture, whisking constantly to combine, then pour the yolk mixture back into the pan, whisking constantly to prevent the eggs from scrambling. Cook, stirring constantly with a silicone spatula, until the mixture is thick enough to coat the back of the spatula, 4 to 6 minutes. Strain the crème anglaise into the canning jar and let cool to room temperature in the ice bath.

5. Place six glasses or serving dishes that hold about 8 ounces each on a baking sheet.

6. Make the mousse: Pour the water into a small heatproof dish and

CRÈME ANGLAISE

161 g / ⅔ cup whole milk

161 g / ⅔ cup heavy cream

1 g / ¼ teaspoon fine sea salt

112 g / ½ cup plus 1 tablespoon granulated sugar

½ vanilla bean, split lengthwise

162 g / 6 large egg yolks

FINISHED MOUSSE

121 g / ½ cup cool water

14 g / 2 packets powdered gelatin

242 g / 1 cup heavy cream

213 g / ½ cup granulated sugar

89 g / 3 large egg whites

sprinkle the gelatin over the top. Let stand for 5 minutes.

7. Meanwhile, in a medium bowl, using a hand mixer, an immersion blender, or a whisk, whip the cream and 50 g / ¼ cup of the sugar to soft peaks. Throw a whisk in the bowl and transfer the bowl to the refrigerator.

8. Transfer 340 g / 1⅓ cups of the crème anglaise to a large bowl. Melt the softened gelatin in the microwave for 30 seconds to 1 minute. Stir to make sure it is fully dissolved.

9. Bring a medium saucepan of water to a bare simmer. In the bowl of a stand mixer fitted with the whisk attachment (or in a large heatproof bowl, using a hand mixer), whisk together the egg whites and the remaining 50 g / ¼ cup sugar. Place the bowl over the pan of barely simmering water and whisk constantly (by hand or with a hand mixer) until the mixture reaches 140°F / 60°C on an instant-read or candy thermometer.

10. Remove the bowl from the heat and whip on medium-high speed until the egg whites reach medium peaks.

11. Stir the melted gelatin into the crème anglaise.

12. Retrieve the whipped cream from the refrigerator and use the cold whisk to whip it to medium peaks. Fold one quarter of the whipped cream into the crème anglaise, mixing well to fully incorporate the whipped cream and lighten the crème anglaise, then gently fold in the remaining whipped cream in 3 additions, mixing just until combined. Fold in one-quarter of the meringue, mixing well, then fold in the remaining meringue in 3 additions, mixing just to incorporate.

13. Divide the mousse evenly among the prepared glasses (you can use a pastry bag or a ladle, or you can pour it from a spouted measuring cup). Chill the mousse until set, at least 30 minutes.

❊ **WHY IT WORKS**

Mousse is all about aeration. This recipe uses both whipped cream and meringue to aerate a classic crème anglaise. While the aerators are largely responsible for the light texture, the mousse would eventually deflate without the structural support provided by the gelatin. (Chocolate mousse is an exception; the chocolate sets firm, so no gelatin is required.)

★ **PRO TIP**

If this recipe intimidates you, make the crème anglaise ahead of time (see Make Ahead and Storage, page 335). Bring it to room temperature before preparing the mousse. Then, when you're ready to make the mousse, it's basically just a matter of whipping cream and making a meringue.

Variations

Orange Mousse: Replace the crème anglaise with 476 g / 2 cups Orange Curd (page 339). Bring the curd to room temperature before making the mousse.

Chocolate Mousse: Replace the crème anglaise with 397 g / 14 oz bittersweet chocolate (I use 60% cacao), melted and cooled for 5 to 10 minutes. Omit the gelatin and water.

Curd, which is a fruit-based custard, is one of a baker's secret weapons. Though traditionally made from lemon, it can be prepared with all kinds of citrus—and, actually, many different kinds of fruit (see the Variations). It's beyond versatile—it's great for spreading on scones, filling cakes and pastries, or mixing into frostings and buttercreams. Plus, it's easy to make and keeps well.

Makes 595 g / 2½ cups

DIFFICULTY: Easy

MAKE AHEAD AND STORAGE: The curd can be stored in an airtight container in the refrigerator for up to 1 week.

Lemon Curd

1. In a medium saucepan, melt 113 g / 4 oz / 8 tablespoons of the butter over medium heat.

2. In medium bowl, whisk together the sugar, lemon zest, lemon juice, salt, and egg yolks.

3. Turn the heat under the saucepan down to low, stir in the egg yolk mixture, and cook, stirring constantly with a silicone spatula and taking care to scrape the sides and bottom of the pan, until the mixture is thick enough to coat the spatula, 6 to 8 minutes. Remove the pan from the heat and stir in the remaining 57 g / 2 oz / 4 tablespoons butter, until it is melted and incorporated.

4. Strain the curd into a shallow dish and cover it with plastic wrap pressed directly against the surface. Refrigerate until thoroughly chilled, at least 2 hours.

❋ **WHY IT WORKS**
Fruit is the flavor star here, but egg yolks are what make the recipe work. The egg proteins slowly coagulate as the mixture is heated, resulting in a glossy, thick spread.

★ **PRO TIPS**
If you're looking for a firmer curd, stir 38 g / ⅓ cup cornstarch into the sugar before you add it to the egg yolks and bring the curd to a simmer over medium-low heat (otherwise, it won't set properly; see page 16). Take care to stir the curd constantly and carefully to avoid scrambling the eggs.

113 g / 6 oz unsalted butter

198 g / 1 cup granulated sugar

6 g / 1 tablespoon finely grated lemon zest

302 g / 1¼ cups freshly squeezed lemon juice (from 5 or 6 lemons)

1 g / ¼ teaspoon fine sea salt

269 g / 10 large egg yolks

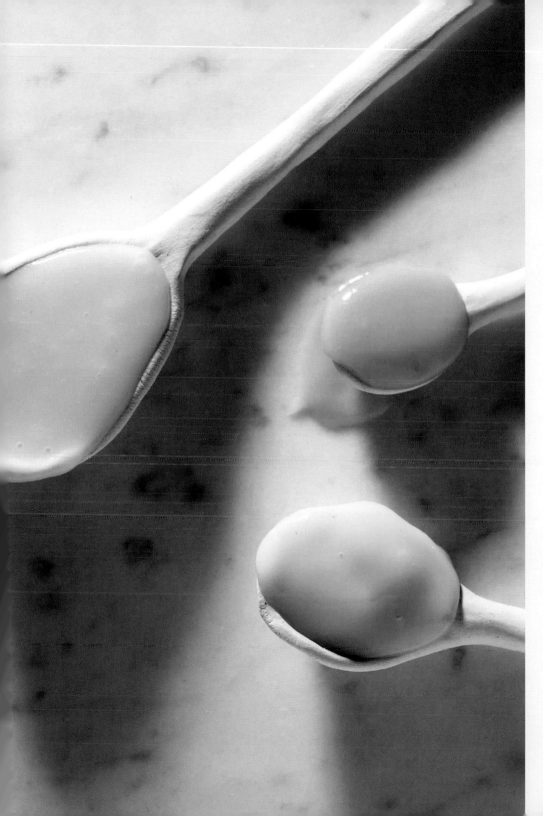

Variations

Grapefruit Curd: Replace the lemon juice with freshly squeezed grapefruit juice. Omit the lemon zest. If you want the curd to be pink, add a drop or two of red food coloring.

Orange Curd: Replace the lemon juice with freshly squeezed orange juice. Replace the lemon zest with orange zest. If you want the curd to be orange, add one drop each yellow and red food coloring.

Lime Curd: Replace the lemon juice with freshly squeezed lime juice. Replace the lemon zest with lime zest. If you want the curd to be green, add a drop or two of green food coloring.

Pear Curd: Replace the lemon juice with pear nectar. Omit the lemon zest.

Passionfruit Curd: Replace the lemon juice with passionfruit nectar. Omit the lemon zest.

Not only is pastry cream crazy delicious, it's useful in so many pastries. You can put it in a crust for a fruit tart, between the layers of a cake, or inside doughnuts or cream puffs. Don't overlook its equally delicious cousins: diplomat cream and chiboust; see the Variations.

Makes 680 g / 3¼ cups

DIFFICULTY: Easy

MAKE AHEAD AND STORAGE: The pastry cream can be stored in the refrigerator for up to 1 week.

Pastry Cream

1. Combine the milk, salt, and 50 g / ¼ cup of the sugar in a medium saucepan. Scrape the seeds from the vanilla bean and add the seeds and pod to the pan. Bring the mixture to a simmer over medium heat.

2. Meanwhile, in a medium heatproof bowl, whisk together the remaining 99 g / ½ cup sugar and the cornstarch.

3. When the milk mixture has come to a simmer, remove the vanilla pod (rinse and dry it to use in vanilla sugar; see Pro Tip, page 97) and turn the heat down to medium-low.

4. Whisk the egg yolks into the sugar-and-cornstarch mixture, then gradually pour in about one third of the hot milk mixture in a slow, thin stream, whisking constantly. Pour the yolk mixture into the pan and cook, stirring constantly with a silicone spatula and taking care to scrape the bottom and sides of the pan, until the mixture gets very thick and comes to "first boil" (a large bubble will rise to the surface in the center), 3 to 4 minutes. Remove the pan from the heat and stir in the butter, mixing until melted and incorporated.

5. Strain the pastry cream into a large heatproof bowl (a shallow one, if you want it to cool faster). Cover with plastic wrap pressed directly against the surface of the cream and refrigerate until thoroughly chilled, at least 2 hours, before using.

726 g / 3 cups whole milk

1 g / ¼ teaspoon fine sea salt

149 g / ¾ cup granulated sugar

½ vanilla bean, split lengthwise

135 g / 5 large egg yolks, at room temperature

38 g / ⅓ cup cornstarch

43 g / 1.5 oz / 3 tablespoons unsalted butter, at room temperature

Variations

Diplomat Cream: For every 1 cup pastry cream, fold in 1 cup heavy cream whipped to medium peaks, mixing just until incorporated.

Chiboust: You'll need 2 cups pastry cream for this recipe. For every 1 cup pastry cream, fold in 1 cup meringue, mixing just until incorporated. To make about 2 cups basic meringue, in the bowl of a stand mixer fitted with the whisk attachment (or in a large bowl, using a hand mixer), whip 120 g / 2 pasteurized egg whites and a pinch of cream of tartar on medium speed until lightly foamy. Raise the mixer speed to high and, with the machine running, gradually add 100 g / ½ cup granulated sugar in a slow, steady stream. Continue whipping until the meringue reaches medium peaks, 5 to 7 minutes.

❋ **WHY IT WORKS**

Pastry cream is thickened by a combination of egg proteins (which must coagulate slowly to achieve a smooth texture) and cornstarch (which is first mixed with the sugar to prevent clumping). Managing all components properly produces a silky custard every time.

★ **PRO TIP**

As if pastry cream weren't delicious, useful, and just generally wonderful enough, two of my other favorite fillings use it as a base—see the Variations. These fillings are a bit more stable than pastry cream and can be piped decoratively as well.

My mama makes this custard every year around the holidays, and it's one of those treats we wait for all year long! It's not quite a traditional panna cotta (see Why It Works), but it has a similar ease, look, and texture. It tastes like Christmas on a spoon, and I can almost hear John Denver and The Muppets singing carols (also part of our tradition) each time I take a bite.

Makes 6 servings

DIFFICULTY: Easy

MAKE AHEAD AND STORAGE: The panna cotta can be kept, tightly covered with plastic wrap, in the refrigerator for up to 3 days. The raspberry sauce will keep airtight in the refrigerator for up to 1 week.

Eggnog Panna Cotta with Raspberry Sauce

1. Set six glasses or serving dishes (see Pro Tip for other ideas) that hold about 8 ounces each on a baking sheet.

2. **Make the custard:** Pour the cold water into a small heatproof dish and sprinkle the gelatin over the top. Let stand for 5 minutes.

3. In the bowl of a stand mixer fitted with the whisk attachment (or in a large bowl, using a hand mixer), whip the cream, sugar, and vanilla to medium peaks.

4. In another large bowl, whisk together the eggnog and rum. Melt the softened gelatin in the microwave, 30 seconds to 1 minute. Stir to make sure it is fully dissolved, then add it to the eggnog mixture, whisking to incorporate.

5. Temper the custard by folding in about one quarter of the whipped cream mixture, mixing well. Add the remaining whipped cream in 2 or 3 additions, gently folding just until incorporated.

6. Divide the custard evenly among the prepared glasses (you can use a ladle or pour it from a measuring cup with a spout). Chill until set, at least 1 hour.

CUSTARD

121 g / ½ cup cold water

7 g / 1 packet powdered gelatin

242 g / 1 cup heavy cream

50 g / ¼ cup granulated sugar

2.5 g / ½ teaspoon vanilla extract

484 g / 2 cups eggnog

30 g / 2 tablespoons dark rum

RASPBERRY SAUCE

170 g / 1 cup raspberries

43 g / 2 tablespoons honey

30 g / 2 tablespoons water

7. **Make the raspberry sauce:** In a medium saucepan, combine the raspberries, honey, and water and cook over medium heat, stirring occasionally, until the fruit breaks down and the mixture resembles a chunky sauce or jam, 4 to 5 minutes. Cool completely.

8. Serve the custards chilled, topped with the raspberry sauce.

❊ WHY IT WORKS

This isn't an entirely traditional panna cotta recipe, thanks to the addition of whipped cream, which gives the finished custard a light, airy texture. But true to panna cotta protocol, it is cold-set, meaning it uses gelatin to set the sweetened liquid base.

★ PRO TIP

You can serve the panna cotta in the containers or you can opt to unmold them. One of my favorite ways to ensure they unmold cleanly is to use disposable molds: cupcake liners, disposable freestanding baking cups, or plastic cups.

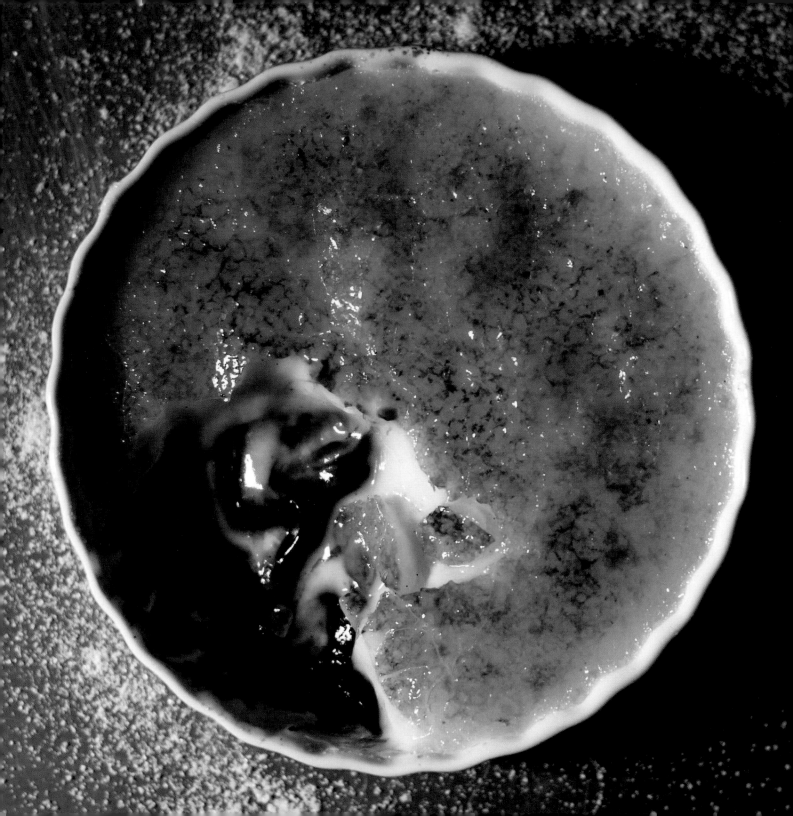

There's a reason crème brûlée is so often on restaurant menus: It tastes over-the-top decadent, but it's actually fairly easy to make. It's also a great opportunity to play with flavors, because you can infuse lots of them into the crème itself. I like to go the triple-layered route: one part crunchy caramel topping, one part silky-smooth custard, and one part melty dark chocolate ganache. Make this the next time you have a dinner party, and prepare for moans around the table.

Makes 6 servings

DIFFICULTY: Medium

MAKE AHEAD AND STORAGE: The un-brûléed crèmes will keep in the refrigerator for up to 3 days.

Black Bottom Crème Brûlée

1. Make the ganache: Place the chocolate in a small heatproof bowl. In a small saucepan, bring the cream to a boil over medium heat. Pour the hot cream over the chocolate and let sit, undisturbed, for 15 to 20 seconds, then stir, beginning in the center of the bowl with small circular motions and widening the circles until the ingredients are uniformly combined and the ganache is smooth.

2. Place six 6-ounce / ¾-cup ramekins or other individual baking dishes on a baking sheet. Spoon 3 tablespoons of the ganache into each ramekin and use a small offset spatula or the back of a teaspoon to spread it into an even layer. Let the ganache stand at room temperature until set.

3. Meanwhile, prepare the crème: Preheat the oven to 325°F / 162°C. Heat a large kettle of water to barely simmering (you can use a pot, but it's a lot easier to pour from a kettle).

4. Combine 181 g / ¾ cup of the cream with the sugar and salt in a medium saucepan. Scrape the seeds from the vanilla bean, add the seeds and pod to the pan, and bring the mixture to a simmer over medium heat.

5. Meanwhile, whisk the egg yolks in a medium heatproof bowl.

6. When the cream mixture has come to a simmer, fish out the vanilla pod (dry it and use it to make vanilla sugar; see Pro Tip, page 97) and slowly pour the hot liquid into the

GANACHE

170 g / 6 oz bittersweet chocolate (I use 60% cacao), chopped

81 g / ⅓ cup heavy cream

CRÈME BRÛLÉE

544 g / 2¼ cups heavy cream

1 vanilla bean, split lengthwise

198 g / 1 cup granulated sugar

1 g / ¼ teaspoon fine sea salt

108 g / 4 large egg yolks, at room temperature

50 g / ¼ cup granulated sugar, or more as needed for finishing

yolks in a thin, steady stream, whisking constantly. Whisk in the remaining 363 g / 1½ cups cream, mixing well.

7. Bake the custard: Transfer the custard to a container with a spout and pour it into the ganache-lined ramekins, filling each one to just below the rim. Transfer the baking sheet to the oven. Carefully pour enough hot water from the kettle into the baking sheet to come about one third of the way up the sides of the ramekins. Bake until the custards are set at the edges but still jiggly in the center, 45 to 55 minutes. Remove the custards from the water bath and cool to room temperature.

8. Caramelize the tops: Sprinkle 8 g / 2 teaspoons of the sugar over each cooled custard and tap and tilt the ramekin to help coat the surface evenly. Use a kitchen torch to caramelize the sugar (at first the sugar will melt, and then it will begin to brown—you're aiming for an even amber color over the entire surface; see page 327 for tips). Serve immediately!

❋ **WHY IT WORKS**
Heating only a portion of the cream to dissolve the sugar means that when you add the remaining cream, it gently cools down the custard, preventing it from melting the ganache too much when you add it to the ramekins and helping to ensure nice clean layers.

★ **PRO TIP**
Traditional crème brûlée can be refrigerated until ready to serve and then caramelized right before serving. Chilling this version will set the chocolate layer firmly. Here's how to resoften it: Just before you caramelize the sugar, use the kitchen torch to warm up the bottom of each dish, or dip each dish in hot water for a few minutes.

Pot de crème is a baked custard that is served cold. It has a silky-smooth texture and is often made with chocolate as the base. It's great served with whipped cream and/or fresh fruit. Caramelized white chocolate will turn any self-proclaimed hater of white chocolate into a serious convert. It takes a little time to make the caramelized chocolate, but the flavor is bonkers good. If you don't want to make it yourself, though, you can replace the white chocolate with an equal amount of Valrhona's Dulcey, which is already caramelized (and so delicious); you can find it online.

Makes 6 servings

DIFFICULTY: Medium

MAKE AHEAD AND STORAGE: The caramelized white chocolate can be stored airtight at room temperature for up to 2 weeks; melt before using. The pots de crème, tightly covered with plastic wrap, can be kept in the refrigerator for up to 3 days.

Caramelized White Chocolate Pots de Crème

1. Preheat the oven to 250°F / 121°C. Line a baking sheet with a silicone baking mat (use parchment paper if you don't have a mat).

2. Spread the white chocolate in a single layer on the lined baking sheet. Transfer the sheet to the oven and bake for 40 to 50 minutes, pulling the baking sheet out every 8 to 10 minutes to stir/spread the white chocolate around. As it melts and then cooks, it will begin to take on a golden color; cook and stir until it's evenly golden brown (it will look like butterscotch). Transfer the caramelized chocolate to a large heatproof bowl and set aside. Increase the oven temperature to 325°F / 162°C.

3. Line the baking sheet with a (fresh) sheet of parchment. Place six 6-ounce ramekins or other individual baking dishes on the baking sheet. Heat a large kettle of water to barely simmering (you can use a pot, but it is a lot easier to pour from a kettle).

4. In a medium saucepan, combine the cream, milk, and salt and bring to a simmer over medium heat.

5. When the cream mixture has come to a simmer, whisk the egg yolks into the warm caramelized white chocolate. Then pour in the hot cream mixture, stirring to combine.

⟶

397 g / 14 oz white chocolate, coarsely chopped

242 g / 1 cup heavy cream

242 g / 1 cup whole milk

4 g / 1 teaspoon fine sea salt

5 g / 1 teaspoon vanilla extract

162 g / 6 large egg yolks, at room temperature

6. Ladle the custard evenly among the prepared ramekins, filling each one to just below the rim. Transfer the baking sheet to the oven and carefully pour enough hot water from the kettle into the baking sheet to come about one third of the way up the sides of the ramekins. Bake until the custards are set at the edges but still jiggly in the center, 45 to 55 minutes.

7. Remove the custards from the water bath and cool for 30 minutes, then transfer to the refrigerator to chill completely, at least 2 hours, before serving.

❄ **WHY IT WORKS**
Pot de crème is thickened by a high ratio of egg yolks and thus requires slow cooking at a relatively low temperature. That way, the egg yolks are slowly coagulated rather than quickly set, resulting in a silky-smooth texture. The white chocolate also firms up the pots de crème as they are chilled, resulting in a custard that's firm but still spoonable.

★ **PRO TIP**
The caramelized white chocolate can be added to any recipe where you might use ordinary white chocolate—and even to many recipes that use milk chocolate or dark chocolate: It's dreamy inside Chewy Oatmeal Cookies (page 36).

I'm a huge rhubarb fan, and I love using it in recipes that traditionally use other tart fruits. Since I usually add lemon zest to my cheesecake, I thought, why not rhubarb? If your rhubarb is very red, the cheesecake will have a gorgeous, blush-pink color; otherwise, you can add a drop or two of red food coloring if you want to get that look.

I borrowed this curl technique for the garnish from my friend Joel Stocks of Holdfast Dining in Portland, Oregon.

I like to make cheesecake at least a day ahead.

Makes one 9-inch cheesecake

DIFFICULTY: Medium

MAKE AHEAD AND STORAGE: The cheesecake can be refrigerated for up to 2 days before serving. Store any leftover slices in an airtight container, refrigerated, for up to 2 days more.

Rhubarb Cheesecake

1. Preheat the oven to 350°F / 175°C, with a rack in the middle.

2. **Make the crust:** In a medium bowl, mix the cookie crumbs and butter together to combine. Press the mixture evenly into the bottom and slightly up the sides of a 9-inch springform pan.

3. Transfer the pan to the oven and bake the crust until lightly golden, 10 to 12 minutes. Let the crust cool to room temperature, then transfer the springform pan to a large roasting pan. Turn the oven temperature down to 325°F / 162°C.

4. **Make the filling:** Heat a large kettle of water to barely simmering (you can use a pot, but it will be a lot easier to pour from a kettle).

5. In a medium saucepan, combine the rhubarb and granulated sugar, tossing to mix. Cook over medium heat, stirring occasionally, until the rhubarb is very tender, 7 to 9 minutes. Let cool slightly, then puree with an immersion blender, or transfer to a regular blender and puree until very smooth. You should end up with 340 g / 1½ cups puree. Let cool to room temperature. (Stir in the vanilla extract, if using.)

CRUST

318 g / 2 cups fine oatmeal cookie crumbs

43 g / 1.5 oz / 3 tablespoons unsalted butter, melted

FILLING

397 g / 3 cups chopped rhubarb

50 g / ¼ cup granulated sugar

907 g / 32 oz cream cheese, at room temperature

248 g / 1¼ cups vanilla sugar (see Pro Tip, page 97), or 298 g / 1½ cups granulated sugar plus 10 g / 2 teaspoons vanilla extract

284 g / 5 large eggs

→

6. Transfer the cooled rhubarb puree to a food processor, add the cream cheese, vanilla sugar, and eggs, and process the mixture until very smooth, 1 to 2 minutes, pausing occasionally to scrape down the bowl.

7. Bake the cheesecake: Pour the custard into the cooled crust. Carefully pour enough hot water from the kettle into the roasting pan to come about halfway up the sides of the springform pan. Transfer the roasting pan to the oven and bake the cheesecake until the edges are set but the center still jiggles slightly when you shake the pan, 60 to 75 minutes.

8. Leave the cheesecake in the water bath to cool for 30 minutes, then transfer the springform pan to the refrigerator and chill thoroughly, at least 2 hours.

9. Meanwhile, make the garnish, if you like: Fill a medium bowl with ice water. Use a sharp peeler to peel long strips from the stalks of rhubarb and transfer them to the ice water—this will help the strips curl up. After about 1 minute in the ice water, drain well on several layers of paper towels.

10. Remove the outer ring of the springform pan and transfer the cheesecake to a platter or cake stand. Just before serving, arrange the rhubarb curls on top of the cheesecake, if desired. Serve the cheesecake chilled.

❋ **WHY IT WORKS**
Cheesecake isn't really a cake at all—it's a baked custard, usually with a crust for textural interest. The eggs slowly coagulate in the oven (protected by a water bath) to set up into the just barely firm, silky-smooth texture cheesecake lovers adore.

★ **PRO TIP**
You can top this cheesecake any way you wish. Make a rhubarb compote or finish it with a layer of lightly sweetened whipped cream.

OPTIONAL GARNISH

4 to 6 stalks rhubarb, trimmed

I like to make rice pudding on rainy days. Something about the starchy-sweet smell of the rice and milk simmering away on the stove puts me in that perfect rainy-day frame of mind. This rice pudding can be served warm (my favorite) or chilled. Just don't skimp on the fruit topping.

Makes 6 servings

DIFFICULTY: Easy

MAKE AHEAD AND STORAGE: The pudding and the peaches can be stored in separate airtight containers in the refrigerator for up to 4 days.

Rice Pudding
with Cardamom Stewed Peaches

1. Make the pudding: Combine the rice, 967 g / 4 cups of the milk, the honey, cardamom pods, star anise, nutmeg, cinnamon stick, and salt in a large saucepan. Scrape the seeds from the vanilla bean and add the seeds and pod to the pan. Bring the mixture to a simmer over medium heat, reduce the heat to low, and cook, stirring frequently, until the rice is tender and has absorbed all the liquid, 15 to 17 minutes.

2. Meanwhile, make the stewed peaches: In a medium saucepan, combine the peaches, honey, cardamom, and water and cook over medium heat, stirring occasionally, until the fruit breaks down and the mixture resembles a chunky sauce or jam, 4 to 5 minutes. Remove from the heat.

3. When the rice is cooked, in a medium bowl, whisk together the egg yolks, sugar, and the remaining 121 g / ½ cup milk. Add the mixture to the pan in a slow, steady stream, stirring constantly to incorporate. Cook the pudding over low heat until it is thick and creamy, 3 to 5 minutes more.

4. The pudding can be served right away. Fish out the vanilla bean, cardamom, star anise, and cinnamon stick

PUDDING

156 g / ¾ cup short-grain rice, such as Arborio or Carnaroli

1.08 kg / 4½ cups whole milk

43 g / 2 tablespoons honey

2 whole cardamom pods

1 whole star anise

Scant 1 g / ¼ teaspoon freshly grated nutmeg

One 2-inch-long cinnamon stick

1 g / ¼ teaspoon fine sea salt

½ vanilla bean, split lengthwise

81 g / 3 large egg yolks

66 g / ⅓ cup granulated sugar

⟶

Variation

Rice Pudding Tarts: The rice pudding can be used to make individual tarts (see the photo on page 198). Preheat the oven to 425°F / 218°C with racks in the upper and lower thirds. Make triple the Whole Wheat Pie Dough recipe on page 192 and divide it into 12 equal disks. Working with one disk at a time, roll out each disk on a lightly floured surface into an oval about ¼ inch thick. Scoop 112 g / heaping ¼ cup rice pudding into the center of each oval, leaving about 1 inch of exposed dough on sides. Fold the exposed dough up around the rice pudding, slide the tarts onto two parchment-lined baking sheets, and bake for 20 to 23 minutes.

from the pudding, and remove the cardamom from the jam. Spoon the pudding into serving dishes and top with the peaches. Or serve the pudding chilled—when it's done, transfer it to a shallow container, cover with plastic wrap placed directly against the surface, and refrigerate until chilled, at least 2 hours. Serve with the peaches, also chilled.

❄ **WHY IT WORKS**

Rice pudding is naturally thickened by the starches in the rice itself, which are released through slow cooking and steady stirring. The last-minute addition of egg yolks also helps thicken the mixture, but it mostly provides richness and creaminess.

★ **PRO TIP**

Rice pudding can be tweaked in a million different ways. Try adding 11 g / 2 tablespoons cocoa powder or 6 g / 1 tablespoon citrus zest to the milk in this recipe, or swapping out some of the spices. I also love infusing the milk with 12 g / 2 tablespoons coffee or tea before adding the rice (see page 325).

STEWED PEACHES

170 g / 1 cup peeled, pitted, and diced peaches

43 g / 2 tablespoons honey

3 or 4 whole cardamom pods

15 g / 2 tablespoons water

Soufflés have a reputation for being harder to pull off than waking up early without pressing the snooze button three times. Truth time: They *are* delicate, but they are totally accessible. This recipe is made the classic way, with a base of pastry cream, which you can make ahead. Then all you have to do at the last minute is whip up the meringue, fold it into the pastry cream, and bake.

Makes 8 individual soufflés

DIFFICULTY: Medium

MAKE AHEAD AND STORAGE: The pastry cream can be refrigerated for up to 3 days.

Honey Soufflés

1. Make the pastry cream: In a medium saucepan, combine the milk and honey. Scrape the seeds from the vanilla bean and add the seeds and pod to the pan. Bring the mixture to a simmer over medium heat.

2. Meanwhile, in a medium heatproof bowl, whisk together the cornstarch and sugar.

3. When the milk has come to a simmer, turn the heat down to medium-low. Whisk the egg yolks into the cornstarch-and-sugar mixture, mixing well to make a thick but smooth paste, then pour one third of the hot milk mixture into the yolk mixture in a slow, thin stream, whisking constantly to combine. Pour the yolk mixture into the pan and cook, whisking constantly (you can switch to a silicone spatula once it begins to thicken), until the pastry cream gets very thick and comes to first boil (a large bubble comes to the surface in the center), 3 to 5 minutes.

4. Strain the pastry cream through a fine-mesh strainer into a large heatproof bowl. Cover with plastic wrap pressed directly against the surface and refrigerate until thoroughly chilled, at least 2 hours. Remove the vanilla bean.

5. Make the soufflés: Preheat the oven to 375°F / 190°C, with a rack in the middle. Generously butter six 4-ounce ramekins. Scoop a few teaspoons of sugar (or granulated honey) into each ramekin, rotating it to coat the bottom and sides. Place the ramekins on a baking sheet.

HONEY PASTRY CREAM

363 g / 1½ cups whole milk

104 g / ⅓ cup honey

½ vanilla bean, split lengthwise

28 g / ¼ cup cornstarch

50 g / ¼ cup granulated sugar

162 g / 6 large egg yolks, at room temperature

FINISHED SOUFFLÉS

Room-temperature butter and granulated sugar or granulated honey (see page 268), to coat the ramekins

179 g / 6 large egg whites

Scant 1 g / ¼ teaspoon cream of tartar

66 g / ⅓ cup granulated sugar

⟶

6. Remove the pastry cream from the refrigerator.

7. In the bowl of a stand mixer fitted with the whisk attachment (or in a large bowl, using a hand mixer), whip the egg whites and cream of tartar on medium speed until slightly foamy. Raise the speed to high, gradually add the sugar in a thin stream, and continue whipping until the meringue reaches medium peaks, 5 to 7 minutes.

8. Temper the pastry cream by folding in about one quarter of the meringue, mixing well. Add the remaining meringue in 2 more additions, gently folding just until incorporated. (Try to use as few strokes as possible to accomplish this, but make sure the mixture is homogeneous.)

9. Divide the mixture among the ramekins (I use a large ladle for this). Transfer the baking sheet to the oven and bake the soufflés, undisturbed, until they have risen about 1 inch above the rims of the ramekins, 30 to 35 minutes. Try your hardest not to open the oven door—use your oven light to check their progress. Pull the soufflés out when they are tall and nicely golden and shiny on top, and serve immediately.

✳ **WHY IT WORKS**

Soufflés rise thanks to the whipped egg whites, which trap tons of air bubbles as they are aerated. In the oven, the meringue pushes up the pastry cream. Eventually the egg white proteins coagulate and set, and the resulting dessert is as gorgeously tall and light as can be!

★ **PRO TIP**

Soufflés are made even better by a drizzle of warm sauce just as they are served. For this soufflé, I use Honey Caramel (page 100—make a double batch), Crème Anglaise (page 335), or warm Ganache (page 345). For bonus points, try a combo!

Want a soufflé that will never, ever fall? Make a frozen soufflé! The base for this light and airy wonder is a curd made from pomegranate juice. It's delicious and very flavorful, but it doesn't have a bright red color, so if you that's what you want, add a drop or two of red food coloring—or just dress it up with plenty of pomegranate arils (seeds).

Makes 6 individual soufflés

DIFFICULTY: Medium

MAKE AHEAD AND STORAGE: The soufflés, once frozen, can be covered with plastic wrap and stored in the freezer for up to 1 week.

Frozen Pomegranate Soufflés

1. Place six 6-ounce ramekins on a baking sheet. Cut six strips of parchment or wax paper long enough to wrap around the ramekins and wide enough to extend 2 inches above the rims. Wrap a strip of paper tightly around each ramekin and secure with tape.

2. In a medium saucepan, combine 198 g / 1 cup of the granulated sugar, the pomegranate juice, egg yolks, and salt and heat over medium-low heat, stirring constantly, until the sugar dissolves. Turn the heat down to low and cook, stirring constantly with a silicone spatula (be sure to get into the corners of the pan), until the mixture is thick enough to coat the back of the spatula, 10 to 12 minutes.

3. Strain the curd into a shallow dish and cover it with plastic wrap pressed directly against the surface. Refrigerate until thoroughly chilled, at least 2 hours.

4. In the bowl of a stand mixer fitted with the whisk attachment (or in a large bowl, using a hand mixer), whip the cream and vanilla to medium peaks. Transfer to another bowl and refrigerate.

5. Wash and dry the bowl and whisk (or beaters). Whip the egg whites on medium speed until slightly foamy, 1 to 2 minutes, then raise the speed to medium-high and whip to soft peaks, 4 to 5 minutes. Gradually add the remaining 99 g / ½ cup granulated

298 g / 1½ cups granulated sugar

242 g / 1 cup pure pomegranate juice

215 g / 8 large egg yolks

2 g / ½ teaspoon fine sea salt

242 g / 1 cup heavy cream

5 g / 1 teaspoon vanilla extract

238 g / 8 large egg whites

Pomegranate seeds, for garnish

Powdered sugar, for dusting

sugar and continue whipping until the meringue reaches medium peaks, 1 to 2 minutes more.

6. Transfer the chilled curd to a large bowl. Gently fold in one quarter of the whipped cream, mixing well, to lighten the curd. Add the remaining cream in 2 or 3 additions, folding gently just until combined. Fold in one quarter of the meringue until thoroughly incorporated. Then add the remaining meringue in 2 or 3 additions, folding more gently.

7. Ladle or scoop the soufflé mixture into the prepared ramekins, filling each one all the way to the top of the parchment paper. Use a small offset spatula to gently level the surface if you want a smooth top.

8. Freeze the soufflés for at least 4 hours.

9. To serve, peel away the parchment paper. Garnish each soufflé with 1 to 2 tablespoons pomegranate seeds and sift some powdered sugar over the surface.

✳ **WHY IT WORKS**

The concept of a frozen soufflé is similar to a baked one—aerators are folded into a custard base to create an airy texture. But freezing, instead of baking, sets them into place.

★ **PRO TIP**

Instead of using individual ramekins, you can make this soufflé in a soufflé dish or other freezer-safe serving dish that holds at least 1½ quarts.

I've long held a soft spot for sweet cream ice cream. Yeah—I'm that girl who really digs simple ice cream flavors. Sweet cream is just sweetened cream and milk turned into ice cream, and it's sinfully rich, yet clean and delicious. I put in a tiny dash of vanilla just to round out the flavor. This ice cream is meant to go with something; it's ideal for pie à la mode or your next really good fruit coulis, or maybe even your new favorite milk shake.

Note that the custard needs to be thoroughly chilled overnight in the refrigerator before it goes into the ice cream machine. (For more ice cream tips, see page 328.)

Makes 1.3 kg / 1½ quarts

DIFFICULTY: Easy

MAKE AHEAD AND STORAGE: The ice cream can be frozen for up to 3 weeks.

Sweet Cream Ice Cream

1. Place a quart-sized canning jar (or similar-size vessel) in a large bowl. Pile ice around the canning jar and pour enough water into the bowl to come about three quarters of the way up the sides of the jar.

2. In a medium saucepan, bring the cream, milk, 99 g / ½ cup of the sugar, and the salt to a simmer over medium heat.

3. Meanwhile, in a medium heatproof bowl, whisk the yolks and the remaining 99 g / ½ cup sugar together.

4. When the cream mixture has come to a simmer, turn the heat down to medium-low. Pour one quarter of the hot cream mixture into the yolk mixture, whisking constantly to combine, then pour the yolk mixture back into the pan, whisking constantly. Cook, stirring constantly with a silicone spatula, until the custard is thick enough to coat the back of the spatula, 3 to 4 minutes. Stir in the vanilla.

5. Strain the mixture into the canning jar and let cool to room temperature in the ice bath. Cover the jar and transfer to the refrigerator to chill overnight.

6. Transfer the chilled custard to an ice cream maker and churn according to the manufacturer's instructions. When the ice cream is thick and frozen, transfer it to storage containers with tight-fitting lids and freeze for at least 1 hour before serving.

846 g / 3½ cups heavy cream

363 g / 1½ cups whole milk

198 g / 1 cup granulated sugar

1 g / ¼ teaspoon fine sea salt

162 g / 6 large egg yolks

1 g / ¼ teaspoon vanilla extract

Variations

Brown Sugar Sweet Cream Ice Cream: Replace the granulated sugar with 213 g / 1 cup packed dark brown sugar. Increase the salt to 3 g / ¾ teaspoon.

Fruity Sweet Cream Ice Cream: When you remove the ice cream from the machine, quickly fold in 425 g / 1¼ cups of your favorite jam or preserves.

Stracciatella: When the ice cream has finished churning, drizzle 85 g / 3 oz / ½ cup melted chocolate (any kind!) into the ice cream maker and churn for a few moments more until the chocolate is distributed and frozen (it will form streaks and chunks throughout the ice cream).

❊ WHY IT WORKS

Like most ice creams, this recipe starts off with a base of crème anglaise, but the custard is churned into a smooth frozen dessert.

★ PRO TIP

If you want to, you can turn this into vanilla ice cream—just scrape the seeds from a split vanilla bean and add the seeds and pod to the cream-and-milk mixture in step 2 (when you strain the custard, rinse and dry the pod and use it for vanilla sugar; see Pro Tip, page 97). Or you can swirl in other ingredients when the ice cream finishes churning—smashed fresh fruit works well.

My first bite of gelato was on the streets of Rome, when I was fifteen years old, and I remember thinking it made ice cream taste like a half-eaten bag of stale, day-old bread. OK, maybe that's not fair to ice cream, but gelato is undeniably denser and richer. (For an explanation of what makes gelato different, see Why It Works.)

Note that the custard needs to chill overnight in the refrigerator before it goes into the ice cream machine. (For more ice cream tips, see page 328.)

Makes 1.3 kg / 1½ quarts

DIFFICULTY: Easy

MAKE AHEAD AND STORAGE: The gelato can be frozen for up to 3 weeks.

Spicy Chocolate Gelato
with Cocoa Nibs

1. Place a quart-sized canning jar (or similar-size vessel) in a large bowl. Pile ice around the jar and pour enough water into the bowl to come about three quarters of the way up the sides of the jar.

2. In a medium saucepan, combine the milk, cream, and 99 g / ½ cup of the sugar. Scrape the seeds from the vanilla bean and add them to the pan (use the pod for Vanilla Sugar; see Pro Tip, page 97). Bring the mixture to a simmer over medium heat.

3. Meanwhile, whisk the remaining 99 g / ½ cup sugar, the cocoa powder, salt, and cayenne together in a medium heatproof bowl. Whisk in the eggs.

4. When the milk mixture has come to a simmer, turn the heat down to medium-low. Pour one quarter of the hot cream mixture into the yolk mixture, whisking constantly. Pour the yolk mixture into the pan and cook, stirring constantly with a silicone spatula, until the mixture is thick enough to coat the back of the spatula, 3 to 4 minutes.

5. Take the pan off the heat and stir in the chocolate until fully melted. Strain the custard into the canning jar and let cool to room temperature in the ice bath, then cover the jar and transfer to the refrigerator to chill overnight.

484 g / 2 cups whole milk

121 g / ½ cup heavy cream

198 g / 1 cup granulated sugar

1 vanilla bean, split lengthwise

64 g / ¾ cup unsweetened cocoa powder

2 g / ½ teaspoon fine sea salt

2 g / ¾ teaspoon cayenne pepper, or more to taste

135 g / 5 large egg yolks

113 g / 4 oz semisweet chocolate, finely chopped

71 g / ½ cup cocoa nibs (see Resources, page 369)

6. Transfer the chilled custard to an ice cream maker and churn according to the manufacturer's instructions. Just before the gelato is finished (5 minutes before the ice cream maker indicates the end of mix time if your ice cream maker dictates times, or when it reaches the fully thick and frozen stage), add the cocoa nibs, then continue churning until the gelato is thick and frozen. Transfer the gelato to storage containers with tight-fitting lids and freeze for at least 1 hour before serving.

❄ **WHY IT WORKS**

Gelato is traditionally made with less cream and more milk than ice cream is, and the lower amount of fat allows the other flavors to really shine. Professionally made gelato is also churned at a slower rate, meaning it's denser and has less incorporated air than ice cream. Some ice cream makers have different speed settings based on the type of ice cream you're churning, but even if yours doesn't, this recipe will make silky-smooth gelato.

★ **PRO TIP**

Pair the gelato with Flourless Cocoa Cookies (page 30) for ice cream sandwiches.

This ice cream is easy to make because there is no custard base—it's just a mixture of sweetened dairy with plenty of fruit. It's the prettiest color ever, and when I'm feeling particularly ambitious, I'll have an ice cream party with multiple fruit variations (see Pro Tip). It's about the best thing to happen to summer since swimming pools.

Note that the custard needs to chill overnight in the refrigerator before it goes into the ice cream machine. (For more ice cream tips, see page 328.)

Makes 1.7 kg / 2 quarts

DIFFICULTY: Easy

MAKE AHEAD AND STORAGE: The ice cream can be frozen for up to 3 weeks.

Blueberry Ice Cream

1. In a medium saucepan, combine the blueberries and sugar. Scrape the seeds from the vanilla bean and add the seeds and pod to the pan. Bring the mixture to a simmer over medium heat, then reduce the heat to medium-low and continue cooking until the blueberries have softened and released their juices, about 10 minutes.

2. Transfer the blueberry mixture to a blender (or use an immersion blender) and puree (vanilla bean and all!) until smooth. Strain the mixture into a large bowl.

3. Stir in the cream and milk, mixing until uniformly combined. Transfer the mixture to the refrigerator to chill overnight.

4. Transfer the chilled mixture to an ice cream maker and churn according to the manufacturer's instructions until the ice cream is thick and frozen. You can serve this immediately, or transfer it to storage containers with tight-fitting lids and freeze until ready to serve.

✳ **WHY IT WORKS**
This type of eggless ice cream is known as Philadelphia style. It's lovely and rich, but a bit icier than traditional ice cream.

★ **PRO TIP**
You can replace the blueberries with other kinds of fruit. Berries and sliced stone fruit work particularly well; raspberries, peaches, and cherries are some of my favorites here.

567 g / 4 cups blueberries

248 g / 1¼ cups granulated sugar

1 vanilla bean, split lengthwise

725 g / 3 cups heavy cream

484 g / 2 cups whole milk

Resources

Here are some of the specialized products I use throughout this book, and where I purchased them. I've used these products a ton and love them—they all have a place in my kitchen. Remember, though, that there are tons of options out there, and you can and should use things you like best!

Black Cocoa: kingarthurflour.com

Black Raspberries (frozen): frankfarms.com

Cake Stands: fishseddy.com

Canelé Molds: amazon.com (DD-life silicone 8-cavity canelé mold)

Cookie Scoops: dreamchefs.com (best 18/8 stainless steel ice cream/cookie dough scoopers, set of 4)

Disposable Pastry Bags: amazon.com (Ateco 18-inch disposable plastic pastry bags)

Espresso Powder: kingarthurflour.com

Freestanding Baking Cups: bakeitpretty.com (mini brown floret baking cups)

Granulated Honey: amazon.com (Barry Farm honey granules)

Heirloom Cake Stands: Aheirloom.com

Ice Cream Maker: brevilleusa.com

Kitchen Scale: amazon.com (Primo digital kitchen scale)

Nordic Ware Cake Pans: nordicware.com

Piping Tip Set: amazon.com (Ateco 55-piece stainless steel decorating set and other smaller sets)

Pizzelle Iron: kingarthurflour.com

Precut Parchment Paper Sheets and Parchment Cake Circles: kingarthurflour.com

Acknowledgments

To **Rux Martin and her team at Houghton Mifflin Harcourt**, thank you for this opportunity and for coaching me to the finish line!

To **Doe Coover**, for everything that's happened from the time we first met in Savannah until right now.

To **Miriam Harris**, for her sharp eye, and to **Judith Sutton**, for her brilliant help in making my book so much better.

To **my leading ladies: Michelle Needham** and **Michelle Holden**, for your support and kindness, and for being the sisters I had always hoped for. To my **Aunt Connee**, who encouraged me to taste the world and appreciate life. To **Sarah and Abby**, for your friendship. To my **Grandma Jeanne**, who was my best friend, confidant, and partner in pie-baking crime all rolled into one—I couldn't have done any of this without her. And to **my mama**, who tested nearly every recipe in this book and provides constant support. Thank you for raising me to be like you: strong, determined, independent, and a little bit of a badass.

To **my main men:** My older brothers, each of whom inspires me more than I can say. To **Matt**, for his photography. To **Jason**, for his always amazing work, especially the illustrations that truly bring this book to life. To **Willie**, for being my friend as well as my sibling, for your general hilarity, and for being my food science consultant. And to **my dad**, for always supporting and guiding me. You made the world seem welcoming and lofty goals seem reachable—you brought me music and poetry and guiding words, and you always, always made me work harder and strive to be better.

To **Maisy, Arlo, Joci, and Lucy**. You bring me joy even when you don't know it. Thank you for your always honest taste-testing.

To **Mary Howe and Rick Stein**, for being wonderful friends, offering great and gentle guidance since grade eight, and sharing countless meals—and to Mary, for naming this book.

To **Dan and Susie Huffman**, for being tireless taste-testers and great friends, and for letting me play in your backyard even though I'm a grown-up.

To **Maggie and Chris Wheeler, Liliana Cabrera, Evan Coben, Sarah "Honey" Daniels, Chris Hurte, Terri Katan, and Rachel Oliver**, for your friendship, counseling, brainstorming sessions, and equally important relaxation sessions.

To **Nathalie Fischer**, for giving me my first job. To **Francesco Tonelli**, for the next. I have learned so much from you both.

To **Ben Fink**, for your friendship and guidance over the past ten years.

To **Rose Levy Beranbaum**, for your counseling, guidance, and friendship. You're the best pen pal I could ever ask for.

To **Irena Chalmers**, an amazing teacher and the best mentor I could have ever hoped for.

To **some amazing instructors** whose wisdom has stuck with me day after day: **Dieter Schorner, Peter Greweling, Fred Brash, Richard Coppedge, Todd Knaster, Eric Kastel, and Francisco Migoya.** I'm so lucky to have been your student!

To **Aubrey Johnson**, for assisting me during the book announcement.

To the brilliant folks behind Food52: To **Amanda Hesser and Merrill Stubbs,** thank you for your support and for creating a place that felt like home from the first time I clicked. To **Marian Bull, Sarah Jampel, and Caroline Lange,** for editing my articles and leading me to great and delicious heights. To **James Ransom, Mark Weinberg, and Bobbi Lin,** for incredible images that make me passionate about my work. To **Kristen Miglore, Kenzi Wilbur, Ali Slagle,** and the rest of the editorial staff, for your support, guidance, and honest taste-testing.

To **Alexis Anderson,** whose timely response to a tentative request played more of a role than she'll ever know.

To **Mary Kate McGrath and Lauren Gniazdowski,** for your never-ending support, enthusiasm, and hunger for more.

To **Josh and Lauren** and their amazing team at Prop Workshop. And to their amazingly talented daughter, **Aliza Simmons** of Henry Street Studio.

To **Amy at AHeirloom,** for a bounty of my favorite cake stands ever.

To **Fishs Eddy,** for lending me a bit of whimsy.

To the lovely **Jennifer May:** Your talent is astounding. I admire your work and feel so lucky to have had you shoot mine.

To **Mandy Maxwell and Kaitlin Wayne,** for dropping your lives and coming to camp cookbook for nearly two weeks. You're aces.

And, finally, to **Derek Laughren.** Thank you for your tireless taste-testing, unwavering confidence in me, and all of the pep talks. I couldn't have done this without you. You make food taste better, light seem brighter, and everything go more smoothly (and no one makes me laugh harder). Thank you—a lot, a lot.

Index

Note: Page references in *italics* indicate photographs or illustrations.

A

all-buttah pie dough, 188–90, *189*
all-purpose flour, about, 14
almond(s)
    brownie pie, *208*, 209
    cream tart, *232*, 233–34
    Danish bread, *298*, 299–300
    dulce de leche ice cream pie, *205*,
        206–7
    pound cake with raspberry swirl, *97*,
        98–99
American buttercream, 134
any-fruit or -nut scones, 256–57, *257*
any-nut tart in phyllo crust, 235–37
apple
    butter, making your own, 225
    butter pie, 225
    cinnamon scones, 257
    pie, cider-caramel, 222–24, *223*
    pie, molasses, 225
    tart, brioche, 288–89, *289*
apricot
    cream cake, 121–23, *122*
    -oat scones, 257

B

baked custards, about, 320
baking powder, about, 18
baking soda, about, 18
baking stones, for pies, 181
baklava muffins, *266*, 267–68
banana cake with cocoa nibs and Nutella
    swirl, 104–5, *110*
bars
    about, 27–28
    butterscotch blondies, 65–67, *66*
    cakey brownies, 70–71
    coconut tres leches, *73*, 74–75
    cream cheese swirl brownies, 69
    fudgy brownies, 68–69, *69*
    glazing, 28
    lining pans for, 27
    peanut butter swirl brownies, 69
    raspberry-ripple crunch, 72–73,
        73
    regular blondies, 67
    salted caramel swirl brownies,
        69
basic glazed doughnuts, *284*, 285

basic yellow sponge cake with dark
    chocolate Italian buttercream,
    148–50
Bavarian cream, defined, 322
beignets
    fried, draining, 252
    frying tips, 252
    ricotta, 281–82, *282*
bench knife, 248
berry(ies)
    black-and-blue scones, 257
    blackberry pavlovas, 274–76, *275*
    black raspberry buttercream, 120
    black raspberry cupcakes, 118–20, *119*
    blueberry cream roulade, 145–47, *146*
    blueberry ice cream, 366, *367*
    eggnog panna cotta with raspberry
        sauce, 342–43, *343*
    galette, double-crust, 200–202, *201*
    glazed waffle cookies, 58–59, *59*
    raspberry-ripple crunch bars, 72–73,
        73
    strawberry cream biscuits, 261–62,
        262

berry(ies) *(continued)*
    strawberry not-so-short cake, 114–16, *115*
    vanilla strawberry mousse cake, 160–62, *161*
biscuits
    buttermilk, 258–59
    crème fraîche, 260, *262*
    cutting out, 252
    drop, 263
    strawberry cream, 261–62, *262*
black-and-blue scones, 257
blackberry(ies)
    black-and-blue scones, 257
    pavlovas, 274–76, *275*
black bottom crème brûlée, *344*, 345–46
black raspberry
    buttercream, 120
    cupcakes, 118–20, *119*
blind-baking
    directions for, 168–69
    a single piecrust, 191
    a tart crust, 197
blondies
    butterscotch, 65–67, *66*
    regular, 67
blueberry(ies)
    black-and-blue scones, 257
    cream roulade, 145–47, *146*
    ice cream, 366, *367*
borders and edges, piping, 92
bourbon-rosemary peach pie, 229–31, *230*
braided lattice, 180–183, *183*
braids, for piecrust edges, 183–84
bread flour, about, 15
breads. *See* brioche
brioche
    almond Danish bread, *298*, 299–300
    apple tart, 288–89, *289*
    figgy pull-apart bread, *290*, 291–92

    rolls, 286–87, *287*
    rolls, faux-laminated maple sugar, 295–97, *296*
    versatility of, 14
brown-butter butterscotch sauce, 67
brownie pie, *208*, 209
brownies
    cakey, 70–71
    cream cheese swirl, 69
    fudgy, 68–69, *69*
    peanut butter swirl, 69
    salted caramel swirl, 69
brown sugar
    preventing from drying out, 41
    shortbread, 40–41
    sweet cream ice cream, 363, *363*
brûléing technique, 327–29
bulk fermentation, 249
Bundt cakes, decorating, 84–85
butter
    cutting up, for pie doughs, 167
    softening, 19
    and sugar, creaming, 78
buttercream
    American, 134
    black raspberry, 120
    caramel pudding, 152
    dark chocolate Italian, 149
    lemon curd, 158
    reconstituting, 151
buttermilk
    biscuits, 258–59
    bringing to room temperature, 19
    lemon loaf, glazed, *97*, 102–3
    making your own, 103
butterscotch
    blondies, 65–67, *66*
    brown-butter sauce, 67
    pudding, salty, 334

C

cake flour, about, 15
cakes
    adjusting recipes for different sized cake pans, 80
    almond pound, with raspberry swirl, *97*, 98–99
    alternating flavor layers, 83
    apricot cream, 121–23, *122*
    banana, with cocoa nibs and Nutella swirl, 104–5, *110*
    basic yellow sponge, with dark chocolate Italian buttercream, 148–50
    blueberry cream roulade, 145–47, *146*
    Bundt, decorating, 84–85
    caramel, 142–44, *143*
    caramel corn layer, 152–55, *153*
    chocolate "high-ratio" sheet, *130*, 131–32
    corn, sweet, 117
    cutting into layers, 82–83
    Dame's Rocket, 139–41, *140*
    decorating, 84–94
    devil's food (my favorite birthday cake), 133–34, *135*
    domed, leveling, 82
    fixing a broken batter, 81
    frosting techniques, 87–88
    ginger pear, 109–11, *110*
    glazed lemon buttermilk loaf, *97*, 102–3
    glazing techniques, 86–87
    grapefruit crepe, 269–70, *271*
    ice cream, about, 330
    lavender petits fours, 129
    layer, assembling, 83–84
    lemon-love chiffon layer, 156–59, *157*
    mini, glazed, 106–8, *107*
    mixing batter for, 78–79

mocha, with coffee–white chocolate
    ganache, *136*, 137–38
mocha, with ganache, 138
orange blossom petits fours, 129
overmixing batter, note about, 79
pb & j whoopie pies, 47–49, *48*
piping frosting on, 89–94
preparing ingredients for, 79
preparing pans for, 78
removing air pockets from batters, 82
rose petits fours, *126*, 127–28
spatula finishes, 88–89
strawberry not-so-short, 114–16, *115*
tomato upside-down, *110*, 112–13
vanilla pound, 96–97, *97*
vanilla strawberry mousse, 160–62,
    161
without frosting, decorating, 84
see also cupcakes
cakey brownies, 70–71
canelés, 272–73, *273*
caramel
    cake, 142–44, *143*
    -cider apple pie, 222–24, *223*
    fudge frosting, 142–44
    -honey glaze, 100–101
    pudding buttercream, 152
    salted, swirl brownies, 69
    salted, –swirled meringues, 53–54, *55*
    sauce, salted, 54
caramel corn layer cake, 152–55, *153*
caramelization process, 17
caramelized white chocolate pots de
    crème, 347–49, *348*
caramel pudding buttercream, 152
cardamom stewed peaches, rice pudding
    with, 353–55, *354*
chalazae, about, 327
Chantilly cream, defined, 322
cheater's whipped cream, *115*, 116

checkerboard edge for crusts, 176, *176*
cheese. *See* cream cheese; mascarpone;
    ricotta
cheesecake, rhubarb, 350–52, *351*
cherry
    -cheese Danish, 312–13, *313*
    cobblers, mini, 264, *265*
chevron fork crimp, 174, *176*
chewy chocolate chip cookies, 32–33, *33*
chewy oatmeal cookies, 36
chiboust
    defined, 322
    recipe for, 341
chiffon foaming method, 78
chiffon pies, about, 173
chocolate
    black bottom crème brûlée, *344*,
        345–46
    brownie pie, *208*, 209
    cakey brownies, 70–71
    chip cookies, chewy, 32–33, *33*
    chip cookies, crispy, 34–35
    cream cheese swirl brownies, 69
    cream pie with whipped peanut butter
        cream, *208*, 210–11
    crust, hazelnut pie with, *208*, 212
    dark, Italian buttercream, 149
    devil's food cake (my favorite birthday
        cake), 133–34, *135*
    devil's food cupcakes, 134
    double, macarons, 44–46, *45*
    dulce de leche ice cream pie, *205*,
        206–7
    flourless cocoa cookies, 30, *31*
    fudgy brownies, 68–69, *69*
    gelato, spicy, with cocoa nibs, 364–65
    -glazed doughnuts, 285
    -glazed 'shmallow grahams, 62–64, *64*
    "high-ratio" sheet cake, *130*, 131–32
    –macadamia nut scones, 257

macaron s'mores, 46, *46*
mocha cake with coffee–white
    chocolate ganache, *136*, 137–38
mocha cake with ganache, 138
mousse, 336, *337*
palmiers, 306, *307*
peanut butter swirl brownies, 69
peppermint–devil's food hi-hat
    cupcakes, 124–25, *125*
pie dough, 192
pizzelle, 56–57, *57*
press-in dough, 197
pudding, *332*, 334
puff pastry, *304*, 305
raspberry-ripple crunch bars, 72–73,
    73
salted caramel swirl brownies, 69
stracciatella ice cream, 363, *363*
sweet cream tartlets, 240–42, *241*
whipped ganache, 132
see also white chocolate
cider-caramel apple pie, 222–24, *223*
cinnamon apple scones, 257
cobblers, mini cherry, 264, *265*
cocoa nibs
    and Nutella swirl, banana cake with,
        104–5, *110*
    raspberry-ripple crunch bars, 72–73,
        73
    spicy chocolate gelato with, 364–65
coconut
    devil's food cake (my favorite birthday
        cake), 133–34, *135*
    devil's food cupcakes, 134
    -glazed doughnuts, 285
    macaroons, peachy, 42–43, *43*
    tres leches bars, *73*, 74–75
coffee
    mocha cake with coffee–white
        chocolate ganache, *136*, 137–38

coffee (*continued*)

mocha cake with ganache, 138

–white chocolate ganache, 137

cold-filled tarts, about, 186

cold foaming method, 78

cold-set custards, about, 320

combination foaming method, 79

Concord grape pie, 226–28, *227*

cookie crusts, press-in, 170

cookies

brown sugar shortbread, 40–41

chocolate chip, chewy, 32–33, *33*

chocolate chip, crispy, 34–35

chocolate-glazed 'shmallow grahams, 62–64, *64*

chocolate pizzelle, 56–57, *57*

cookie scoops for, 23

cut-out, about, 22–23

double chocolate macarons, 44–46, *45*

drizzling icing over, 28

drop, about, 22

drop, how to stuff, 25

dunking, in icing, 28

enrobing, with icing, 28

fillings for, 26–27

flourless cocoa, 30, *31*

icebox, about, 23–24

Italian custard (genovesi), 50–52, *51*

lemon-rosemary madeleines, 60–61, *61*

lime sablé sandwiches, 37–38, *39*

macaron s'mores, 46, *46*

makeshift molds and stamps for, 24

making ice cream sandwiches with, 330

mixing doughs and batters, 22

oatmeal, chewy, 36

pb & j whoopie pies, 47–49, *48*

peachy coconut macaroons, 42–43, *43*

salted caramel–swirled meringues, 53–54, *55*

sandwich, about, 26–27

shaped, about, 24–25

vanilla macarons, 46

vanilla pizzelle, 57

waffle, glazed, 58–59, *59*

see also bars

corn

cakes, sweet, 117

caramel, layer cake, 152–55, *153*

cream cheese

cheater's whipped cream, *115*, 116

cherry-cheese Danish, 312–13, *313*

Dame's Rocket cake, 139–41, *140*

lime sablé sandwiches, 37–38, *39*

pie dough, 192

raspberry-ripple crunch bars, 72–73, *73*

rhubarb cheesecake, 350–52, *351*

swirl brownies, 69

cream pies, about, 173

cream puffs, 277–80, *278*

cream(s)

bringing to room temperature, 19

and custards, types of, 322–24

(basic custard) defined, 322

whipped, defined, 324

crème Anglaise, defined, 322

crème brûlée

black bottom, *344*, 345–46

brûléing, 327–29

defined, 322

crème caramel, defined, 322

crème fraîche biscuits, 260, *262*

cremeux, defined, 322

crepe cake, grapefruit, 269–70, *271*

crispy chocolate chip cookies, 34–35

crisscrossing fork crimp, 174, *176*

croissants, spiced, *313*, 314–17, *315*

crumb crusts, 169–70

cupcakes

black raspberry, 118–20, *119*

decorating, 85

devil's food, 134

honey pound, with honey-caramel glaze, 100–101, *119*

peppermint–devil's food hi-hat, 124–25, *125*

curd

defined, 323

grapefruit, 339, *339*

lemon, 338, *339*

lemon, buttercream, 158

lime, 339, *339*

orange, 339

passionfruit, 339

pear, 339

custard

-based desserts and ices, frozen, types of, 325

cookies, Italian (genovesi), 50–52, *51*

pies, about, 171–73

piping, 327

tarts, about, 186

custards

basic methods, 320

brûléing, 327–29

and creams, types of, 322–24

decorating with drizzles and splatters, 329

determining doneness, 323

dressing up, 326

infusing with flavor, 325

preparing, guidelines for, 321

sifting powder over surface, 329

starch-thickened, notes about, 16, 320

straining, 327

unmolding, 326–27
cut-out cookies, about, 22–23
cutouts, for pies, 184–86

D

Dame's Rocket cake, 139–41, *140*
Danish, cherry-cheese, 312–13, *313*
decorative fork crimp, 174, *176*
devil's food cake (my favorite birthday
    cake), 133–34, *135*
devil's food cupcakes, 134
diagonal lattice, 180, *182*
digital scales, 79
diplomat cream
    defined, 323
    recipe for, 341
DIY sprinkles, 95, *95*
dots, piping, 90–91
double chocolate macarons, 44–46, *45*
double-crust berry galette, 200–202,
    201
doughnuts
    basic glazed, *284*, 285
    chocolate-glazed, 285
    coconut-glazed, 285
    fried, draining, 252
    fruit-glazed, 285
    frying tips, 252
    yeast, 283–85, *284*
drips, for decorating cakes, 86
drizzles
    decorating cakes with, 86–87
    decorating custards with, 329
    decorating tarts with, 186
drop biscuits, 263
drop cookies
    about, 22
    stuffing, with ingredients, 25
dulce de leche ice cream pie, *205*, 206–7

E

edible garnishes, 94
eggnog panna cotta with raspberry sauce,
    342–43, *343*
egg(s)
    amylase enzyme in, 16
    bringing to room temperature, 19
    leavening ability, 16
    "peak" whipping stages, 16
    and sugar, foaming, 78–79
    unique properties of, 16
    whites of, whipping, 16
    white strands (chalazae), in custards,
      327
    whole, whipping, 16
    yolks of, whipping, 16
egg wash
    for pastries, 255
    preparing, 168
even-flakier piecrust, 192

F

fat lattice (fattice), 180, *181*
faux-laminated maple sugar brioche rolls,
    295–97, *296*
fermentation
    bulk, description of, 249
    slowing down (retarding), 250
figgy pull-apart bread, *290*, 291–92
finger crimp, basic, 174, *176*
five-spice pumpkin pie, 218
flan, defined, 323
floats, made with ice cream, 330
flourless cocoa cookies, 30, *31*
flours
    all-purpose, about, 14
    bread, about, 15
    cake, about, 15

graham, about, 15
    pastry, about, 15
    rye, about, 15
    semolina, about, 15
    whole wheat, about, 15
    whole wheat pastry, about, 15
foaming methods, 78–79
foldover edge for crusts, 176, *176*
fork crimp, 174, *176*
frostings
    American buttercream, 134
    applying crumb coat, 87–88
    applying to cakes, 87–88
    black raspberry buttercream, 120
    buttercream, for devil's food cake,
      134
    caramel fudge, 142–44
    caramel pudding buttercream, 152
    coffee–white chocolate ganache, 137
    dark chocolate Italian buttercream,
      149
    lemon curd buttercream, 158
    peppermint seven-minute, 124–25
    reconstituting buttercream, 151
    spatula finishes, 88–89
    whipped ganache, 132
frozen custard, defined, 325
frozen custard-based desserts and ices
    preparing, tips for, 328
    types of, 325
frozen soufflés
    defined, 325
    pomegranate, 359–61, *360*
frozen yogurt, defined, 325
fruit
    any- , or -nut scones, 256–57, *257*
    arranging, on top of tarts, 187
    -glazed doughnuts, 285
    pies, about, 171
    pies, reheating, 184

fruit (*continued*)
    vanilla mascarpone cream pie, *195*, 203–4, *205*
    see also berry(ies); *specific fruits*
fruity sweet cream ice cream, 363, *363*
frying pastries, 252
fudgy brownies, 68–69, *69*
full glaze, for decorating cakes, 86

G

galette, double-crust berry, 200–202, *201*
ganache
    coffee–white chocolate, 137
    mocha cake with, 138
    whipped, 132
garnishes, edible, 12, 94
gelato
    defined, 325
    spicy chocolate, with cocoa nibs, 364–65
genovesi (Italian custard cookies), 50–52, *51*
ginger pear cake, 109–11, *110*
glass pie pans, 169
glazed lemon buttermilk loaf, *97*, 102–3
glazed mini cakes, 106–8, *107*
glazed waffle cookies, 58–59, *59*
glazes
    drip technique, 86
    drizzle technique, 86–87
    drizzling cookies with, 28
    dunking cookies in, 28
    enrobing cookies with, 28
    flooding technique, 29
    full glaze technique, 86
    honey-caramel, 100–101
    medium, about, 29
    partial glaze technique, 86

thick, about, 29
thin, about, 29
gluten development, 248–49
graham flour, about, 15
grahams, chocolate-glazed 'shmallow, 62–64, *64*
grape, Concord, pie, 226–28, *227*
grapefruit
    crepe cake, 269–70, *271*
    curd, 339, *339*
    meringue pie, 219–20, *220*

H

hand pies, jammy, *198*, 199
hazelnut pie with chocolate crust, *208*, 212
hi-ratio foaming method, 79
honey
    baklava muffins, *266*, 267–68
    -caramel glaze, 100–101
    pound cupcakes, with honey-caramel glaze, 100–101, *119*
    soufflés, *356*, 357–58

I

icebox cookies, about, 23–24
ice cream
    blueberry, 366, *367*
    brown sugar sweet cream, 363, *363*
    defined, 325
    dulce de leche pie, *205*, 206–7
    fruity sweet cream, 363, *363*
    fun things to do with, 330
    stracciatella, 363, *363*
    sweet cream, 362–63, *363*
icing, royal, 163
inclusions, for recipes, 18
ingredients, basic, for baking
    bringing to room temperature, 19

eggs, 17
flours, 14–15
inclusions, 18
leaveners, 15–18
liquefiers, 15
measuring by weight, 79
preparing, for cakes, 79
stabilizers, 15
sugar, 17
Italian custard cookies (genovesi), 50–52, *51*

J

jammy hand pies, *198*, 199
jimmies, DIY, 95, *95*
just fruit scones, 257
just nuts scones, 257

K

kolaches, poppy seed, 293–94

L

laminated doughs, working with, 303
lamination method for pastries, 251
lattice crusts, 177–83
    braided lattice, 183, *183*
    diagonal lattice, 180, *182*
    fat lattice (fattice), 180, *181*
    random lattice, 180, *182*
    skinny lattice, 180, *182*
    slattice, 180, *183*
    tightly woven lattice, 180, *182*
    tips for, 177–78
    unwoven, 179, *179*
    woven, 178, *180*
lavender petits fours, 129
leaveners, for recipes, 15, 18

lemon
    buttermilk loaf, glazed, *97*, 102–3
    curd, 338, *339*
    curd buttercream, 158
    -licorice meringue pie, 221, *221*
    -love chiffon layer cake, 156–59, *157*
    –poppy seed tartlets, 243–45, *244*
    ricotta turnovers, 310–11, *311*
    -rosemary madeleines, 60–61, *61*
licorice-lemon meringue pie, 221, *221*
lime
    curd, 339, *339*
    sablé sandwiches, 37–38, *39*
liquefiers, for recipes, 15

M

macadamia nut–chocolate scones, 257
macarons
    double chocolate, 44–46, *45*
    s'mores, 46, *46*
    vanilla, 46
macaroons, peachy coconut, 42–43, *43*
madeleines, lemon-rosemary, 60–61, *61*
maple sugar brioche rolls, faux-laminated,
    295–97, *296*
marshmallow crème, for chocolate-glazed
    'shmallow grahams, 63–64
marshmallows, in macaron s'mores, 46,
    46
mascarpone
    orange tart, 238–39, *239*
    vanilla cream pie, *195*, 203–4, *205*
meringue(s)
    blackberry pavlovas, 274–76, *275*
    pie, grapefruit, 219–20, *220*
    pie, lemon-licorice, 221, *221*
    preparing, 341
    salted caramel–swirled, 53–54, *55*
    versatility of, 14

milk, bringing to room temperature, 19
milk shakes, making, 330
mini cherry cobblers, 264, *265*
mocha cake with coffee–white chocolate
    ganache, *136*, 137–38
mocha cake with ganache, 138
molasses
    apple pie, 225
    sweet potato pie, 216–17
molded and stamped cookies, about, 24
molds and stamps, makeshift, 24
(more) traditional scones, 257
mousse
    about, 320
    chocolate, 336, *337*
    defined, 323
    layering colors and flavors, 329
    orange, 336
    piping, 327
    preparing, tips for, 324
    vanilla bean, 335–36
mousseline, defined, 323
muffins, baklava, *266*, 267–68

N

Nutella swirl and cocoa nibs, banana cake
    with, 104–5, *110*
nut(s)
    any- , or fruit scones, 256–57, *257*
    any- , tart in phyllo crust, 235–37
    baklava muffins, *266*, 267–68
    ginger pear cake, 109–11, *110*
    hazelnut pie with chocolate crust,
    208, 212
    macadamia, –chocolate scones, 257
    pies, about, 173
    pistachio pithiviers, 308–9, *309*
    tarts, about, 186
    see also almond(s)

O

oat(s)
    -apricot scones, 257
    chewy oatmeal cookies, 36
    ginger pear cake, 109–11, *110*
orange
    curd, 339
    mousse, 336
    tart, 238–39, *239*
orange blossom petits fours, 129

P

palmiers, chocolate, 306, *307*
panna cotta
    defined, 324
    eggnog, with raspberry sauce, 342–43,
    343
    layering colors and flavors, 329
parbaking
    directions for, 168–69
    a single piecrust, 191
    a tart crust, 194
partial glaze, for decorating cakes, 86
passionfruit curd, 339
pastries
    almond Danish bread, *298*, 299–300
    any-fruit or -nut scones, 256–57, *257*
    apple cinnamon scones, 257
    apricot-oat scones, 257
    baklava muffins, *266*, 267–68
    basic glazed doughnuts, *284*, 285
    black-and-blue scones, 257
    blackberry pavlovas, 274–76, *275*
    brioche apple tart, 288–89, *289*
    brioche rolls, 286–87, *287*
    buttermilk biscuits, 258–59
    canelés, 272–73, *273*
    cherry-cheese Danish, 312–13, *313*

pastries (*continued*)

chocolate-glazed doughnuts, 285

chocolate–macadamia nut scones, 257

chocolate palmiers, 306, *307*

chocolate puff pastry, *304*, 305

coconut-glazed doughnuts, 285

cream puffs, 277–80, *278*

crème fraîche biscuits, 260, *262*

cutting biscuits, scones, and other pastries, 252

determining doneness, 255

drop biscuits, 263

faux-laminated maple sugar brioche rolls, 295–97, *296*

figgy pull-apart bread, *290*, 291–92

fruit-glazed doughnuts, 285

frying tips, 252

grapefruit crepe cake, 269–70, *271*

just fruit scones, 257

just nuts scones, 257

laminated doughs, working with, 303

lamination method, 251

lemon ricotta turnovers, 310–11, *311*

making them beautiful, 255

mini cherry cobblers, 264, *265*

(more) traditional scones, 257

piping, 254

pistachio pithiviers, 308–9, *309*

poppy seed kolaches, 293–94

puff pastry, 301–5

ricotta beignets, 281–82, *282*

shaping, 253–54

spiced croissants, *313*, 314–17, *315*

straight-dough method, 248–51

strawberry cream biscuits, 261–62, *262*

yeast doughnuts, 283–85, *284*

yeasted puff pastry, 305

pastry bags

best sizes for, 91

disposable, 91

filling, note about, 89–90

how to hold, 90

tip shapes and sizes, 93

pastry cream, 340–41, *341*

bringing to a boil, note about, 16

defined, 323

variations, 341

versatility of, 14

pastry flour, about, 15

pastry wheel, 253

pâte à bombe, defined, 324

pâte à choux

recipe for, 277–79, *278*

versatility of, 14

pavlovas, blackberry, 274–76, *275*

peach(es)

cardamom stewed, rice pudding with, 353–55, *354*

peachy coconut macaroons, 42–43, *43*

pie, bourbon-rosemary, 229–31, *230*

peanut butter

cream, whipped, chocolate cream pie with, *208*, 210–11

pb & j whoopie pies, 47–49, *48*

pie dough, 192

swirl brownies, 69

pear

cake, ginger, 109–11, *110*

curd, 339

peppermint

–devil's food hi-hat cupcakes, 124–25, *125*

seven-minute frosting, 124–25

petits fours

lavender, 129

orange blossom, 129

rose, *126*, 127–28

phyllo

baklava muffins, *266*, 267–68

crust, any-nut tart in, 235–37

piecrusts

basic finger crimp, 174, *176*

braids for, 183–84

checkerboard edge, 176, *176*

chevron fork crimp, 174, *176*

crisscrossing fork crimp, 174, *176*

crumb crusts, 169–70

cutouts for, 184–86

decorative edges for, 173–76

decorative fork crimp, 174, *176*

foldover edge, 176, *176*

fork crimp, 174, *176*

lattice, 177–83

rope crimp, 174–76, *176*

scalloped edge for, 174, *176*

single, blind-baking, 191

single, parbaking, 191

spoon crimp, 174, *176*

pie doughs

all-buttah, 188–90, *189*

blind-baking, 168–69

chilling, 166–68

chocolate, 192

cream cheese, 192

cutting butter into flour, 167

egg wash for, 168

even-flakier, 192

freezing, 168

parbaking, 168–69

peanut butter, 192

rolling out, 166

size of butter pieces for, 167

versatility of, 14

whole wheat, 192

see also piecrusts

pie pans

glass, 169

with wide rims, note about, 169
pies
    apple butter, 225
    baking stones for, 181
    bourbon-rosemary peach, 229–31, *230*
    brownie, *208*, 209
    chiffon, about, 173
    chocolate cream, with whipped peanut butter cream, *208*, 210–11
    cider-caramel apple, 222–24, *223*
    cold-filled, about, 173
    Concord grape, 226–28, *227*
    cream, about, 173
    custard, about, 171–73
    dulce de leche ice cream, *205*, 206–7
    five-spice pumpkin, 218
    fruit, about, 171
    fruit, reheating, 184
    glass pie pans for, 169
    grapefruit meringue, 219–20, *220*
    hand, jammy, *198*, 199
    hazelnut, with chocolate crust, *208*, 212
    lattice crusts for, 177–83
    lemon-licorice meringue, 221, *221*
    molasses apple, 225
    nut, about, 173
    purple sweet potato, 217
    sugar, 213, *215*
    sweet potato, 216–17
    vanilla mascarpone cream, *195*, 203–4, *205*
piped cookies, about, 24
piping frostings, 89–94
    borders and edges, 92
    dots, 90–91
    rosettes, 91
    ruffles, 92
    stripes, 91–92

    technique for, 90
piping mousse and custard, 327
piping pastries, 254
pistachio(s)
    baklava muffins, *266*, 267–68
    pithiviers, 308–9, *309*
pithiviers, pistachio, 308–9, *309*
pizzelle
    chocolate, 56–57, *57*
    vanilla, 57
pomegranate soufflés, frozen, 359–61, *360*
poppy seed
    kolaches, 293–94
    –lemon tartlets, 243–45, *244*
portion scoops, 23
pots de crème
    caramelized white chocolate, 347–49, *348*
    defined, 324
pound cakes
    almond, with raspberry swirl, *97*, 98–99
    vanilla, 96–97, *97*
    versatility of, 14
pound cupcakes, honey, with honey-caramel glaze, 100–101, *119*
press-in cookie crusts, 170
press-in tart dough, 196–97
press-in tart dough, chocolate, 197
pudding
    caramel, buttercream, 152
    chocolate, *332*, 334
    defined, 324
    rice, tarts, *198*, 355
    rice, with cardamom stewed peaches, 353–55, *354*
    salty butterscotch, 334
    vanilla, *332*, 333–34
puff pastry, 301–5
    chocolate, *304*, 305

    cutting, 252
    yeasted, 305
pumpkin pie, five-spice, 218
purple sweet potato pie, 217

R

random lattice, 180, *182*
raspberry
    black, buttercream, 120
    black, cupcakes, 118–20, *119*
    -ripple crunch bars, 72–73, *73*
    sauce, eggnog panna cotta with, 342–43, *343*
raspberry jam
    almond pound cake with raspberry swirl, *97*, 98–99
    pb & j whoopie pies, 47–49, *48*
    sweet cream tartlets, 240–42, *241*
recipes
    adjusting, for different cake pan sizes, 80
    basic, to know and master, 14
    bringing ingredients to room temperature, 19
    flour types for, 14–15
    four basic baking ingredients, 15–18
    looking for baking/chilling/resting visual cues, 12
    making components ahead, 12
    taking advantage of shortcuts, 12
    using edible garnishes, 12
    "why it works" tips, 12
regular blondies, 67
rhubarb cheesecake, 350–52, *351*
rice
    pudding tarts, *198*, 355
    pudding with cardamom stewed peaches, 353–55, *354*

Rice Krispies, in raspberry-ripple crunch
    bars, 72–73, *73*
ricotta
    beignets, 281–82, *282*
    lemon turnovers, 310–11, *311*
rolls
    brioche, 286–87, *287*
    faux-laminated maple sugar brioche,
        295–97, *296*
rope border for tarts, 186, *187*
rope crimp, 174–76, *176*
rosemary
    -bourbon peach pie, 229–31, *230*
    -lemon madeleines, 60–61, *61*
rose petits fours, *126*, 127–28
rosettes, piping, 91
roulade, blueberry cream, 145–47,
    146
royal icing, 163
ruffles, piping, 92
rum
    canelés, 272–73, *273*
    eggnog panna cotta with raspberry
        sauce, 342–43, *343*
rye flour, about, 15

S

sabayon, defined, 324
sablé sandwiches, lime, 37–38, *39*
salted caramel sauce, 54
salted caramel swirl brownies, 69
salted caramel–swirled meringues, 53–54,
    55
salty butterscotch pudding, 334
sandwich cookies, about, 26–27
sauces
    brown-butter butterscotch, 67
    raspberry, 342–43, *343*
    salted caramel, 54

scales, digital, 79
scalloped edges for crusts, 174, *176*
scones
    any-fruit or -nut, 256–57, *257*
    apple cinnamon, 257
    apricot oat, 257
    black-and-blue, 257
    chocolate–macadamia nut, 257
    cutting, 252
    just fruit, 257
    just nut, 257
semolina, about, 15
separation foaming method, 78–79
shaped cookies, about, 24–25
sherbet, defined, 325
shortbread
    brown sugar, 40–41
    versatility of, 14
skinny lattice, 180, *182*
slattice, 180, *183*
soft-serve, defined, 325
sorbet, defined, 325
soufflés
    defined, 324
    frozen, defined, 325
    frozen pomegranate, 359–61, *360*
    honey, *356*, 357–58
spiced croissants, *313*, 314–17, *315*
spicy chocolate gelato with cocoa nibs,
    364–65
splatters, decorating custards with,
    329
sponge cake, versatility of, 14
spoon crimp, 174, *176*
sprinkles, DIY, 95, *95*
stabilizers, for recipes, 15
stirred custards, about, 320
stracciatella ice cream, 363, *363*
straight-dough method for pastries,
    248–51

strawberry
    cream biscuits, 261–62, *262*
    not-so-short cake, 114–16, *115*
    vanilla mousse cake, 160–62, *161*
stripes, piping, 91–92
sugar
    and butter, creaming, 78
    caramelization properties, 17
    crystallization properties, 17
    and eggs, foaming, 78–79
    hygroscopic properties, 17
    pie, 213, *215*
    sprinkling pastries with, 255
    syrups, cooking, note about, 17
    unique properties of, 17
    vanilla, how to make, 97
    see also brown sugar
sundaes, making, 330
sweet corn cakes, 117
sweet cream ice cream, 362–63, *363*
sweet cream tartlets, 240–42, *241*
sweet potato
    pie, 216–17
    purple, pie, 217

T

tart crusts
    blind-baking, 197
    crumb crusts, 169–70
    parbaking, 194
    press-in cookie crusts, 170
tart dough, 193–94
    blind-baking, 168–69
    chilling, note about, 168
    chocolate press-in, 197
    mixing methods, 167
    parbaking, 168–69
    press-in, 196–97
    versatility of, 14
    see also tart crusts

tarts
    almond cream, *232*, 233–34
    any-nut, in phyllo crust, 235–37
    apple brioche, 288–89, *289*
    arranging fruit on top of, 187
    cold-filled, about, 186
    custard, about, 186
    drizzles on top of, 186
    lemon–poppy seed tartlets, 243–45, *244*
    nut, about, 186
    orange, 238–39, *239*
    piping toppings onto, 186–87
    rice pudding, *198*, 355
    rope border for, 186, *187*
    special looks for, 186–87
    sweet cream tartlets, 240–42, *241*
    swirling fillings in, 187
tightly woven lattice, 180, *182*
tomato upside-down cake, *110*, 112–13
tres leches coconut bars, *73*, 74–75
turnovers
    lemon ricotta, 310–11, *311*
    shaping, 253

U

unwoven lattice, 179, *179*

V

vanilla
    bean mousse, 335–36
    macarons, 46
    mascarpone cream pie, *195*, 203–4, *205*
    pizzelle, 57
    pound cake, 96–97, *97*
    pudding, *332*, 333–34
    strawberry mousse cake, 160–62, *161*
    sugar, how to make, 97

W

waffle cookies, glazed, 58–59, *59*
walnuts
    baklava muffins, *266*, 267–68
    ginger pear cake, 109–11, *110*
warm foaming method, 78

whipped cream
    cheater's, *115*, 116
    defined, 324
whipped ganache, 132
white chocolate
    caramelized, pots de crème, 347–49, *348*
    –coffee ganache, 137
    lime sablé sandwiches, 37–38, *39*
whole wheat flour, about, 15
whole wheat pastry flour, about, 15
whole wheat pie dough, 192
whoopie pies, pb & j, 47–49, *48*
woven lattice, 178, *181*

Y

yeast
    doughnuts, 283–85, *284*
    instant, working with, 248
yeasted puff pastry, 305
yogurt, frozen, defined, 325

ERIN JEANNE McDOWELL

is a food writer and food stylist. She serves as Baking Consultant at Large for Food52.com and is the Recipe Editor for PureWow.com. Her work has appeared in newspapers, such magazines as *Fine Cooking* and *Sift,* and ad campaigns for print and television. *The Fearless Baker* is her first cookbook.

Originally from Lawrence, Kansas (a state she loves so much that she has it tattooed on the back of her neck), she trained at The Culinary Institute of America in Hyde Park, New York. She lives in North Bergen, New Jersey. Her Westie terrier, Brimley, is an enthusiastic taste-tester.